AF655213

BUSINESS LEGISLATION

(TEXTBOOK WITH SUGGESTED ANSWERS)

BUSINESS LEGISLATION

(TEXTBOOK WITH SUGGESTED ANSWERS)

An Exclusive & Comprehensive Book
Covering Revised UGC Syllabus

FOCUS:

MBA, M.Com., BBA, BCA, B.Com., B.E. and other Professional Courses

CA. C. RAMA GOPAL

F.C.A., F.C.S., CAIIB. A.I.B.
(London - Part-1)

Professor and Head
Department of Finance
VNS Institute of Management
Bhopal
Former Executive Director (Finance), MPSCSC Ltd., Bhopal
Former Deputy Regional Manager, Bank of India
(sandhyaramagopal@yahoo.com)

Author : *Export-Import Procedures, Documentation & Logistics*
Financial Management

PUBLISHING FOR ONE WORLD

NEW AGE INTERNATIONAL (P) LIMITED, PUBLISHERS

New Delhi • Bangalore • Chennai • Cochin • Guwahati • Hyderabad
Jalandhar • Kolkata • Lucknow • Mumbai • Ranchi

Visit us at **www.newagepublishers.com**

Copyright © 2008, New Age International (P) Ltd., Publishers
Published by New Age International (P) Ltd., Publishers
First Edition: 2008

All rights reserved.
No part of this book may be reproduced in any form, by photostat, microfilm, xerography, or any other means, or incorporated into any information retrieval system, electronic or mechanical, without the written permission of the copyright owner.

ISBN 13: 978-81-224-2232-0

ISBN 10: 81-224-2232-2

Rs. 150.00

C-07-12-2151

Printed in India at Ramprintograph, Delhi.
Typeset in-house

PUBLISHING FOR ONE WORLD
NEW AGE INTERNATIONAL (P) LIMITED, PUBLISHERS
4835/24, Ansari Road, Daryaganj, New Delhi - 110002
Visit us at **www.newagepublishers.com**

Dedicated to

Lord Venkateswara

PREFACE—SHARING MY THOUGHTS

Teaching law to management students, rather than students of law, is a challenge. This would, indeed, be a bigger challenge when the students do not have any rudimentary knowledge about law. Now, majority of students who join MBA are from non-commerce background so they would not have had any opportunity to study even the fundamentals of law. The problem is where to start. I have the answer. The UGC syllabus of "Business Legislation" has been taken as the basis for writing this book. The compelling force behind me to take up this task is my students. They have approached me to make a tailor-made book available to them to meet the needs of UGC syllabus as no book is available to cater their total needs, all at one place. This book crisply covers the syllabus and even the chapters are dealt in the same order of the UGC syllabus of MBA. In this process, many university students' requirements are covered, to a large extent, as a greater number of institutions have, involuntarily, chosen same topics in their syllabus too.

The second aspect is the treatment of explanation. Many consider law is complicated and nothing is said, directly. I intend to give a different treatment for the subject. I have chosen the straight way to explain in an easy and direct method. Language is not to stand as a barrier as many Hindi medium students have been joining MBA, of late. They want the subject to be dealt in an easy way to understand, with practical and professional approach, but not in a legal way. This book is meant for managers of tomorrow. They require understanding of law for managing the business and not to practise as lawyers. Legal concepts are explained in a layman's language.

The best compliment I have enjoyed on my earlier book "Export-Import Procedures, Documentation and Logistics" is from Hindi medium students, pursuing MBA. They have complimented "No difficult words are in the book, which we have not understood". I thank them for making the book to go for reprint, within six months of its first appearance. This book has been accepted as a recommended reading book at IIM, Indore too.

During my interaction and long observation, majority of students and, in particular, working executives, busy with their employment start preparing, a couple of weeks before the commencement of examinations. To facilitate them for quick and easy understanding, Descriptive Questions provide the necessary clues (reference to paragraphs, broadly) for finding answers, quickly, and also serving as a ready suggested answer book.

I have my family members Sandhya-wife, Radhi, Kalyan, Dheera and Kish, and my lovely little American grandsons –Theer and Tarkh– not preventing me to write, who have extended their support in one way or other to steer the book to a happy ending.

CA. C. Rama Gopal

CASE LAWS — DECISIONS

S. No.	*Name of Case Law*	*Matter-Decided*	*Page No.*
1.	Solomon Vs A. Solomon & Co. Ltd.	A company has a separate and independent legal existence. Company is, altogether, a different person, even from its directors and members.	2
2.	Life Insurance Corporation of India Vs Escorts Ltd.	In the case of dishonest and fraudulent use of the facility – separate legal entity -given to company, the law lifts the corporate veil and identifies the persons who are behind the scene and responsible for the perpetration of the fraud.	3
3.	Egyptian Salt and Soda Co. Ltd. Vs Port Said Salt Association Ltd.	Purpose of Memorandum of Association is to enable the shareholders, creditors and those who deal with the company to understand the permitted range of the objects of the enterprise.	12
4.	Ashbury Railway Carriage Co. Ltd. Vs Riche	Any act done outside the objects clause of the Memorandum of Association is void. Even the shareholders cannot ratify that act.	13
5.	Moosa Goolam Ariff Vs Goolam Ariff	Certificate of Incorporation is a conclusive proof and regularity of such Certificate cannot be questioned by any one, at any time.	20
6.	Mothey Krishna Rao Vs Grandhi Anjaneyulu	Articles of Association does not constitute a contract between an outsider and the company.	21

S. No.	Name of Case Law	Matter-Decided	Page No.
7.	Carlil Vs Carbolic Smoke Ball Co.	Any one who complies with the conditions contained in the General Offer can bind the person who has made the offer. General Offer is of continuous nature.	30
8.	Lalman Shukla Vs Gauri Datt	No person can accept the offer unless he has knowledge of the offer made.	31
9.	Mohiri Bibee Vs Dharmodas Ghosh	Agreement with the minor is absolutely void and contract cannot be enforced.	32
10.	Devi Shivaji Vs Karsandas Ramji	Court is not concerned with adequacy of consideration and it is for the contracting parties to settle. For validity of contract, presence of consideration is sufficient.	32
11.	Balfour Vs Balfour	Intention to create legal relationship is necessary for formation of a valid contract.	33
12.	Rose & Frank Co. Vs Crompton & Brothers Ltd.	Normally, intention to create legal relationship is presumed in business contracts. However, a specific mention in business contracts that the contract does not create legal relationship is also valid.	33
13.	C. Srinivas Vs K. Raja Ram Mohan	Agreement is void if the object is unlawful.	54
14.	Pearce Vs Brooks	Agreement is void if the object is unlawful.	54
15.	Lowe Vs Peers	Agreement in restraint of marriage is void.	54
16.	Mahabir Prasad Vs Dutta	In business contracts, time for delivery of goods is deemed to be essence of contract.	61
17.	Dominion of India Vs Gaya Prashad	Timely delivery of goods has been considered as essence of the contract and its failure results in payment of damages.	61

S. No.	Name of Case Law	Matter-Decided	Page No.
27.	Laxmi Engineering Works Vs P.G.S. Industrial Institute	A person who buys goods and uses for himself, exclusively, for the purpose of earning livelihood, by self-employment, falls within the definition of 'Consumer' under Consumer Protection Act.	92
28.	Kody Elcot Ltd. Vs Dr. C. P. Gupta	Doctor is a 'Consumer' under Consumer Protection Act for the equipment purchased by him for earning livelihood.	92
29.	Secretary, Consumer Guidance and Research Society of India Vs B.P.L. India Ltd.	Purchase of photocopier by a lady for earning her livelihood has been held as a 'Consumer', not for commercial purpose under Consumer Protection Act.	92
30.	HCL Ltd. Vs Krishna Nanu Naik and Sons & Another	Purchase of a computer by a large commercial firm has been held to be for commercial purpose under Consumer Protection Act.	92
31.	Thiruvalluvar Transport Corporation Vs Consumer Protection Council	Person who has sustained accident and made a claim for compensation has been held not as a 'consumer' under Consumer Protection Act.	94
32.	Indian Medical Association Vs V.P. Shantha	Service rendered by employee to his employer has been held not as a 'Consumer' under Consumer Protection Act.	94
33.	Indian Medical Association Vs V.P. Shanta	When free service is rendered to patients by medical practitioner, then patients do not become 'Consumers' under Consumer Protection Act.	94
34.	Dr. Sr. Louie & Anr. Vs Kannolil Pathumma	Legal heirs/representative of a deceased consumer, entitled to the estate of the deceased, have a *locus standi* and can file a complaint under Consumer Protection Act.	94
35.	Byford Vs S.S. Srivasthava	Absence of consideration for any item of purchase does not make a 'consumer' and so is not eligible for relief under Consumer Protection Act.	105

S. No.	Name of Case Law	Matter-Decided	Page No.
36.	Vishwa Jyoti Printers Vs Moklins of India	Warranty for free service was part of a composite contract and does not deprive one to be a 'Consumer' for relief under Consumer Protection Act.	105
37.	Bank of Maharashtra Vs Mrs. Jyoti Satya	Bank has been held liable for deficiency of service, while providing locker service, under Consumer Protection Act.	105
38.	Church of God (Full Gospel) in India Vs K.K. of Majestic Colony Welfare Association	Religious and social activities should not create any noise and such activities fall in the purview of environmental pollution under "The Environment (Protection) Act, 1986".	113
39.	Gramophone Co. India Ltd. Vs Shanti Films Corp., AIR 1997 Calcutta	Copyright is a beneficial interest and need not be registered for protection under the Copyright (Amendment) Act.	131
40.	Mankam Investments Ltd.	Shareholders in a company can decide whether Amalgamation or Merger is beneficial or not for them.It is not the job of the court to decide so long as the Merger is not manifestly unfair.	153
41.	Miheer H. Mafatlal Vs Mafatlal Industries Ltd.	When provisions of the statute have been complied with, court has no jurisdiction to decide on the commercial wisdom of the class of persons, even if the court feels better scheme could have framed for the Merger.	153
42.	Hindustan Lever Employees' Union Vs Hindustan Lever Ltd.	Obligation rests with the Court to be satisfied that the scheme for Amalgamation or Merger is not contrary to public interest.	154

CONTENTS

1

FORMATION AND INCORPORATION OF COMPANIES

1.1 INTRODUCTION

The Companies Act of 1956 sets down rules for the establishment of both public and private companies. The most commonly used corporate form is the limited company, unlimited companies being relatively uncommon.

1.2 MEANING OF COMPANY

In common usage, 'Company' means an association of persons associated for some common purpose. The common object may be business, charity, research etc. The persons are united for achieving a common objective, normally, for earning profits, which are shared by the investors.

Definition of Company: Section 3 (1) (i) of the Companies Act, 1956 defines a company as:

> **"A company registered and formed under this Act or an existing company."**

The above definition does not give clear description about the company. The definition provided by Haney gives a better view about the essential elements of a company. According to Haney,

> **"A company is an incorporated association which is an artificial person created for by law, having a separate entity, with a perpetual succession and a common seal."**

The characteristics of the company give a better picture about the essential elements mentioned in the above definition. Let us discuss those characteristics that describe the company, comprehensively.

1.3 CHARACTERISTICS OR ESSENTIAL FEATURES OF A COMPANY

1. **Registration:** A company is to be compulsorily registered under the Companies Act.
2. **Artificial Person: A company is an artificial person. "Company is an artificial person, invisible, intangible and existing only in the eyes of law."** It is created under the law, not itself a human being. It is called a person as it is clothed with certain rights and obligations.
3. **Separate Legal Entity:** A company can enter into contracts with its directors, its shareholders and outsiders. It functions through its board of directors. **A company is a distinct person, with its own independent identity.**

   One Man Company: When a single person holds almost all the shares of the company, it is called 'One Man Company'. Such a company has a legal personality, if it complies with the necessary requirements of registration **(Solomon Vs A. Solomon & Co. Ltd.).** Such companies may be public or private companies. Usually, they are private companies.

Solomon Vs A. Solomon & Co. Ltd.: In Solomon Vs A. Solomon & Co. Ltd. (1897) AC 22, it has been held that in common law, a company is a 'legal person or has a legal entity separate from its members and is capable of surviving beyond the lives of its members.'

In this case, one Solomon was a shoe manufacturer. He incorporated a company named Solomon and Co. Ltd. He took over the entire business of a running concern. Solomon and the seven subscribers to the memorandum were he and his family members. Solomon and his two sons were the Directors of the Company. The business of the company was transferred for £30,000. Solomon took 20,000 share of 1 £ each and debentures worth 10,000 in consideration.

The Company went into liquidation, within a year. On winding up, the unsecured creditors contended that the company was not having independent existence as Solomon was the Managing Director of the company and the entire company was under his control. They further contended that Solomon was holding majority of the shares and therefore, the company was merely a sham. Their contention was that the limited firm was only a guise to conceal the real identity of the persons who own. However, it was held that Solomon and Co. Ltd. fulfilled all the requirements of the legislature. Further, it was held that the company cannot be equated with the members comprising it. The company was not the agent of Solomon. It was therefore, treated as a company, distinct and independent corporation.

A company has, therefore, a separate legal existence, and is altogether a different person even from its directors and members.

Corporate Veil: On incorporation, a company assumes a separate personality of its own, called the 'Corporate veil'. On incorporation, the veil is drawn between the company and its members. The advantages of the incorporation –separate entity – were allowed only to those who make an honest use of the 'company'.

Lifting Corporate Veil: There may be circumstances in which the privileges of 'separate entity, may be misused. In such cases, the court, may disregard the corporate veil.

Ignoring separate entity or overlooking corporate personality is known as the phenomenon of **lifting corporate veil'**. Lifting corporate veil is an exception to the decision in Solomon's case.

In the case of dishonest and fraudulent use of the facility of corporation, the law lifts the corporate veil and identifies the persons who are behind the scene and responsible for the perpetration of the fraud. **(Life Insurance Corporation of India Vs. Escorts Ltd. (1986).**

Overlooking the corporate personality or separate entity is known as "the phenomenon of lifting the corporate veil."

4. **Common Seal:** Common seal is the signature of the company. As company is an artificial person, it is not bestowed with the body of a human being. The company has a separate legal existence through its common seal. The use of common seal is provided in the articles of association of the company.
5. **Separate Property:** A company can open a bank account in its name. It can exercise the entire powers incidental to the attainment of the objects of the company. A company can enter into contracts, through its board of directors. Shareholders are not, in the eyes of the law, part owners of the company.
6. **Company to Sue and be Sued:** A company can sue and be sued in its name. The company's right to sue arises as and when some loss is caused to the company. In case of breach of performance by any third party, the company can sue the third party in its name.

1.4 TYPES OF COMPANIES

Companies can be classified into three categories, based on their mode of incorporation.

(1) **Chartered Companies:** A chartered company is created under a charter, granted by the king or queen in exercise of the powers vested in the crown. A chartered company is regulated by its charter. For example, the East India Company has come into existence by the grant of Royal charter. The Companies Act is not applicable to them. Since independence, chartered companies have no place in India.

(2) **Statutory Companies:** These are the companies incorporated under a Special Act, passed by the Central or State Legislatures. Statutory companies are like Reserve Bank of India, Life Insurance Corporation of India, Food Corporation of India or State Bank of India, which are created by the special acts of parliament or legislature. The statutory bodies are governed by the Act under which they are constituted or formed. Companies Act is not totally applicable to statutory companies. The provisions of Companies Act are applicable only to the extent they are not inconsistent with the provisions of the Special Act. They do not have either Memorandum or Articles of Association. The word "Limited" is not a part of their name.

(3) **Registered Companies:** Apart from statutory government owned concerns, the most prevalent form of large business enterprises is a company, incorporated with limited liability. Companies limited by guarantee and unlimited companies are relatively uncommon.

A company can be a public or a private company and could have limited or unlimited liability. A company can be limited by shares or guarantee.

(A) Company Limited by Shares

In the case of company limited by shares, the personal liability of a member is limited to the face value of the share or amount unpaid on the share, whichever is lower.

(i) Private Companies

A private company is defined under Section 3 (i) (iii) under the Act. It has the following characteristics:

- **Right to Transfer:** The right to transfer shares is restricted.
- **Number of Shares:** The maximum number of its shareholders is limited to 50 (excluding employees) and the minimum number of shares is 2.
- **Invitation to Public:** No offer can be made to the public to subscribe for its shares and debentures.
- **Regulation:** Private companies are relatively less regulated than public companies as they deal with relatively smaller amounts of public money.

Deemed Public Company: The concept of deemed public companies was introduced in the Companies Act to check the misuse of private companies. A private company is deemed to become a public company in the following situations:

- When 25 percent or more of the private company's paid-up capital is held by one or more public company.
- The private company holds 25 percent or more of the paid-up share capital of a public company.
- The private company accepts or renews deposits from the public.
- The private company's average annual turnover is not less than Rs. 10 crores during the relevant period of three years.

The above provisions of Section 43(A) shall not apply on or after 31st December, 2000. Deemed concept of a public company on account of the above four factors is abolished.

(ii) Public Companies

A public company is defined as one which is not a private company. In other words, to a public company the restrictions of a private company do not apply.

(B) Company Limited by Guarantee

In the case of company limited by guarantee, the personal liability is limited by a pre-decided nominated amount. This guaranteed amount is fixed by the members and specified in the memorandum of association, which they respectively undertake to pay, in the event of the winding up of the company. The guaranteed amount can be called upon by the company only at the time of winding up, if the liabilities exceed its assets.

(C) Unlimited Company

In the case of an unlimited company, the liability of its members is unlimited. Its members are liable to contribute to the debts of the company in proportion of their respective interests.

(4) Foreign Companies: A foreign company is a company incorporated outside India and under the law of that country. Foreign investors can enter into the business in India either as a foreign company in the form of a liaison office/representative office, a project office and a branch office. It has to register with Registrar of Companies (ROC), New Delhi, within 30 days of setting up a place of business in India or as an Indian company in the form of a Joint Venture and wholly owned subsidiary. For opening of the foreign company, specific approval of Reserve Bank of India is also required. The foreign company must conspicuously exhibit on the outside of every office or business the name of the company, whether it is a public company or a private company and where incorporated.

Where 50% of the paid up of share capital of the foreign company is held by Indian citizens and /or companies incorporated in India, the foreign company is treated as an Indian company with respect to its Indian business. This is designed to protect the interests of the Indian citizens and Indian companies as substantial portion of their share capital is raised from them.

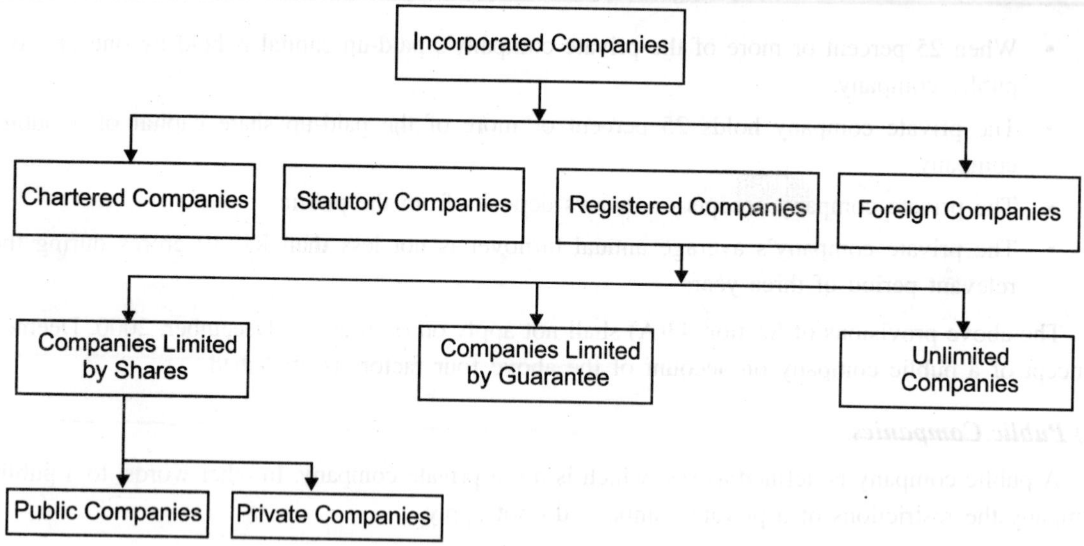

Types of Companies
(Diagram No. 1)

1.5 FORMATION OF COMPANY

The whole process of formation of a company is divided into four steps for convenience.

A. Promotion of Company
B. Incorporation or Registration of Company
C. Floatation of Company
D. Commencement of Business

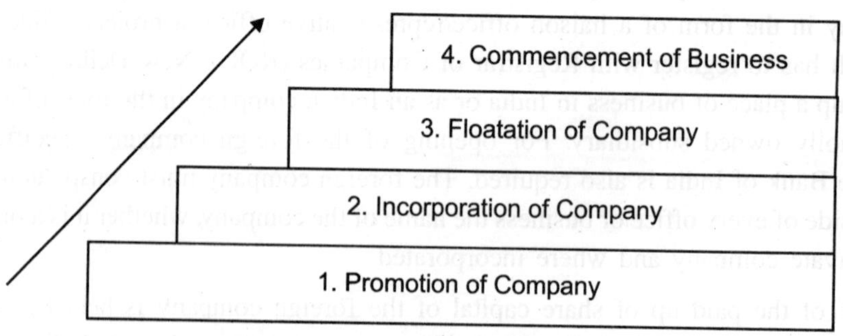

Steps in Formation of Company
(Diagram No. 2)

1.6 PROMOTION OF COMPANY

Promoter: Promoter is a person who initiates the process of formation of company. He undertakes to form a company with reference to a given project and takes the necessary steps to accomplish the purpose. Promoter assumes responsibility for all the matters relating to the formation of the company.

The term "Promotion" refers to the process of by which a company is 'incorporated' or brought into existence.

Fiduciary Position of Promoter

The promoter takes the necessary steps for the registration and floatation of the company. A promoter occupies a fiduciary position [Relationship of trust and confidence] with the company and the persons whom he induces to be the shareholders of the company. On account of this relationship, the promoter has to make a full disclosure of all material facts relating to the formation of the company. A promoter is not forbidden from making a profit in the formation of the company, but the profit is not to be secret.

"A promoter is neither the trustee nor the agent of the company, he promotes." Reason is neither a company has been formed nor a principal is in existence. In the absence of the principal, an agent cannot represent the principal. Similarly, the beneficiary has not yet born for the trustee to act. Yet, the responsibility of an agent and trustee is placed upon the promoter. Consequently, a promoter must act honestly and must not make money, directly or indirectly, at the expense of the company. He has to account and give to the company, whatever money is secretly received by him.

Remuneration to Promoter: Promoter gets remuneration for the work he does in the form of a lump sum. One of the usual ways of getting remuneration is sale of one's own property to the company, at an inflated price. He must disclose all the facts relating to the property to an independent and competent Board of Directors. If he sells the property to the company, without making a disclosure, the company may rescind the contract. The promoter may be required to pay back the price he has received from the company. Where rescission is not possible, the promoter may be required to pay damages to the company to the extent of the undisclosed profits.

Where remuneration is paid to the promoter, it must be disclosed in the prospectus, if paid within two years preceding the date of issue of prospectus.

1.7 INCORPORATION OR REGISTRATION OF COMPANY

For a public company, the minimum number of members is seven, while it is two in the case of a private company. The promoter has to gather the required number for subscribing to the Memorandum of Association.

The following are the steps for the incorporation of a company:

1. **Application for Availability of Name:** A company cannot be registered in the name of an existing company. It also cannot be registered in a name, which is undesirable in the opinion of the Central Government. Therefore, it is necessary for the promoters to find out the availability of the name of the company from the Registrar of Companies. The first step in the formation of a company is the approval of the name by the Registrar of Companies (ROC) in the State/Union Territory in which the company is to be registered. This approval is provided subject to certain conditions. For instance, there should not be an existing company by the same name. Further, the last words in the name are required to be "Private Ltd." in the case of a private company and "Limited" in the case of a Public Company.

Finalisation of name: The application for approval of name should mention at least four suitable names of the proposed company, in order of preference. The ROC, generally, informs the applicant within seven days from the date of submission of the application, whether or not any of the names applied for is available. Once a name is approved, it is valid for a period of six months, within which time Memorandum of Association and Articles of Association together with miscellaneous documents should be filed. If one is unable to do so, an application may be made for renewal of name, by paying additional fees. After obtaining the name approval, it normally takes approximately two to three weeks to incorporate a company, depending on where the company is registered.

2. **Filing of Documents:** The following three documents are required to be filed with the Registrar of Companies of the State in which the registered office of the company is to be situated:
   (i) Memorandum of Association,
   (ii) Articles of Association, and
   (iii) Agreement with the company for the proposed appointment of the managing director, whole-time director or manager.

The above documents (i) and (ii) are required to be signed by the seven persons in the case of the public company and two persons in the case of private company.

3. **Payment of Stamp Duty and Filing Fee:** The company has to pay the necessary stamp duty and filing fee, according to the authorized share capital of the company.
4. **Declaration of Compliance of Act and Rules:** A declaration that the requirements of the Act and the rules framed there under have been complied. This declaration is to be signed by an advocate of the Supreme Court or High Court or attorney or a pleader having the right to appear before High Court. Alternatively, this declaration can be signed by a Company Secretary or Chartered Accountant in whole time-practice, who is engaged in the formation of a company or a person named in the articles as a director. This declaration is also to be filed with the Registrar of Companies, where the registered office of the company would be located. - Section 33(2).

5. **Additional Requirement, in Case of a Public Company:** The following further requirements are to be complied with:
   (i) A list of persons who have consented to act as directors.
   (ii) Written consent of the directors to act in that capacity.
   (iii) An undertaking by the directors to take up and pay for the qualification shares.
6. **Certificate of Incorporation or Registration:** If the Registrar is satisfied that the requirements under the Act for the purpose of registration of a company have been complied with, he shall register the company and issue a certification of incorporation, under his hand and seal.

1.8 ADVANTAGES OF CERTIFICATE OF INCORPORATION

1. **Corporate Existence:** After certificate of incorporation, company obtains independent existence. The company enjoys a distinct legal personality. It becomes capable of functioning, independently, as a corporate individual, distinct from its members.
2. **Liability:** The liability of the members is limited to the extent of the nominal amount of the shares subscribed. In the case of a company limited by guarantee, the liability of the member is limited to the amount guaranteed by him.

The liability of partners in a partnership firm is unlimited. However, the liability of the members in a limited company is limited to the face value of the shares held by him. In case, the face value of a share is Rs. 10 and an individual holds 100 shares, his total liability, at any time, is only Rs. 1,000. If he has already paid, Rs. 400, his balance liability is limited to Rs. 600 only. Even, in the event of winding up of the company and the company does not have sufficient assets to pay the total liabilities, still, the individual member cannot be called upon to pay beyond Rs. 600 as he has already paid Rs. 400. In case, the member has paid the total amount of his liability Rs. 1,000, he has no further liability to the company, at all. The novel idea of limited liability has encouraged the people to invest in a company, with limited liability, unlike in a partnership firm.

3. **Transferability of Shares:** Shares in a company can be transferred easily, without the consent of other members of the company.

The greatest advantage of company is transferability of shares, unlike in a partnership firm. In a partnership firm, without the consent of the other partners, a partner cannot transfer his share to others. A member can transfer his shareholding, without the consent of the other members, in the manner provided by the Articles Association of the company. However, there are certain restrictions on the transferability of shares, in a private limited company. Certain restrictions can be imposed in a private limited company, but not in a public limited company about the transferability of shares.

In a public limited company, Articles of Association states the procedure to be followed, but cannot impose any restriction in respect of transferability of shares.

4. **Perpetual Existence and Succession:** A company incorporated never dies. The members of the company change with the transfer of shares. The death or insolvency of the members does not affect the corporate existence of the company. Only on winding up of the company, it ceases to exist.

Prof. Grover in his book on Modern Company Law says that "A company continues to exist even if all the members are dead. During the war, all the members of one private company, while in general meeting, were killed by a bomb. But, the company survived. Not even a hydrogen bomb could destroy it."

5. **Members and the Company:** A company enjoys separate legal entity. So, it can enter into contracts with its members and sue them in the ordinary way.
6. **Separate Property:** Capital of the company is contributed by its members. However, company owns the assets in its name and the members do not have any ownership right on the property of the company.
7. **Capacity to Sue and be Sued:** A company being a body corporate, it can sue and be sued in its own name.

1.9 EFFECT OF CERTIFICATE OF INCORPORATION

The certification of incorporation is conclusive evidence about registration and compliance of all the legal requirements. Date of certificate of incorporation is date of birth of a company.

Once a company is registered, the certificate of incorporation cannot be challenged, though there may be irregularities prior to registration.

A company obtains separate legal existence only after it is registered under the Companies Act. By virtue of this legal existence, the company comes into being as a separate person, distinct from the persons who form it. The company becomes a body corporate, with perpetual succession. Once company is registered, the only method to end it is through the process of winding up. **The certificate of incorporation cannot be cancelled by the Registrar of Companies, even if irregular.**

1.10 FLOATATION OF COMPANY

Once the Certificate of Incorporation is received, it means the company is registered. Then the next step is to raise the required finances for running the company. The company is ready for floatation.

Floatation means raising the required finances for commencing and carrying on the business, satisfactorily.

In other words, the company can go ahead, with raising capital sufficient to commence the business and carry on it, satisfactorily.

Prospectus & 'Statement in lieu of Prospectus': A private company is prohibited from raising funds from the public. It can arrange the capital, privately, from its friends and relatives. In the case of public companies, it has the option to raise the funds from the public or through private sources, without raising funds from the public. In case, it decides to invite the public to subscribe to its capital, the public limited company has to issue prospectus. In case, the funds are arranged privately, the public company has to file a 'Statement in lieu of Prospectus' with the Registrar of Companies.

1.11 CERTIFICATE OF COMMENCEMENT OF BUSINESS

A public company, having share capital, cannot commence the business, without obtaining the certificate of commencement of business. The certificate of commencement of business can be obtained, only after completing the floatation process. In other words, a public limited company has to file either prospectus or statement in lieu of prospectus and comply with the required legal requirements, relating to the capital requirements. Thereafter only, Certificate of Commencement of Business is issued by ROC.

A Public Company, having share capital, cannot commence the business, without obtaining the Certificate of Commencement of Business.

However, a private limited company can commence the business, without obtaining the 'Certificate of Commencement of Business'. There is no need for a private company to obtain Certificate of Commencement of Business. After obtaining the Certificate of Incorporation, it can immediately commence business. It is the privilege a private limited company enjoys.

1.12 MEMORANDUM OF ASSOCIATION

Public Documents: Memorandum of Association and Articles of Association are public documents. Any one who deals with the company are presumed to be aware of the contents of those documents.

Memorandum of Association is a document, which contains the fundamental conditions regarding constitution, objects or activities and powers of the company. It is a charter of the company. It is a principal document without which a company cannot be registered. It is a life-giving document.

Memorandum of Association is a document based on which the relations of the company is governed with outsides and members of the company.

Purposes: Memorandum of Association serves the following purposes:

(A) It contains the fundamental conditions on which the company is formed.

(B) It sets the boundaries of the company.

Lord Macmillan has rightly observed that the purpose of Memorandum of Association is to enable the shareholders, creditors and those who deal with the company to know the permitted range of the enterprise. **(Egyptian Salt and Soda Co. Ltd. Vs Port Said Salt Association Ltd. -1931).**

1.13 CONTENTS OF MEMORANDUM OF ASSOCIATION

According to Section 13 of the Act, the Memorandum of Association of every company should contain the following contents:

(A) Name Clause: Once the name of the company is approved and registered by the Registrar of Companies, the name of the company must be painted or affixed outside of every office or place of business. The name and address of registered office of the company has to be mentioned in letter-heads, business letters, notices and common seal of the company.

(B) Registered Office: Every company must have a registered office from the date of commencement of business, or 30th day of the incorporation date, whichever is earlier. All the notices have to be sent to this address.

(C) Objects Clause: The objects clause of the company indicates the sphere of activities and powers of the company.

The purpose of the objects clause is two-fold:

(i) To inform the members and creditors of the company in what kind of business their capital and funds may be used, and

(ii) To inform the persons dealing with the company what its powers are.

The objects are divided into two parts. Now, it is compulsory to specify in clear terms the main and other objects of the company.

(i) **The Main objects** to be pursed by the company on its incorporation and the ancillary objects incidental to the attainment of the main objects. The ancillary objects must have reasonable proximity or connection with the main objects.

(ii) **Other objects:** These are the objects which are not included in the above.

A company is prohibited from commencing any new business, though stated in the other objects, without passing the special resolution passed in the general meeting.

Doctrine of *Ultra Vires*

'Ultra' means 'beyond. 'Vires' means 'powers'. So, the term *"Ultra vires"* means 'beyond the powers of the Company'. A company exists only to carry on the objects which are expressly stated in the objects clause. It means the company can perform those objects only. It can also do such acts, which are incidental or consequential to the specific objects of the company. A trading company has implied power to borrow and this power need not be stated, separately.

This doctrine has been first explained in the leading case of **Ashbury Railway Carriage Co. Ltd. Vs Riche LR HL 653 (1875)**. The object of the company as contained in the Memorandum of Association has been "to make, sell or lend on hire, railway carriages and wagons of all kinds ..... to carry on the business of mechanical engineers and contractors. The directors of the company, however, have contracted for financing the construction of a railway line in Belgium. The company has endorsed the act of directors by passing a special resolution in the general meeting. However, the contract has been held to be ultra vires of the objects of the company because the word 'general contractors' does not authorize the company to make contract of every description. The doctrine has been confirmed by the Supreme Court in **Lakshmana Sami Mudaliar Vs LIC of India 1963 AIR Sc 1185.**

An act done outside the express or implied objects is *ultra vires*. The *ultra vires* acts are null and void *ab initio*.

> **The object of the ultra vires doctrine is to protect the interests of the investors and creditors by ensuring that the company does not invest or utilize the money in those acts, which is not contemplated by the shareholders or creditors of the company.**

Effect of *Ultra Vires* Acts

1. **Void ab initio:** These acts are void from the beginning.
2. **Injunction:** A member of the company can bring an injunction (order of the court refraining to do) against the company to prevent from proceeding with the ultra vires act.
3. **Personal Liability of Directors:** The directors of the company may be personally held liable to outsiders for those *ultra vires* acts. This is made on the ground of breach of warranty or authority.
4. **No Ratification: If an act is *ultra vires* the company, it does not create legal relationship.** It is violation of the law and diversion of the assets of the company to purposes, not contemplated by the members and creditors of the company. As it is an act outside the powers of the company, even the whole body of shareholders cannot ratify it and make it binding on the company.
5. **Company Can Neither Sue or be Sued:** The company cannot sue the contracting party. Equally, the contracting party cannot sue the company.

Various Types of Ultra Vires Acts: It is necessary to distinguish the acts, outside the powers of the company and Board of Directors.

Acts beyond the scope of Memorandum of Association cannot be ratified by the company, even by the total body of the shareholders as they are outside the powers of the company. However, if the acts are only beyond the powers of the directors, but within the powers of the company, those acts can be ratified by the company.

(D) Capital Clause: In the case of a company having a share capital, the capital clause has to state the nominal or authorized capital of the company. The nominal capital is divided into different classes of shares. The capital clause has to state the values of the different classes of shares such as equity share capital and preference share capital and their division into shares of a fixed amount.

In the case of a company limited by guarantee, the amount promised by each member to be contributed by them in the event of winding up of the company, is to be mentioned.

(E) Liability Clause: The liability of the members is limited to the extent of the shares subscribed by the members of the company, in the case of a company having share capital. It means no member can be called upon to pay more than the nominal value of the shares held by him or the amount remaining unpaid. In case the shares are fully paid, the liability is nil.

In the case of a company by guarantee, the liability is limited to the extent of guarantee given by the members. This can be called only when the liabilities exceed the assets of the company.

(F) Subscription or Association Clause: In the case of a public company, at least, there must be seven subscribers although two are sufficient in the case of a private company. All the subscribers must sign the Memorandum of Association. Each subscriber must take at least one share in a company. Normally, the declaration of association reads like this "We, the several persons whose names, addresses and occupations are subscribed, are desirous of being formed into a company in pursuance of the Memorandum of Association and respectively agree to take the number of shares in the capital of the company, set opposite of our respective names."

After incorporation, no subscriber can withdraw his name on any ground whatsoever.

1.14 ARTICLES OF ASSOCIATION

Articles of Association lays down the rules and regulations framed for the purpose of its internal management of the affairs of the company.

They facilitate the way for carrying out the objects, specified in the Memorandum of Association.

Relationship between Memorandum of Association and Articles of Association

1. **Ranking:** Articles of Association is subordinate and controlled by the Memorandum of Association.

2. **Subordinate:** The Articles of Association are subordinate to Memorandum of Association. Articles of Association cannot contain any provision which is inconsistent with the Memorandum of Association. Articles of Association may the supplement the Memorandum of Association.
3. **Scope:** The Memorandum of Association lays down the scope or powers of the company, while the Articles of Association govern the way in which the objects of the company can be carried out. As regards the contents, Articles of Association resembles a partnership deed.

Adoption of Table A: A public company limited by shares may have its own Articles of Association. In the absence of its own Articles of Association, the company can adopt Table A. In other words, preparation of Articles of Association is not compulsory. Even if Table A is adopted, if the company's Articles of Association is silent on any matter, provisions of Table A would be applicable.

Contents of Articles of Association: Some of the contents of Articles of Association are here under:

(i) Allotment of shares
(ii) Procedure for Transfer of Shares
(iii) Powers of Directors
(iv) Forfeiture of shares
(v) Common seal of the company
(vi) Accounts and audit
(vii) Voting rights and proxies

The Articles of Association spells out the way the affairs of the company would be conducted.

1.15 ALTERATION OF MEMORANDUM OF ASSOCIATION AND ARTICLES OF ASSOCIATION

Alteration of Memorandum of Association is much difficult and strictly regulated. Articles of Association can be easily altered by passing a special resolution in the general meeting.

Check Your Understanding

State whether the following statements are True or False

1. A company is a distinct person, with its own independent identity.
2. The liability of the members in a company is unlimited, similar to a partnership firm.
3. The greatest advantage of company is transferability of shares, unlike in a partnership firm.
4. Common seal is the signature of the company.
5. In the eyes of law, shareholders of the company are part owners.

6. The term “Promotion” refers to the process of by which a company is ‘incorporated’ or brought into existence.
7. A promoter is both a trustee and agent of the company, before and after formation of the company.
8. In the case of company limited by shares, the personal liability of members is limited to the amount unpaid on their shares, at any time.
9. The Companies Act is totally applicable to statutory companies.
10. ‘One Man Company’ is not a company registered under the Act.
11. The person who assumes the task of promotion of the company is called ‘Promoter’.
12. Promoters occupy a fiduciary relationship, relationship of trust and confidence, with the company.
13. For a public company, the minimum number of members is two, while it is seven in the case of a private company.
14. A company obtains separate legal existence only after it is registered under the Companies Act.
15. Articles of Association can be altered, while Memorandum of Association cannot be altered at all.
16. “One Man Company” means a limited company with only one member as its shareholder.
17. Once a company is registered, the certificate of incorporation cannot be challenged, though there may be irregularities prior to registration.
18. Floatation means raising the required finances for commencing and carrying on the business, satisfactorily.
19. A private company is allowed to raise funds from the public.
20. A public limited company enjoys the privilege of commencing the business, without obtaining the ‘Certificate of Commencement of Business’.
21. The objects clause in the Memorandum of Association of the company indicates the sphere of activities and powers of the company.
22. An act done outside the express or implied objects of the company is *ultra vires.*
23. Even after the shares are fully paid, the liability of the member continues to remain to the face value of the shares held by him.
24. Articles of Association are the regulations or bye-laws, which govern the internal management and conduct of the company.
25. The Companies Act is applicable only to public companies, but not to private companies.
26. The directors of the company may be personally held liable to outsiders for the *ultra vires* acts, beyond the scope of the powers contained in Memorandum of Association.
27. The Memorandum of Association lays down the scope or powers of the company, while the Articles of Association govern the way in which the objects of the company can be carried out.
28. The certificate of incorporation can be cancelled by the Registrar of Companies, when the certificate is found irregular.

29. The ancillary objects stated in the Memorandum of Association need not have reasonable proximity or connection with the main objects.
30. The object of the ultra vires doctrine is to protect the interests of the investors and creditors by ensuring that the company does not invest or utilize the money in unauthorised acts, not contemplated by the shareholders or creditors of the company.
31. Acts which are within the powers of the company, but beyond the powers of the directors, can be ratified by the company.
32. It is necessary for every public company to have its own Articles of Association.
33. Articles of Association does not constitute a contract between the company and an outsider.

Answers:

1. True	2. False	3. True	4. True	5. False
6. True	7. False	8. True	9. False	10. False
11. True	12. True	13. False	14. True	15. False
16. False	17. True	18. True	19. False	20. False
21. True	22. True	23. False	24. True	25. False
26. True	27. True	28. False	29. False	30. True
31. True	32. False	33. True		

Pick up the Right Answer

Q.1 The person who initiates the process of formation of company is known is:
- (a) Director.
- (b) Shareholder.
- (c) Promoter.
- (d) Registrar.

Q.2 Company may start its business in the following circumstances:
- (a) When it is registered, in case of a public company.
- (b) On presentation of an application for registration on requisite form.
- (c) When the private limited company obtains certificate of incorporation.
- (d) When Memorandum of Association of the company is presented before the Registrar of Companies.

Q.3 The company may appoint the following as director:
- (a) An individual.
- (b) A body corporate.
- (c) An association of individuals.
- (d) A partnership firm.

Q.4 Company is a:

(a) Natural person.

(b) Artificial person.

(c) Natural and artificial person.

(d) None of the above.

Q. 5 Based on the following document, the relations of the company is governed with outsides and members of the company:

(a) Articles of Association

(b) Prospectus

(c) Memorandum of Association

(d) Statement in lieu of Prospectus

Q.6 This document is called as the charter of the company.

(a) Articles of Association

(b) Prospectus

(c) Memorandum of Association

(d) Statement in lieu of Prospectus

Q.7 The Companies Act is applicable to the following categories of companies:

(a) Statutory companies

(b) Companies registered under the Companies Act

(c) Partnership firms

(d) Chartered Companies

Q.8. The following document lays down the rules and regulations for internal management of the company:

(a) Articles of Association

(b) Prospectus

(c) Memorandum of Association

(d) Statement in lieu of Prospectus

Q.9 Floatation of Company means

(a) raising required finances at the initial starting and carrying on business, satisfactorily.

(b) registration of a company.

(c) running business efficiently and profitably.

(d) situation before winding up of the company.

Q. 10 This form of business enjoys corporate form

(a) limited company,

(b) unlimited company

(c) partnership firm

(d) proprietorship concern

Q.11 Name the company which is not a statutory company from the following:

(a) Reserve Bank of India

(b) Life Insurance Corporation of India

(c) Food Corporation of India

(d) HDFC

Q.12. Articles of Association lays down

(a) relationship between company and outsiders.

(b) rules and regulations for internal management of the company.

(c) relationship between company and employees.

(d) relationship between company and shareholders of the company.

Q.13 If there is any contradiction between Memorandum of Association and Articles of Association, the following document prevails.

(a) Memorandum of Association.

(b) Articles of Association

(c) Both (a) and (b)

(d) Company cannot perform that act.

Q.14 Memorandum of Association is

(a) a public document

(b) a private document

(c) a confidential document

(d) none

Q.15 When Articles of Association of a public company, limited by shares, is silent on any matter, then

(a) company cannot do any act on that matter.

(b) company cannot do till its Articles of Association is altered.

(c) Table A is applicable to that extent.

(d) provision of Memorandum of Association is applicable on that matter.

Answers:

1. (c)	2. (c)	3. (a)	4. (b)	5. (c)
6. (c)	7. (b)	8. (a)	9 (a)	10 (a)
11. (d)	12. (b)	13. (a)	14. (a)	15. (c)

Discuss Legal Implications

(A) Memorandum of Association of a public company has been signed by six majors and a guardian of a minor. The Certificate of Incorporation has been issued by the Registrar of Joint Stock Companies, without noticing the defect. Is the Certificate of Incorporation valid? Can the Registrar of Joint Stock Companies cancel the certificate, once the irregularity is found out? Does it make any difference if only one adult has forged the signatures of the rest of four members?

Answer: In the case of a public company, the signatories to the Memorandum of Association should be seven. In the relevant case, seven members have signed, but out of seven one is a minor. Minor has been signed by the guardian. Minor is incompetent to enter into a contract. Any contract with a minor is void. But, the Certificate of Incorporation has been issued by the Registrar of Joint Stock Companies. With the issue of Certificate of Incorporation, the company has been formed. The date of the certificate is the date of birth of the company.

According to Section 35 of Companies Act, once the Certificate of Incorporation is issued, it is a conclusive proof that the requirements of the Companies Act have been complied with, in full. The regularity of the certificate cannot be questioned. **(Moosa Goolam Ariff Vs Goolam Ariff ILR(1913) 40 CAL PC)**

Registrar of Joint Stock Companies has no authority to cancel the certificate. Winding up of the company is the normal way for the closure of the company.

Any irregularity such as forgery does not affect the validity of the Certificate of Incorporation.

(B) A promoter has approached Registrar of Joint Stock Companies to register a new company with the name "New Bata Ltd." to carry on shoe manufacturing activity. Can the company secure the approval for the name requested? Would the Registrar of Companies be justified in disallowing the proposed name?

Answer: No company is allowed to be registered in the name of any existing company or with such a misleading name which would confuse the public that the new company is connected to the existing company. Here, the proposed name "New Bata Ltd." is also engaged in the shoe manufacturing activity, similar to the existing company "Bata Ltd." This would naturally create misleading impression and confusion that the proposed company is connected with the existing company. So, Registrar of Companies would be justified in disallowing the new proposed name.

(C) The Articles of Association has contained a clause that A should be the Financial Advisor of the company for a period of five years and he should not be removed for misconduct. Vinod acted as Financial Advisor for a period of two years. Later, the company has removed him. Vinod sues the company for damages. Decide.

Answer: Vinod cannot succeed because the Articles of Association does not constitute a contract between the company and an outsider. Moreover, the right has been conferred on Vinod other than as a member. The leading case on this matter is **Eley Vs Positive Life Assurance Co. (1876) 1 Ex. Div.88 and Mothey Krishna Rao Vs Grandhi Anjaneyulu (AIR 1954) Madras 113).**

Descriptive Questions

1. Define 'Company'. Write the essential features of a company. **(1.2 and 1.3)**

2. "Company is an artificial person, invisible, intangible and existing only in the eyes of law." Explain. **(1.2 and 1.3)**

3. "A company has a separate legal existence, and is altogether a different person from its directors and members." –Discuss. **(1.2 and 1.3)**

4. Discuss the facts and principles of law laid down in Soloman Vs Soloman.**(1.2 and 1.3)**

5. Discuss the concept of 'One man Company'. **(1.2 and 1.3)**

6. State the principles of law laid down in "Solomon Vs. Solomon and Co. Ltd. What are the exceptions to the decision in Solomon's case? **(1.3)**

7. Define company and describe the different types of companies. **(1.2 and 1.4)**

8. Who is a promoter? "A promoter is neither the trustee nor the agent of the company, he promotes." Discuss. Can a promoter be paid remuneration? **(1.6)**

9. Explain the term "Company". Discuss the various steps involved in Formation of Company. **(1.2, 1.5, 1.6, 1.7, 1.10 and 1.11)**

10. Write the advantages of Incorporation of Company. What is the effect on incorporation of a company? **(1.7, 1.8 and1.9)**

11. Discuss the importance and contents of Memorandum of Association and Articles of Association. **(1.2, 1.12 and 1.13)**

12. What are the clauses to be stated in the Memorandum of Association? **(1.2, 1.12 and 1.13)**

13. "The Memorandum of Association is the fundamental law or charter defining the objects and limiting the powers of the company." Explain. **(1.2, 1.12 and 1.13)**

14. Explain the doctrine of 'Ultra Vires'. What are the effects of the ultra vires transaction? Can a company ratify such transactions? **(1.13 –Point C)**

15. Write short notes on:

(A) One-man company **(1.3)**

(B) Corporate veil **(1.3)**

(C) *Ultra vires* of Memorandum of Association **(1.13 –C)**

(D) Common seal **(1.3 –Point 4)**

(E) Commencement of business **(1.11)**

2

CONTRACT—ESSENTIAL ELEMENTS

- Introduction
- Importance of Understanding Contract Law
- Meaning of Contract
- The Law of Contracts is Neither the Whole Law of Agreements Nor the Whole Law of Obligations
- Distinction between an Agreement and a Contract
- Essential Elements of a Valid Contract
- All Essential Elements Necessary to Form a Contract
- Check Your Understanding
- Discuss Legal Implications
- Pick up the Right Answer
- Descriptive Questions

2.1 INTRODUCTION

The law in India owes its origin to the British legal system. Our country has been ruled by the British regime for a very long period. British colonial system has lasted long and its influence, despite their exit from the country and our independence, is still noticeable in our legal system.

2.2 IMPORTANCE OF UNDERSTANDING CONTRACT LAW

In our daily life, we enter into contracts, knowingly and at times, unknowingly. A commercial transaction, be it purchase or sale of goods and services, results into a contract. These are the contracts we get into, knowingly. Contract law governs the formation and performance of contracts. Additionally, there are several instances, where we enter into contracts, unknowingly. These instances are numerous. When we enter into an auto and ask him to reach for a specified destination, at an agreed price, unknowingly, we have entered into a contract with the driver of the auto. The auto driver is entitled to receive the fare, once he performs the obligation on his part i.e. after reaching to the specified place. It is necessary to understand the law as ignorance of law is no excuse. If we are caught driving without the requisite driving license, we cannot plead ignorance of the law. We cannot avoid payment of penalty for not holding the required license.

Businessmen and managers have to manage the affairs of the business, in consonance with the applicable laws.

While performing the managerial functions, it is necessary for managers to have knowledge of contract law to understand the implications of non-performance and rights to enforce a contract, in case, the other party is the defaulter. A smart manager may take advantage of the law to his strategic advantage, once he is aware that the chances of failure to perform are more than the performance by incorporating higher penalty for failure of performance.

2.3 MEANING OF CONTRACT

Section 2(h) of Indian Contract Act, 1872 defines the term 'Contract'. As per the definition, contract is as an agreement enforceable by law. The definition of the contract must have the following two elements:

(A) An agreement, and

(B) Enforceability of agreement, i.e., it should be enforceable under law.

From the definition, it is clear that there should be two components to constitute a contract. There should be existence of an agreement and enforceability of the agreement.

Now, the question arises 'What is an agreement'? and 'What is the enforceability of an agreement'?

What is an Agreement?

An agreement consists of an offer by one party and its acceptance by the other. In the form of an equation, it can be shown as under:

Agreement = Offer or Proposal + Acceptance of Offer or Proposal

The first step is that one person has to make a proposal or offer to the other person, with a view to obtain his acceptance. When the proposal is accepted, it becomes an agreement. **So, an agreement is an accepted proposal.**

Example: Theer offers to sell his car for Rs. 2,00,000 to Tarkh and proposal of the former is accepted by the later. The offer, followed by acceptance, between Theer and Tarkh becomes an agreement.

What is Enforceability of an Agreement?

An agreement that can be enforced in law is a contract. If there is a legal obligation, it is enforceable at law. An agreement becomes enforceable when it gives rise to legal obligations. Obligation is a restraint which one party exercises over another.

> **By virtue of the legal obligation, one party can compel the other to do something or refrain from doing something.**

In other words, the sufferer can go to a court of law, in case of default, for redressal of the grievance. **The law of contracts deals only with those agreements, which are enforceable at law.** In the former example, if Tarkh pays the agreed amount, Theer has to deliver the car to him. If Tarkh refuses to pay, after taking delivery of the vehicle, Theer has a legal right to recover the amount. In other words, if there is a breach of performance of promise made, the other party has a legal remedy, which can be enforced in a court of law.

However, there are some agreements, which are not enforceable in a court of law. Such agreements do not give raise to contractual obligations and are not contracts. So, they cannot be enforced in a court of law.

Example: Kalyan invites Kishore for a dinner. Kalyan does not turn up at the agreed restaurant, to the utter surprise of Kishore. Alternatively, Kalyan appears there, but refuses to entertain Kishore. Kishore has no remedy.

After the acceptance of invitation, Kishore refuses to dine with Kalyan. Kalyan cannot sue him, though he has incurred expenditure for booking the table and placing the order, in advance.

Why the parties cannot sue each other for breach? What is the reason behind?

> **In case of domestic or social agreements, the usual presumption is the parties do not intend to create legal relationship.**

Every contract is an agreement plus something. That 'something' is the availability of the 'right to enforce performance', legally. While, it is a right of one person, the same is the 'obligation' of another. So, every contract is an agreement, but all agreements need not be contracts.

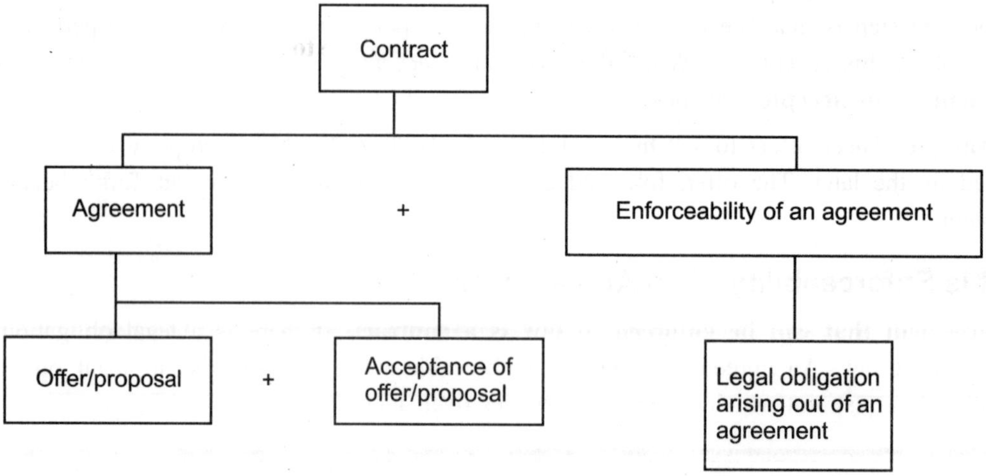

Difference between Agreement and Contract
(Diagram No. 3)

2.4 THE LAW OF CONTRACTS IS NEITHER THE WHOLE LAW OF AGREEMENTS NOR THE WHOLE LAW OF OBLIGATIONS

2.4.1 The Law of Contracts is not the Whole Law of Agreements

The law of contracts is concerned with those agreements that can be enforced in a court of law. The law of contracts is not concerned with those agreements, where the parties do not have the intention to create legal obligations. In social or domestic agreements, the parties do not intend to create legal obligations.

Difference between Agreement and Contract: The true test between an agreement and contract is its enforceability under law or not. If the agreement can be enforced in a court of law, it is a contract. In case, the agreement cannot be enforced in a court of law, it is not contract.

Example: Father promises to give son a pocket allowance of Rs. 1,000 per month. After giving the pocket allowance for a couple of months, father discontinues the allowance to son, afterwards, without assigning any reason, what so ever. The son cannot sue the father for non-payment of allowance. The reason is it does not constitute a contract; it is only a social obligation.

Here, there is an agreement. But, this agreement cannot be enforced in a court of law as it is based only on social obligation that father has to support son. So, there is no contract.

The term 'Agreement' is wider than the term 'Contract'.

An agreement can become a contract or may not become a contract. It is this argument which has given rise to the popular saying **"All contracts are agreements but all contracts need not be contracts."**

An Agreement to become a Contract must give raise to Legal Obligations.

In other words, it should result into a duty, enforceable under law. If an agreement is incapable of creating a duty enforceable under law, it is not a contract. **"All contracts are agreements but all agreements are not contracts."** Agreements of moral, religious or social nature e.g. promise to have dinner together or to take a walk together are not contracts as they are not likely to create a duty, enforceable by law. An agreement of a purely social or domestic nature is not a contract. The simple reason is that the parties never intend to have legal consequences for the failure to perform.

In business agreements, the presumption is usually to create legal relationship. If there is no presumption of such nature in business, no business can be executed. For breach of performance, there is always a penalty to compensate for the loss sustained.

The Act restricts the use of the word 'contract' to only those agreements which give rise to legal obligations.

If Agreement is enforceable under law, it is a Contract, otherwise, it is not a Contract. All Contracts are Agreements, but all Agreements are not Contracts.

Similarly, agreements to do an unlawful act, immoral or illegal act, for example smuggling or murdering a person, cannot be enforceable at law.

It can be said that the law of contracts is not the whole law of agreements. It is the law which deals with those agreements that can be enforced, legally.

Thus, the position can be summarized, as under:

Type of Agreements	***Whether Law of Contract Covers Such Agreements***
1. Agreements, where parties intend to create legal obligations.	YES
2. Agreements where the parties do not intend to create legal obligations. e.g. social agreements result into social engagements.	NO

2.4.2 The Law of Contracts is not the Whole Law of Obligations

It is important to note that the law of contract deals only with such legal obligations which spring from agreements. In other words, the agreement should result into legal obligation. Obligation is a restraint which one party exercises over another. By virtue of this obligation only, one can compel the other to do something or refrain from doing something. Here, obligation means legal obligation, not social or religious obligation. Legal obligation involves money, while social obligation does not involve money.

It should be remembered that obligations arise even without agreements. Sources of such obligations are:

(A) Torts or civil wrongs
(B) Quasi-contracts
(C) Decrees by courts etc.

An agreement must create legal obligation. If there is no legal obligation, there is no contract.

Contractual relationship creates rights and obligations. **Contractual rights and obligations are correlative.** An example explains the picture, better.

Example: Suresh enters into a contract for sale of his car with Vasu for Rs. 50,000. Both agree to exchange payment against delivery of vehicle, on a specified date. Vasu makes the agreed payment on the due date, but Suresh does not deliver the car on the agreed date and delays the delivery, for no specific reason. During the intervening period of delivery, Vasu is forced to use a hired vehicle. Vasu claims compensation from Suresh for the delayed delivery of the vehicle in the form of hire charges paid by him.

Here, the following rights and obligations have been created:

(i) Suresh is under an obligation to deliver the car to Vasu. He has a correlative right to receive the amount for Rs. 50,000.

(ii) Vasu is under an obligation to pay Rs. 50,000 to Suresh. He has a correlative right to receive the vehicle from Suresh.

In other words, each party has a right as well as an obligation in a contract.

More so, the performance is expected to be executed on the same date. The aggrieved party, Vasu has rendered his performance on the due date. So, he is entitled for compensation, which has been paid by him in the form of hire charges of alternative vehicle.

Obligation which is not contractual in nature is outside the purview of the law of contract. For example, obligation to observe the law of the land, obligation to enforce the court order, obligation to maintain wife and children, depending upon the status of husband, do not fall with in the scope of the Contract Act.

The whole position may be summarized as under:

Type of obligations	*Whether the Law of Contract can cover such obligations*
1. Obligations which arise out of agreements.	YES
2. Obligations which do not arise out of agreements.	NO

Every contract creates a legal obligation on both the parties. But, it is not necessary that the source of every obligation is only from a contract. There are various obligations, which may arise from sources other than contracts.

Salmond has rightly observed: "The law of contracts is not the whole law of agreements, nor is it the whole law of obligations. It is the law of those agreements which create obligations, and those obligations, which have their source in agreements."

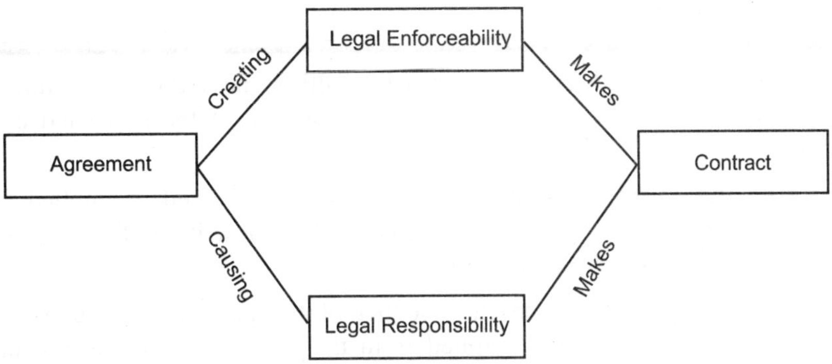

Relationship between Agreement and Obligation with Contract (Diagram No. 4)

2.5 DISTINCTION BETWEEN AN AGREEMENT AND A CONTRACT

	Basis of Distinction	*Agreement*	*Contract*
1.	What constitute?	Offer and its acceptance together constitute an agreement.	Agreement and enforceability together constitute a contract.
2.	Creation of legal obligation	Agreement may or may not create a legal obligation.	A contract necessarily creates a legal obligation.
3.	One in another	All agreements are not contracts.	All contracts are necessarily agreements.
4.	Binding	Agreement is not a binding contract.	Contract is binding on both the parties.
5.	Width	An agreement is wider than contract. Agreement can be enforceable or not enforceable.	A contract is narrower as it is specie of agreement only.

2.6 ESSENTIAL ELEMENTS OF A VALID CONTRACT

The essential elements of a valid contract can be summed up as under:

(i) **Offer & Acceptance:** An agreement is composed of two elements –offer and acceptance. The party making the offer is known as offeror. The party to whom the offer is made is called the offeree. Thus, essentially, there are two parties to a contract.

(A) Offer May be Specific or General: An offer is said to be 'specific' when it is made to a definite person or persons. When Kiran offers to sell his cycle to Kirti for Rs. 500, the offer is specific. A stranger like Komal cannot accept the offer.

A 'general offer', on the other hand, is made to the whole world, at large or public, in general.

This offer can be accepted by a person who fulfills the requisite conditions. No separate written communication is needed for acceptance. Compliance of the stipulated conditions itself is the acceptance.

Express Offer and Implied Offer: An offer may be expressed or implied from the conduct of the parties. An express offer is made by words, spoken or written. The offer can be through a letter, telegram or fax or even through e-mail.

An implied offer is gathered from the conduct of the parties or circumstances of the case. When a person goes to a doctor, it is implied from the conduct of the person that he would pay the usual charges, once treatment is given.

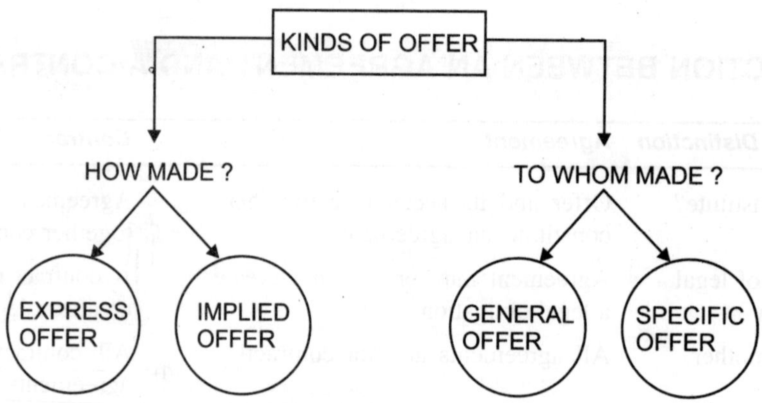

Kinds of Offer
(Diagram No. 5)

Case of Carlill Vs Carbolic Smoke Ball Company: The leading case on the subject of 'general offer' is that of Carlill Vs. Carbolic Smoke Ball Co. (1893), 1 Q B 256.

In the above case, the Carbolic Smoke Ball Company issued an advertisement in which the company offered to pay £ 100 to any person who contracts influenza, after having used their smoke ball three times, daily, for two consecutive weeks, according to the printed directions. Mrs. Carlill, on the faith of the advertisement, bought and used the balls according to the directions. Nevertheless, she subsequently suffered from influenza. She sued the company for the promised reward.

The company was held liable. Here, the offer was a general offer of continuous nature. Any person who complies with the conditions was entitled to claim the compensation.

(B) Offer Must be Communicated to the Offeree: An offer is effective only when it is communicated to the offeree. Doing anything, in ignorance of the offer can never be treated as an acceptance. In the absence of knowledge of the offer, there is no acceptance.

Case of Lalman Shukla Vs Gauri Datt: The defendant's nephew absconded from home. The defendant sent his servant in search of the missing nephew. After the servant left for searching, the defendant announced an award of Rs. 501 to anybody giving information relating to the boy. The servant located the nephew and informed the defendant. At the time of informing, the servant was not aware of the reward. Later, on reading the notice of reward, the servant claimed the award.

Held the servant was not entitled to claim the award. The suit was dismissed on the ground that he could not accept the offer, unless he had knowledge of the offer.

(C) No Confusion on Identity of Subject: There should be no confusion in their thinking about the matter, they are dealing. The terms of acceptance must coincide with the terms of offer. Acceptance has to be communicated to the offeror in the mode prescribed.

Example: Kalyan is having two cars of Maruti brand –Maruti 800 and Alto. While discussing the sale of vehicle with Kishore, Kalyan proposes to sell Maruti, without mentioning further details, and plans to sell Maruti 800 while Kishore thinks that the discussion for sale is about Maruti Alto. Kishore gives his acceptance to buy the same which is on his mind. There is no contract because the contracting parties have not agreed on the same thing. Here, there is no consensus of mind. There must be *consensus-ad-idem.*

Further, it is necessary to distinguish between offer and invitation to offer.

Window display is an invitation to offer, not offer itself.

Another distinction is to be noted between offer and counter offer. When the terms of acceptance are different from the offer, then it is called counter offer. The counter offer has to be accepted by the offeror.

(ii) **Free Consent:** There must be free and genuine consent of the parties. The consent of the parties should not be obtained from misrepresentation, undue influence, mistake, coercion and fraud. In other words, the consent has to be free from these flaws. If the consent is obtained by any of these flaws, then the contract is not valid.

Example: A threatens to kill B unless he enters into an agreement to sell his house. In this case, consent of B has been obtained by coercion. So, it cannot be regarded as free consent.

(iii) **Contractual Capacity:** The parties should be competent to contract. The capacity of the parties is an important element for the validity of the contract. The contracting parties should be

(i) Major in age,

(ii) Sound in mind, and

(iii) Not disqualified from entering into contract by any law to which he is subject to like insolvency or alien status.

A minor is incompetent to enter into contract.

It has to be referred to the age and mental state of the contracting parties, at the time of entering into the contract.

If the disqualification occurs after the formation of the contract, the contracts that have been entered into, before the disqualification, are not affected, in any manner. In other words, the contracts continue to be binding as the important point is the status of the parties, at the time of formation of the contract. The subsequent events do not influence. Similarly, agreement with a person of unsound mind, at the time of creation of the contract, is not enforceable.

An agreement with a minor is void *ab-initio*. The leading case is **Mohiri Bibi Vs Dharmodas Ghosh.**

Facts: D, a minor borrowed money by executing a mortgage of his property. Subsequently, the mortgagee has filed a suit for recovery of the debt and sale of mortgaged property, due to default in payment. Held that the Sections 10 and 11 of the Indian Contract Act make the minor's agreement absolutely void. Therefore, the mortgagee neither could recover the mortgage money nor compel the sale of property for repayment of debt.

(iv) Lawful Consideration: The agreement must be supported by consideration on both sides. Each party to the agreement must give or promise to give something and receive something or promise to receive something, in return. A promise is made in return of a promise.

As a general rule, agreement without consideration is void.

Normally, consideration is expressed, in terms of money. However, consideration need not be in terms of money. Further, consideration need not be adequate too.

Example: Radhi agrees to sell her car to Dheera for Rs.1,00,000. Here, payment of Rs. 1,00,000 is the consideration from the side of Dheera, while delivery of car is the consideration from the side of Radhi.

Alternatively, instead of Rs. 1,00,000 the contract could be entered into Dheera giving her ring to Radhi in exchange of her car. In fact, the cost of ring may be lower than the value of car.

The inadequacy of consideration is immaterial for the validity of the contract.

The court is not concerned with the inadequacy of consideration. What is important, the contract must be supported with consideration. Its adequacy or otherwise is the look out of the parties. The court can hardly assume the role for settling about the right amount of consideration for a promise.

This is the principle followed in the case **Devi Shivaji Vs Karsandas Ramji (1954).** In this case, the transfer of goodwill and the whole of the assets have been made for a mere sum of Rs.1, 000, which has upheld by the court.

Inadequacy of consideration is not a valid ground, but if the consent is obtained by coercion or other vitiating element, the later would be a valid ground to the court to invalidate the agreement.

Example: Suresh agrees to sell the horse worth of Rs. 20,000 for Rs. 10. If Suresh is in sound mind at the time of entering into the contract and there is no coercion and his consent has been freely obtained, the court does not interfere in respect of inadequacy of the consideration.

(v) **Intention to Create Legal Relationship:** Both the parties to the contract should have the intention to create legal relationship. An agreement to attend a dinner party does not create legal relationship. It is only a question of social relationship. There must be common intention of the parties to create legal relation to constitute a legal contract.

Balfour Vs Balfour (1919)2 K.B. 571]: A husband promises to pay 30 pounds, every month, during the period while he is abroad. The husband failed to pay the promised amount and the wife has sued for recovery of the amount. Held that the parties did not intend to create legal relationship.

> **Normally, in commercial and business transactions, an intention to create legal relations is presumed.**

However, this presumption is rebuttable by giving evidence to the contrary. This is possible by showing that the intention of the parties has not been to create legal obligations. Even a business agreement does not amount to a contract, if the parties have specifically resolved that the agreement does not create legal obligations. This was held in the case **Rose & Frank Co. Vs Crompton & Brothers Ltd. (1923), 2 K.B.261.**

(vi) **Lawful Object and not Illegal:** The object of the agreement must be lawful. The agreement should not be for illegal purpose or illegal.

Example: After the Government has banned lottery, a lottery has been floated. As the object is illegal and not approved by the Government, the agreement is illegal and cannot be enforced.

The object of agreement must be lawful, otherwise the agreement is void. Any act forbidden by the law is unlawful.

Example: Sharma, a married person, has entered into a marriage agreement with his tenant, an unmarried girl. This agreement is void as the second marriage is forbidden by law.

> **Even voluntary payment of dowry is unlawful as it would defeat the provisions of law.**

Legal Formalities: Oral contract is a valid contract. No particular form of writing is necessary to constitute a contract. Intentions of the parties to enter into a contract and give effect to it only are required. If, however, certain acts, under law, may require that the contract has to be in writing, it must comply with the necessary formalities as to writing, registration and attestation.

For example, under Indian Registration Act, 1908 registration is compulsory for gifts and mortgages. In such a case, unless they are registered, the agreements are not valid contracts.

(vii) Certainty of Terms: The terms of a contract should be clear. In other words, the contract must not be vague. Contracts which are vague cannot be enforced. If any of the parties proves that there is ambiguity in material terms of the contract, the contract can be avoided.

(viii) Enforceable by Law: In order to be a valid contract, the agreement must be enforceable. This element of enforceability only distinguishes between agreement and contract. If it is enforceable, it is a contract otherwise, it is only an agreement. The aggrieved party should be able to obtain relief through law, in the event of breach of contract.

(ix) Possibility of Performance: The terms of the agreement must be capable of performance. According to Section 56, "An agreement to do an impossible act is void."

Example: Ram and Krishna enter into an agreement whereby Ram agrees to produce treasure by magic for which Krishna promises to give Rs. 10,000. This agreement is void because it is an agreement to do an impossible act.

(x) Agreement not Expressly Declared Void: The agreement must not have been expressly declared void under the Indian Contract Act. Under the provisions, agreement in restraint of marriage, agreement in restraint of legal proceedings and agreement in restraint of trade are void.

Example: A promises to marry none else except B and in default agrees to pay Rs. 10 lakhs. A marries Z, without the consent of B. B sues A for the amount. It was held that B was not entitled to recover the amount as this agreement was in restraint of marriage and as such void.

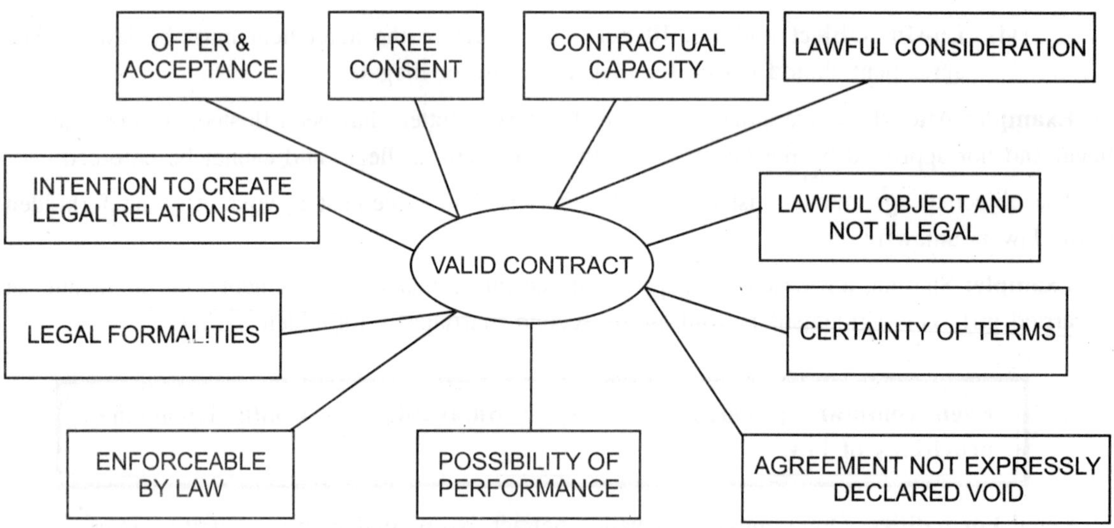

Essential Elements of a Valid Contract
(Diagram No.6)

2.7 ALL ESSENTIAL ELEMENTS NECESSARY TO FORM A CONTRACT

Section 10 of Contract Act lays down that all agreements are contracts, provided the above conditions or elements are complied with.

The above elements must exist together. If only certain elements exist and other elements do not exist, then it is not a valid contract. In such circumstances, the agreement is not enforceable. In other words, when any element is missing, it ceases to be a contract though it may be a valid agreement.

Check Your Understanding

State whether the following statements are True or False

1. In commercial and business agreements, the presumption is that the parties intend to create legal obligations.
2. All agreements are contracts.
3. An agreement, not supported by enforceability, is not a valid contract.
4. Law of contract is the whole law of agreements.
5. All contracts have to be in writing to become binding on both the parties.
6. A gift deed has to be in writing to become an enforceable contract.
7. Law of contract is not the whole law of obligations.
8. Contract between two minors is a valid contract as both the parties stand on the same footing.
9. All contracts are agreements.
10. At the time of entering into the contract, the contracting party has been in sound health, but later has become mentally unsound so it is a ground for the invalidity of the contract.
11. In social agreements, the usual presumption is that the parties intend to create legal obligations.
12. Adequacy of consideration is necessary to be a contract.
13. In business agreements, the usual presumption is that the parties do not intend to create legal obligations.
14. Contract and agreement mean the same.
15. All kinds of obligations between the parties form part of the contracts.
16. A proposal when accepted becomes a contract.
17. An agreement with intention to create legal liability is not enforceable under law.
18. A person who is usually of unsound mind but casually of sound mind can always enter into a valid contract.
19. An agreement entered into by a minor cannot be enforced by law.
20. No consideration, no contract.
21. If the unsound mind occurs after the formation of the contracts, the contracts that have been entered into, before the disqualification- unsound mind, are not binding, in any manner.

22. Contract can be inferred from the conduct of the parties too.
23. Inadequacy of consideration is a valid ground for making the contract void.
24. Acceptance of offer need not always be in writing, can also be in compliance of the stipulated conditions of the offer made.
25. If there is no legal obligation, there is no contract.
26. Company law governs the formation and performance of contracts.
27. All contracts are agreements but all agreements need not be contracts.
28. There is no difference between general offer and special offer.
29. Awareness of offer is not a primary requirement for a valid acceptance.
30. For formation of contract, consideration has to be necessarily in money.
31. Dowry provided, voluntarily, by the father of a divorced daughter is not unlawful.
32. Inadequacy of consideration is not a valid ground, but if the consent is obtained by coercion or other vitiating element, the later would be a valid ground to the court to invalidate the agreement.
33. An unenforceable contract can be enforced, if the technical defect is removed.

Answers:

1. True	2. False	3. True	4. False	5. False
6. True	7. True	8. False	9. True	10. False
11. False	12. False	13. False	14. False	15. False
16. True	17. False	18. False	19. True	20. True
21. False	22. True	23. False	24. True	25. True
26. False	27. True	28. False	29. False	30. False
31. False (dowry is against the law)			32. True	33. True

Discuss Legal Implications

Question 1: A patient medicine company advertised that it would give a reward to anyone who is contracted by influenza after using the medicine for a certain period, according to the printed conditions. A patient used and not finding the advertised relief, sued the medicine company. The company has refused to pay on two grounds. The first ground is that the offer has not been made to her. The second ground is that patient has not communicated its acceptance, separately, to the company. Discuss the stand and liability of the company. **(B.U. 2007)**

Answer: The facts of the case are similar to the case of **Carlill Vs Carbolic Smoke Ball Co. (1813) 1 Q.B. 256.** In that case, the company has advertised that it would give a reward of 100 pounds to anyone who contracts influenza, in spite of using the smoke ball of the company, according to the printed instructions on the product. The company has raised the same objections that the offer has not been made to the patient and the patient has not communicated the acceptance, separately, to the company.

Held that the patient could recover the award as she has accepted the offer by complying with conditions of offer. This is not a specific offer, but a case of general offer. It is sufficient for the offeree to comply with the conditions, stated in the general offer made. It is not necessary for the offeree to be known to the offeror, when the offer is made. The aggrieved may be a stranger, but by complying with the conditions of the offer, he or she is deemed to have accepted the offer.

Question 2: Ramesh promises his wife to bring a beautiful sari if she sings a song. The wife obliges and sings a song. But, Ramesh refuses to buy the sari for her. His wife Ruchi wants to sue her husband for his failure. Decide.

Answer: Ruchi, wife of Ramesh cannot bring legal action against her husband Ramesh for failure of performance. The agreement lacks the intention to create legal relationship. In the family relationship of husband and wife, there is no legal relationship.

Question 3: Srinivas agrees to pay Rs. 1,000 to Mahesh if the later brings God before him. Mahesh agrees to pay the same amount, in the event of his failure. This agreement is executed on a stamped paper, with two witnesses. Mahesh has failed to perform. Srinivas plans to go to a court of law for recovering the amount, executed on a stamped paper. Decide.

Answer: The agreement between Srinivas and Mahesh is not a valid contract. It is a void agreement as per Section 56 of Indian Contract Act, 1872 as "An agreement to do an impossible act in itself is void." The agreement is void from the beginning as bringing God in physical form is an impossible act.

Question 4: Discuss formation of contract in the following cases:

(A) When taxi is called on phone.

(B) When one rupee coin is inserted in the slot of a weighing machine.

(C) When you board a public bus.

(D) When you dine in a hotel.

(E) When you invite your girl friend for dinner and she does not turn up, after accepting the invitation.

Answer: Contract is formed in all cases: A to D. An offer and acceptance is made either by words or conduct which results in agreement and the agreement is binding on both the parties for performance.

No contract is formed in case of E. Here, the matter relates to social arrangement and the parties involved have not contemplated on any legal relationship, at the time of entering into the contract.

Question 5: In a public meeting, Akhilesh announces a donation of rupees one lakh for the repairs of a temple. After a month, the trustees of the temple approached him for payment of donation. Akhilesh refuses to pay any amount of donation. Decide if the trustees

(i) plan to make repairs, after collecting all the assured donations.

(ii) have initiated repair works, based on the announcement of Akhilesh as his donation is the biggest amount and he has been in the habit of paying donations, frequently.

Answer: In the first case, the trustees cannot recover the donation amount from Akhilesh.

Reason: The agreement is void, in the absence of consideration.

In the second case, the trustees can recover the promised amount.

Reason: There is consideration in the form of detriment to the trustees as they have incurred liability on the faith of the promise made by the person.

Question 6: Vasu has sold his brand new Maruti 800 car, worth more than Rs. 2 lakhs, for Rs. 100 to Kumari. After the sale, Vasu contends in a court of law that the consideration is grossly inadequate and has been forced by Kumari to sign the transfer of papers for registration, while he is drunk. Decide the validity of the agreement.

Answer: Mere inadequacy of consideration is not a valid ground for the invalidation of the agreement. Court is not concerned to settle what the adequacy of consideration for every promise is. It is the look out of the parties to decide the amount of consideration. Every agreement has to be supported by consideration and the quantum of amount is immaterial for the validity of the contract. Inadequacy of consideration is not a valid ground.

However, if the contention of drinking at the time of entering into the contract and he has not been in a position to exercise thinking power and on that ground of coercion- a vitiating element for formation of contract- the agreement can be set aside by the court.

Pick up the Right Answer

1. For formation of contract:
   (a) There must be an agreement.
   (b) Agreement should be enforceable by law.
   (c) None of the above.
   (d) All the above.

2. An offer cannot be accepted unless and until it has been brought to the knowledge of the person to whom made, was decided in the case of:
   (a) Lalman Shukla Vs. Gauri Datt.
   (b) Carlill Vs. Carbolic Smoke Ball Company.
   (c) Soloman Vs. Soloman.
   (d) Mohiri Bibi Vs. Dharmodas Ghosh.

3. An agreement requires
   (a) offer
   (b) acceptance
   (c) offer and acceptance
   (d) consideration

4. An agreement becomes a contract if it has
   (a) offer
   (b) acceptance
   (c) offer and acceptance
   (d) enforceability

5. The term 'Agreement' is ....than the term 'Contract'.
   (a) narrower
   (b) wider
   (c) scope is equal
   (d) The term 'Contract' is wider than 'Agreement'.

6. In the formation of contract, consideration should
   (a) exist
   (b) be adequate
   (c) be sufficient to the value of the goods exchanged
   (d) not an important element

7. This is not an essential element of a valid contract.
   (a) offer
   (b) acceptance
   (c) consideration
   (d) materiality

8. If the consent is obtained with the following quality, then only a valid contract is formed.
   (a) fraud
   (b) free from vitiating elements
   (c) undue influence
   (d) mistake

9. This is not a kind of offer
   (a) express offer
   (b) implied offer
   (c) silent offer
   (d) none of the above

10. This is not a proper acceptance to form an agreement
    (a) acceptance in writing
    (b) acceptance in oral form

(c) fulfilling all the requisite conditions of offer

(d) no communication

11. The objective of agreement has to be for
 (a) illegal purpose
 (b) legal purpose
 (c) immoral purpose
 (d) achieving anything
12. An usual presumption in business under the Contract Act, while entering into a contract, is the parties want to create the following relationship:
 (a) business relationship
 (b) legal relationship
 (c) friendship
 (d) matrimonial relationship
13. The law of contracts is the whole law of obligations.
 (a) True
 (b) False
 (c) Can be true or false
 (d) none
14. Under the Contract Act, obligation means
 (a) legal obligation
 (b) social obligation
 (c) religious obligation
 (d) friendly obligation
15. The person to whom the offer is made is called
 (a) offeree
 (b) offeror
 (c) acceptance
 (d) contract
16. Total number of persons involved in a contract is
 (a) one
 (b) two
 (c) three
 (d) four

17. The contract is not valid if entered with
    (a) major in age
    (b) an insolvent
    (c) a person, sound in mind
    (d) a person, not disqualified from entering into contract by any law
18. Contract is invalid if the disqualification, in respect of contractual capacity, occurs
    (a) after formation of contract
    (b) at the time of formation of contract
    (c) at any time
    (d) contract is not affected
19. The following law governs the formation and performance of contracts.
    (a) Company law
    (b) Indian Contract Act
    (c) Mercantile law
    (d) Negotiable Instruments Act
20. Window display is a/an
    (a) offer
    (b) acceptance
    (c) invitation to offer
    (d) contract
21. 'An agreement with the minor is void' was held in the following case:
    (a) Lalman Shukla Vs. Gauri Datt
    (b) Carlill Vs. Carbolic Smoke Ball Company
    (c) Soloman Vs. Soloman
    (d) Mohiri Bibi Vs. Dharmodas Ghosh

Answers:

1. (d)	2. (a)	3. (c)	4. (d)	5. (b)
6. (a)	7. (d)	8. (b)	9. (c)	10. (d)
11. (b)	12. (b)	13. (b)	14. (a)	15. (a)
16. (b)	17. (b)	18. (b)	19. (b)	20. (c)
21. (d)				

Descriptive Questions

1. Define contract. When an agreement becomes a contract. **(2.3)**
2. Define the terms "Agreement" and "Contract" and bring out their distinction. **(2.3 and 2.5)**
3. "All contracts are agreements but all contracts need not be contracts." –Discuss. **(2.3 and 2.4.1)**
4. "The law of contracts is neither the whole law of agreements, nor the whole law of obligations." –Discuss. **(2.3, 2.4.1 and 2.4.2)**
5. "The law of contracts is not the whole law of obligations." –Discuss. **(2.3 and 2.4.2)**
6. Define the essential elements of a valid contract. **(2.6 and 2.7)**
7. If some elements are missing, it is only an agreement, not a contract. –Discuss. **(2.6 and 2.7)**

3

CLASSIFICATION OF CONTRACTS

- Introduction
- Contracts on the Basis of Formation
  - Express Contract
  - Implied Contract
  - Contracts of Mixed Character
  - Quasi Contract
- Contracts on the Basis of Performance or Execution
  - Executed Contract
  - Executory Contract
  - Partly Executed and Partly Executory Contract
- Contracts on the Basis of Validity or Enforceability
  - Valid Contract
  - Voidable Contract
  - Void Agreement
  - Void Contract
  - Illegal or unlawful Contract, and
  - Unenforceable Contract
- Distinction between Void Agreement and Voidable Contract
- Agreements Declared Void by Law
- Check Your Understanding
- Discuss Legal Implications
- Pick up the Right Answer
- Descriptive Questions

3.1 INTRODUCTION

There are different kinds of contracts. Contracts may be classified in terms of their mode of formation, performance or execution and validity of enforceability.

3.2 CONTRACTS ON THE BASIS OF FORMATION

On the basis of formation or creation, the contracts may be classified as under:

(A) Express Contract: Express contract is one which is made by words spoken or written. In this type of contract, the concerned parties have made an oral or written declaration of their intention to enter into a contract.

Example: Over telephone, Suresh offers to sell his scooter to Srinivas, description and condition of vehicle are known, for Rs. 10, 000 and in the conversation Srinivas accepts his proposal and agrees to pay the amount on the next date. This is an express contract as the offer is followed by acceptance, turning into contract.

(B) Implied Contract: An implied contract is one in which the evidence of the agreement is not shown by words, spoken or written, but by acts and conduct of the parties concerned. The contract is inferred from the conduct or circumstances of the particular case.

Example: A porter, in uniform, takes up the luggage and the passenger mentions the name of the train to which the luggage is to be boarded. Here, the law implies that the passenger agrees to pay for the services of the porter. An implied contract has been formed and the passenger has to pay the charges to the porter for the luggage, carried by him.

A professional shoe shiner starts to polish the shoes of the passenger, removing the shoes of the passenger and he allows him for polishing. The passenger cannot refuse to pay the charges for shining, taking the plea that the shoe shiner did not ask for his specific consent. His consent is his behaviour and an implied contract has been formed.

(C) Contracts of Mixed Character: A mixed character contract is a mixture of 'express' and 'implied' contracts. There are two components of an agreement, namely offer and acceptance. One of the components is expressed in words and the other is implied from the acts and circumstances. Such contracts may be called as 'contracts of mixed character'.

Example: Sandhya, a readymade garment designer and dealer phones about the new gagra dresses she has designed for sale to the cinema actress Rani and sends them, price tags showing their respective prices. The actress chooses two dresses and sends the amount in cash towards the price of two dresses. Here, a contract of mixed character has been formed with the phone call as offer (spoken words) and acceptance in the form of conduct (remittance of money towards the price of dresses).

(D) Quasi Contracts: It is not a contract in the strictest legal sense. But it resembles a contract. Such a contract does not arise by virtue of any agreement, express or implied between the parties. The law infers or recognizes a contract under special circumstances. The law imposes certain peculiar obligations on a person in some circumstances.

Such obligations are:

(i) Claim for necessaries supplied: Minors and lunatics are not capable of entering into contracts. If a person has supplied necessaries, suited to the conditions in life of such persons, the person who has supplied is entitled for reimbursement from the property of such incapable person.

(ii) Finder of lost goods: For example, when Renu finds some goods belonging to the other person, Apeksha, a duty is cast on Renu to restore the goods to the rightful owner as she has taken possession of the goods. If Renu does not take possession of other's goods, no duty or responsibility is imposed on her. Renu cannot retain other's goods with her and the law recognizes an obligation on her part as a contract.

(iii) Obligation of person enjoying benefit of a non-gratuitous act: Radhi, a garment dealer, leaves her garments, meant for sale with Rani for two days. Rani takes some of the garments for her personal consumption. Rani is bound to pay the cost of the garments taken by her.

(iv) Person paying money owed by another: Suresh is bound to make payment to Vasu. His well wisher Bobji is interested in such payment and pays the amount. There is a quasi contractual obligation on the part of Suresh to reimburse the amount to Bobji.

(v) Payment by mistake: A and B jointly owe Rs. 10,000 to Z. A repays the total amount to Z. B is not aware of the repayment by A. So, B again pays the amount to Z and Z coolly takes the amount, again. Here, Z has a duty to pay back the amount, paid twice, by mistake. It is immaterial whether the payment is made by mistake of fact or law.

In all the above case, the person who has received the benefit has an obligation to compensate the person paying the benefit. Law recognizes this obligation as a contract though there is no explicit or agreed agreement between giver and receiver of the benefit.

> **The rationale behind quasi contract is the principle that the law as well as justice does not allow any person to take undue advantage, at the cost of another, and is meant to prevent "unjust enrichment."**

3.3 CONTRACTS ON THE BASIS OF PERFORMANCE OR EXECUTION

From the view point of the extent of execution, a contract may be classified as under:

(A) Executed Contract: A contract is said to be executed contract, when both the parties have fulfilled their respective obligations under the contract. In this type of contract, both the parties have completely performed their share of obligations and nothing remains to be done by either party of the contract.

Example: X contracts to buy a bicycle for from Z for cash Rs. 10,000. X has paid cash and Z has delivered bicycle to the former. Here, both the parties have performed their respective obligations and nothing remains to be done, further.

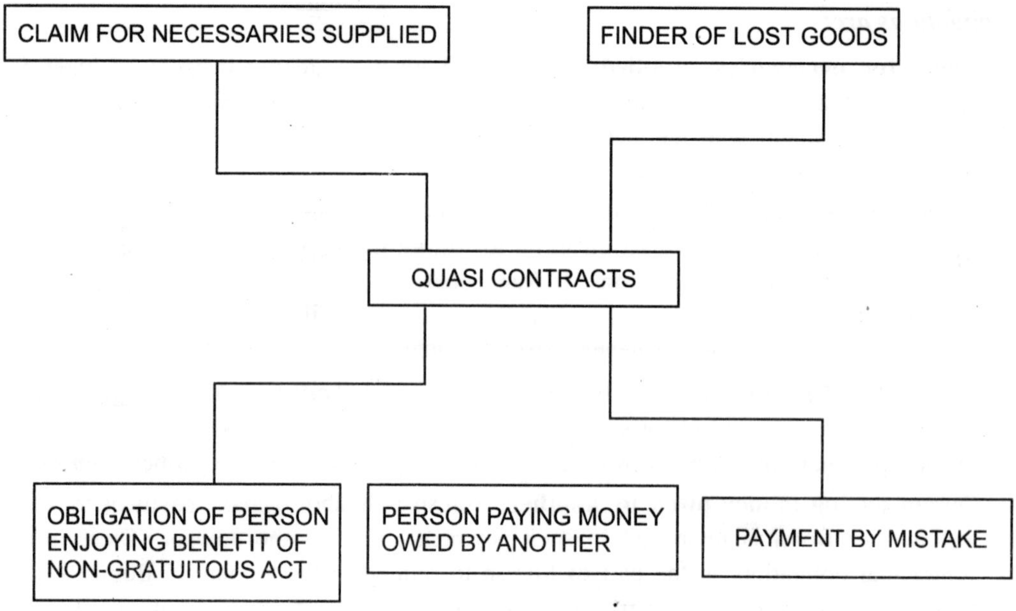

Types of Quasi Contracts
(Diagram No.7)

(B) Executory Contract: It is a contract where both the parties to the contract are still to perform their respective obligations.

Example: Sameer offers to sell his car for Rs. 30,000 to Sumeet and the offer has been accepted by the later. Neither Sameer has delivered the car nor did Sumeet pay the price to Sameer. Here, both the parties are to perform their respective obligations.

(C) Partly Executed and Partly Executory Contract: It is a contract where one of the parties has fulfilled his obligations and the other party is yet to perform the obligation on his part.

Example: In the above example, Sameer has delivered the car to Sumeet while Sumeet is yet to pay the price though he has taken delivery of the vehicle and even using the same. Here, Sameer has fulfilled the obligation on his part while Sumeet is yet to fulfill the obligation. Alternatively, Sumeet has paid the price while Sameer has not yet delivered the car to him.

3.4 CONTRACTS ON THE BASIS OF VALIDITY OR ENFORCEABILITY

On the basis of validity, the contracts may be classified as under:

(i) Valid contract
(ii) Voidable contract
(iii) Void agreement
(iv) Void contract
(v) Illegal or unlawful contract, and
(vi) Unenforceable contract

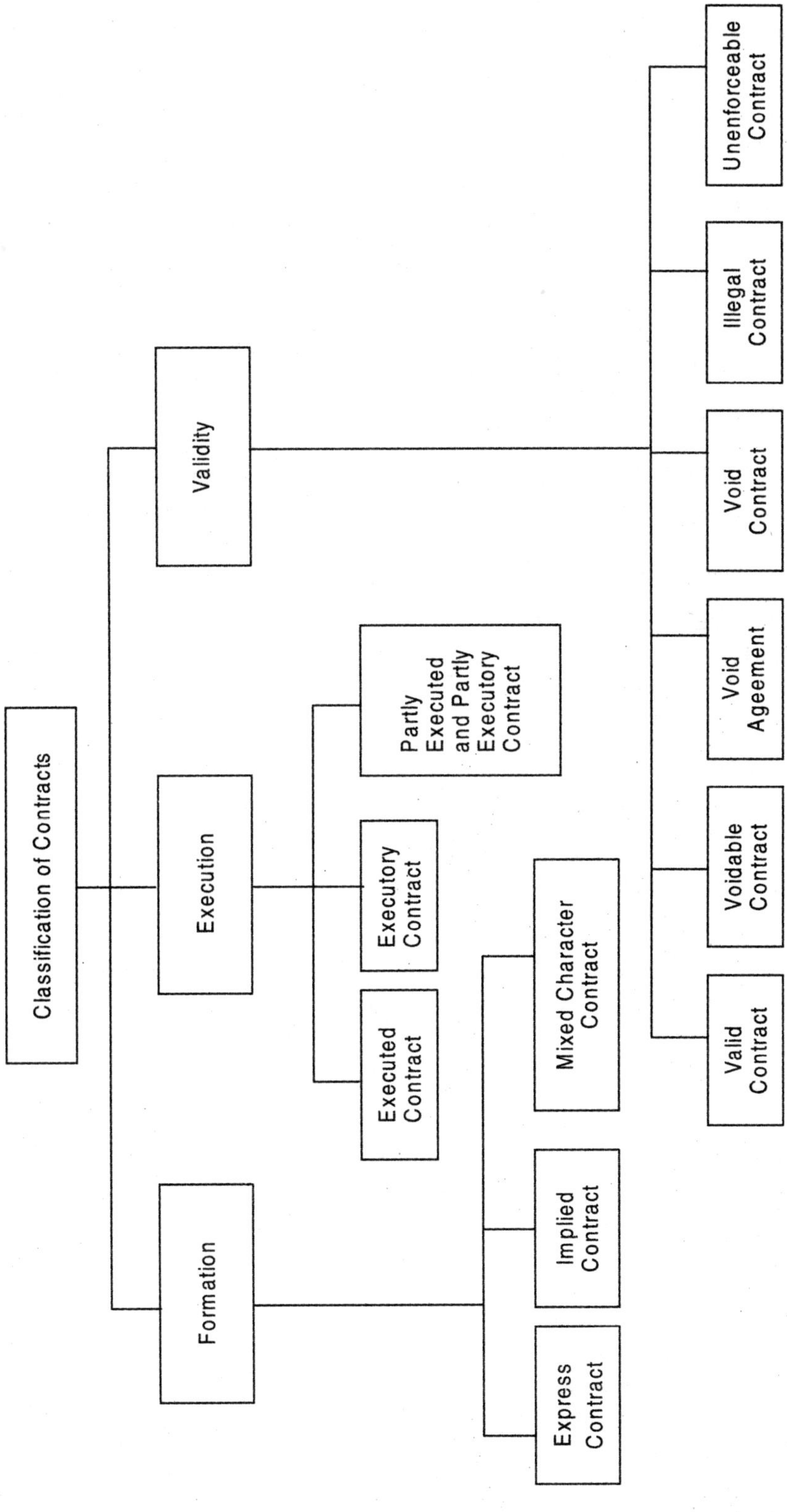

Classification of Contracts (Diagram No.8)

(i) **Valid contract:** A contract which satisfies all the essential elements prescribed by law is a valid contract. It is an agreement which is binding and enforceable. The essential elements for the formation of a valid contract have been spelt out already in the earlier chapter.

Example: X makes an offer to sell his house for 10 lakhs to Y and Y accepts the offer. Both X and Y set out agreement, spelling all the conditions of sale, including the remedies available to both the parties, in case of non-performance by either party. This is a valid and binding contract between both the parties.

(ii) **Voidable contract:** According to Section 2 (i) of the Indian Contract Act, 1872, an agreement which is enforceable at the option of one or more of the parties to the contract, but not at the option of the other or others, is a voidable contract. In other words, "A voidable contract is one which can be set aside or repudiated or avoided at the option of the aggrieved party."

Until the contract is repudiated or set aside by the aggrieved party, it remains a valid contract.

The contract is binding till it is repudiated. For example, a contract is treated as voidable at the option of the party whose consent has been obtained by coercion or undue influence or fraud or misrepresentation.

The presence of the flaw (coercion, undue influence, fraud and misrepresentation) has affected the validity of the contract. This defect enables the aggrieved party to take steps to repudiate the contract. The important point is till the steps are taken by the aggrieved, the contract is binding. The aggrieved party must exercise the option of rejecting the contract

(A) within a reasonable time, and

(B) before the rights of third parties intervene

In case, the aggrieved party does not choose to repudiate, the contract becomes binding and enforceable.

Restoration of benefit in case of voidable contracts: The aggrieved party has a right to reject the contract, within a reasonable period, as stated above. He also has an obligation to restore any benefit received under the contract. In other words, he cannot rescind the contract and retain the benefit.

Example: X threatens to shoot his father-in-law if he does not sell his new Ikon car for Rs. 50,000 to him. X pays an advance of Rs. 10,000 towards the sale and obtains receipt for the amount paid. His father-in-law signs the sale agreement.

The contract has been executed through coercion. So, the contract is voidable at the option of the father-in-law. The party rescinding the contract must restore the benefit received by him under the contract. In case, father-in-law chooses to avoid the contract, he is free to do so, within a reasonable time. In case of his repudiation, he has to refund the amount Rs. 10, 000 to his son-in-law. It is not possible to retain the amount and repudiate the contract.

(iii) **Void agreement: According to Section 2 (g), "An agreement not enforceable by law is said to be void."** Such agreements are *void-ab-initio.* This means that the agreements are unenforceable from the beginning, the time they are made. In other words, in the eyes of law, such an agreement is not agreement, at all, from its very inception.

Example: An agreement with a minor or a person of unsound mind is *void-ab-initio* as a minor or person of unsound mind is incompetent to contract.

It is important to understand the difference between an unlawful (illegal) agreement and void agreement. An unlawful agreement is one which is forbidden by law. An agreement to give dowry, at the time of marriage, is unlawful. This type of agreement is against the law. On the other hand, a void agreement although not forbidden, is unenforceable. For example, an agreement with minor is unenforceable, though not forbidden. Thus an illegal agreement must be necessarily void but a void agreement need not be illegal.

Every individual enjoys the freedom to marry.

> **According to Section 26 of the Contract Act, "every contract in restraint of marriage of any person, other than a minor, is void."**

An agreement agreeing not to marry at all, or a particular person, or a class of persons or for a fixed period is void. **It is interesting to note that a promise to marry a particular person does not imply restraint of marriage. So, it is a valid contract.**

Example: Dheera agrees with Kishore that she will marry him only. It is a valid contract of marriage.

Example: Chandra promises Rahul for a consideration that she will not marry Mahesh. It is a void agreement.

(iv) **Void contract:** A void contract should be distinguished from a void agreement. An agreement not enforceable at law is a void agreement. Agreement with a minor is void as the minor is not competent to enter into a contract. A void agreement never amounts to a void contract as the former is void from the beginning.

> **A void contract is valid when it is entered into, but subsequent to its formation, something happens which makes it unenforceable by law.**

It is important to note that a contract cannot be void *abinitio* and only an agreement can be void *abinitio.*

An example explains the difference between the two, better.

Example: Surekha and Sudhir contract to marry each other. Before the fixed time for marriage, Surekha becomes mad. The contract becomes void.

Example: Suresh promises to take Vasu to Pakistan on a fixed date. Before the promised date, war has been declared against Pakistan. The contract becomes void, when the war is declared.

In both the examples, the contract is valid at the time of formation. The impossibility of performance has happened after the formation of the contract. The contracts have become void afterwards, by the subsequent happenings.

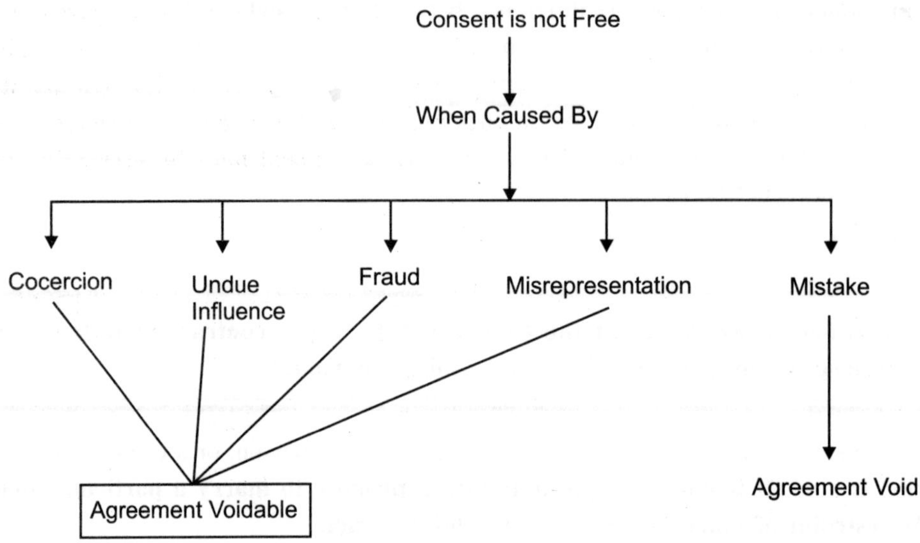

Void & Voidable Agreement
(Diagram No.9)

Obligation of person who has received advantage under void agreement or contract that becomes void:

Section 65 of the Contract Act lays down that when an agreement is discovered to be void or when a contract becomes void, any person who has received any advantage under such agreement or contract is bound to restore it or make compensation for it, to the person from whom the benefit has been received.

Example: Ram enters into a contract with Rahim for purchase of his horse for Rs. 10,000 and pays an advance of Rs. 5,000. It turns out that the horse has been dead, before the date of the contract and the fact is not known to both the parties. The agreement is void, due to impossibility of performance. Rahim has to refund the advance received from Ram. Rahim cannot retain the benefit of advance. In this case, no contract ever existed at all.

Let us discuss another situation. On the date of entering into the contract, the horse is alive. But before the scheduled date of delivery, the horse dies. Here too, the contract is void, due to impossibility of performance. The contract is valid as the horse is alive on the date of formation of the contract. But, later, with the death of the horse, the contract has become void.

(v) **Illegal or unlawful contract:** The word 'illegal' means contrary to law. The term contract means 'an agreement enforceable by law'. Illegal contract gives a contradictory meaning something like 'an agreement enforceable by law, contrary to law'. Thus, it is proper to say illegal agreement, rather than illegal contract. An illegal agreement is void *abinitio.*

An agreement is illegal and void if the object or consideration is forbidden by law. Even if permitted, it would defeat the provisions of law or the court regards it as immoral or opposed to public policy. Thus, an agreement to commit murder or assault and robbery or a gift in consideration of illicit intercourse is illegal and void *abinitio.*

Example: X and Y enter into an agreement whereby X promises to pay Rs. 1,00,000 if Y kills Z. X gives an advance of Rs. 10, 000 to Y for the proposed murder. Y kills Z and claims the balance amount. Can Y recover the balance from X?

Y fails to kill Z and so X wants to recover the advance paid from X. Is recovery of amount possible?

Y cannot recover the balance amount from X.

Equally, X cannot get back the advance paid. The reason is, in both the cases, the agreement between X and Y is illegal as the object is unlawful.

Public Policy: Public Policy is a principle of law. It is not possible to give a precise or exact definition of the term 'Public Policy'. An agreement is unlawful if the court regards it as opposed to public policy. According to this principle, no citizen can lawfully do which is injurious to the public or is against the interests of the society or state.

Example: A promises B to drop the prosecution charges for the robbery in his house and B assures to restore the goods stolen.

Here, the agreement is void.

(vi) **Unenforceable contract:** It is a contract which is actually valid but cannot be enforced due to some technical defect. The defect may be that the agreement is not in writing or not stamped or under stamped.

Example: An oral arbitration agreement is not enforceable as arbitration agreement has to be in writing. If the oral arbitration agreement is reduced to writing, it becomes enforceable.

3.5 AGREEMENTS DECLARED VOID BY LAW

All the agreements which are or declared by the Contract Act to be void are summed up here for the convenience of the reader.

1. Contracts by a minor or a person of unsound mind. (Sec. 11).
2. Contract made under a mistake of fact material to the agreement on the part of both the parties. (Sec. 20).
3. An agreement of which the consideration or object is unlawful. (Sec. 23).

4. If any part of a single consideration for one or more objects, or one or more considerations for a single object, is unlawful, the agreement is void. (Sec. 24).
5. An agreement made without consideration (Subject to certain exceptions). (Sec. 25).
6. An agreement in restraint of marriage. (Sec. 26).
7. An agreement in restraint of trade. (Sec. 27).
8. An agreement in restraint of legal proceedings. (Sec. 28).
9. Agreements, the meaning of which is not certain, or capable of being made certain. (Sec. 29).
10. Agreements by way of wager. (Sec. 30).
11. An agreement to enter into an agreement in the future.
12. An agreement to do an act impossible in itself. [Sec.56(1)

3.6 DISTINCTION BETWEEN VOID AGREEMENT AND VOIDABLE CONTRACT: VOID AGREEMENT DIFFERS FROM VOIDABLE CONTRACT IN THE FOLLOWING RESPECTS

Basis of Distinction	*Void Agreement*	*Voidable Contract*
1. Void ***abinitio***	It is void from the very beginning.	It is valid when it is made. It continues to be valid till it is repudiated by the aggrieved party.
2. Which essential element is missing?	Essential elements (other than free consent) of valid contracts are missing.	Voidable as the free consent is missing.
3. Enforceability	No party can enforce the agreement.	It continues to be enforceable, if the aggrieved party does not repudiate.
4. Right of Third Party	Third party does not acquire any right.	A third party who purchases goods, in good faith, and for consideration acquires good title, if the purchase is made before repudiation of the contract.
5. Effect of lapse of reasonable time	Even after the expiry of reasonable time, it can never become a valid contract.	On the expiry of reasonable time, it may become a valid contract, if the aggrieved party does not repudiate.
6. Damages	Question of damages does not arise.	The aggrieved party can claim damages.

Check Your Understanding

State whether the following Statements are True or False

1. Express contract is one which is made by words spoken or written.
2. Implied contract is made by words spoken only.
3. The implied contract is inferred from the conduct of the parties.
4. A mixed character contract is a mixture of 'express' and 'implied' contracts.
5. Express contract is made by words in writing only.
6. A contract is said to be executed contract when both the parties have fulfilled their respective obligations under the contract.
7. There is no difference between executory contract and executed contract.
8. In executory contract, only one of the parties is still to perform his obligation.
9. A voidable contract is binding till the contract is repudiated by the aggrieved party.
10. In a voidable contract, both the parties to the contract have a right to rescind, at their choice.
11. A void contract is valid when it is entered into, but subsequent to its formation, something happens which makes it unenforceable by law.
12. A contract can be void *ab-initio.*
13. A void agreement never amounts to a void contract as it is void from the beginning.
14. An agreement in restraint of marriage is void.
15. In an unenforceable contract, the contract can be enforced by the parties after the technical defect is removed.
16. A voidable contract continues to be enforceable, if the aggrieved party does not repudiate.
17. In a void agreement, third party can acquire right, before the aggrieved party repudiates the contract.
18. A voidable contract is not enforceable at law.
19. A contract is not void from its inception.
20. A contract is usually treated as voidable when the consent of a party has not been free.
21. There is no difference between an unlawful (illegal) agreement and void agreement.
22. An unlawful agreement is one which is forbidden by law.
23. The rationale behind quasi contract is the principle that the law as well as justice does not allow any person to take undue advantage, at the cost of another, and is meant to prevent "unjust enrichment."
24. Finder of lost of goods has no obligation.

Answers:

1. True	2. False	3. True	4. True	5. False
6. True	7. False	8. False	9. True	10. False

11. True	12. False	13. True	14. True	15. True
16. True	17. False	18. False	19. True	20. True
21. False	22. True	23. True	24. False	

Discuss Legal Implications

1. **Question:** Ram has given a loan to his friend Samboo to celebrate his minor daughter's marriage. At the time of giving the loan, Samboo is aware of the fact of her minority as Ram has told him that he wants her to get married before she attains majority. Can Ram recover the loan from his friend Samboo?

   Answer: Ram cannot recover the loan amount from his friend Samboo as the agreement is void as its object is unlawful (i.e. minor's marriage is in contravention of the Child Marriage Restraint Act). **Leading case: C. Srinivas Vs K. Raja Ram Mohan.**

2. **Question:** Krishna and Kishore are the rival traders in Bhopal and are engaged in trade in T.T. Nagar and their shops are located opposite to each other. Krishna's business has become dull, due to keen competition and drastic reduction of prices by Kishore. Krishna enters into an agreement with Kishore. As per the agreement, Kishore has to close his business, permanently and Krishna would pay him Rs. Five lakhs. Kishore closes the business, as per the agreement. Later, Krishna refuses to pay the amount to Kishore. Can Kishore recover the amount from him?

   Answer: No. The agreement between Krishna and Kishore is void as agreement in restraint of trade is void under Section 27 of Indian Contract Act, 1872.

3. **Question:** A lets out his house to a prostitute, knowing that it would be used for immoral purposes. The prostitute has not paid the agreed rent. Can the landlord A sue her for the rent that has not been paid?

   Answer: No. The landlord cannot recover the rent as the agreement is void. The reason is the object of the agreement is immoral. **Leading case: Pearce Vs Brooks.**

4. **Question:** Raman has promised to marry Reeta only and pay a sum of Rs. One lakh if he marries some one else. Examine the validity of the agreement entered into between Raman and Reeta.

   Answer: The agreement is void. Agreement in restraint of marriage, other than a minor, is void and therefore unenforceable. So, the agreement between Raman and Reeta is void. The leading case in this context is **Lowe Vs Peers (1768)**.

Pick up the Right Answer

1. An agreement is voidable at the option of the parties:
   (a) When agreement is without consideration.
   (b) When agreement is in restraint of trade.
   (c) Agreement is in restraint of legal proceeding.
   (d) When consent is caused by undue influence.

Answer:

1. (d)

Descriptive Questions

1. Distinguish between the following:
   (A) Implied contract and Express contract **(3.2)**
   (B) Executory contract and Executed contract **(3.3)**
   (C) Void contract and voidable contract **(3.4)**
2. Explain the different types of contracts on the basis of formation, with suitable examples. **(3.2)**
3. Explain the classification of contracts, in terms of creation, execution and enforceability. **(3.2, 3.3 and 3.4)**
4. Detail the agreements, which are declared void by law. **(3.5)**
5. Bring out the distinction between void agreement and voidable contract. **(3.6)**

4

PERFORMANCE OF CONTRACTS

- ❖ Introduction
- ❖ Meaning – Performance of Contract
- ❖ Types of Performance and Effect on Relationship
  - Actual Performance
  - Attempted Performance or Tender
- ❖ Essentials of Valid Tender of Performance
- ❖ Persons who can demand Performance
- ❖ Who has to Perform
- ❖ Rules for Appropriation of Payments by Debtor
  - Appropriation by Debtor
  - Appropriation by Creditor
  - Appropriation by Law
- ❖ Contracts which need not be Performed
- ❖ Check Your Understanding
- ❖ Pick up the Right Answer
- ❖ Discuss Legal Implications
- ❖ Discriptive Questions

4.1 INTRODUCTION

The rights and obligations of the parties, created by a contract, continue as long as the contract is in force.

Performance of contract is one of the most usual ways of discharge of a contract. This is the normal conclusion of a contract as planned, originally, by the parties while entering into a contract. The contract can be discharged in either of the six ways.

Different ways of discharge of contract are shown in the diagram.

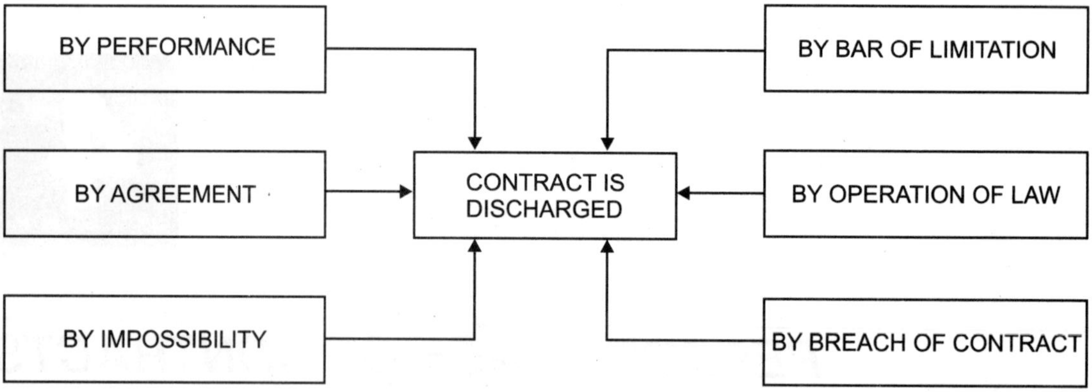

Discharge of A Contract
(Diagram No.10)

4.2 MEANING – PERFORMANCE OF CONTRACT

The parties to a contract must perform or offer to perform their respective promises. On the performance of the obligations undertaken by both the parties, the contract is automatically discharged. This is the happy ending of the contract and nothing more remains. If only one party performs his promise, he, alone, is discharged. The other party to the contract is not discharged. He acquires a right of action against the other party, who is guilty of breach of performance.

> **"Performance of Contract" means fulfilling the respective legal obligations created under the contract by both the promisor and the promisee.**

According to Section 37 of Contract Act, the parties to the contract must either perform their respective promises or offer to perform the same, unless such performance is dispensed with or excused under the provisions of the Contract Act or any other law.

4.3 TYPES OF PERFORMANCE AND EFFECT ON RELATIONSHIP

Every contract consists of reciprocal promises. As a general rule, the parties to the contract must perform their obligations.

(A) Actual Performance: When every party has done what is required to do under the contract and nothing is left out to do, it is called an actual performance.

Example: Kalyan has entered into a contract with Kishore for selling his vehicle for Rs. 50,000 and performance by both the parties is scheduled on 20th July, 2007. Kalyan delivers his vehicle and

Kishore pays the amount Rs. 50,000 on the specified date. Here, both the parties have actually performed their duties and so the contract is discharged with performance. Nothing is left, further, for completion by any party.

Performance in accordance with the terms of Contract: To complete the performance, the actual performance must be made in accordance with the terms of the contract. It is the duty of the seller to deliver the goods. Buyer has to pay the price, in accordance with the terms of the contract.

Both delivery and payment are concurrent unless otherwise agreed.

In other words, both promisor and promisee have to do their duties, simultaneously (Section 32).

(B) Attempted Performance or Tender: When a promisor has made an offer of performance and the promisee does not accept the offer, it is called as attempted performance. Tender means offer to deliver goods or services or payment by the promisor to the promisee, strictly, in terms of the contract.

Offer of Performance is called Tender of Performance.

Example: In the above example, Kalyan offers to deliver the vehicle to Kishore on the specified date. However, Kishore refuses to take delivery and does not make the payment. In this case, Kalyan has attempted to perform, but the actual performance could not take place due to refusal of Kishore to take delivery and on his part, he has failed to pay the amount too. Kalyan acquires the right against Kishore for breach of performance.

Effect of Refusal to Accept Performance: The effect of refusal on both the parties is as follows:

Type of Performance	*Effect on Promisor*	*Effect on Promisee*
1. Delivery of goods and services	Once promisor offers and promisee has refused to accept, the promisor is discharged. Goods and services need not be offered, again. Promisor is discharged from his responsibility or duty, required under the terms of the contract. Promisor may sue the promisee for damages.	Promisee cannot demand delivery of goods and services, again, at his convenience. Promisee is liable for damages to the promisor.

Contd...

2. Delivery of money	When promisor offers to repay debt and promisee refuses to accept, the promisor is not discharged from debt. Promisor is not liable for the payment of interest from the date of refusal to accept repayment of debt.	Promisee can get the payment of debt, but not interest from the date of refusal.

4.4 ESSENTIALS OF VALID TENDER OF PERFORMANCE

The essentials of a valid tender are shown in the diagram.

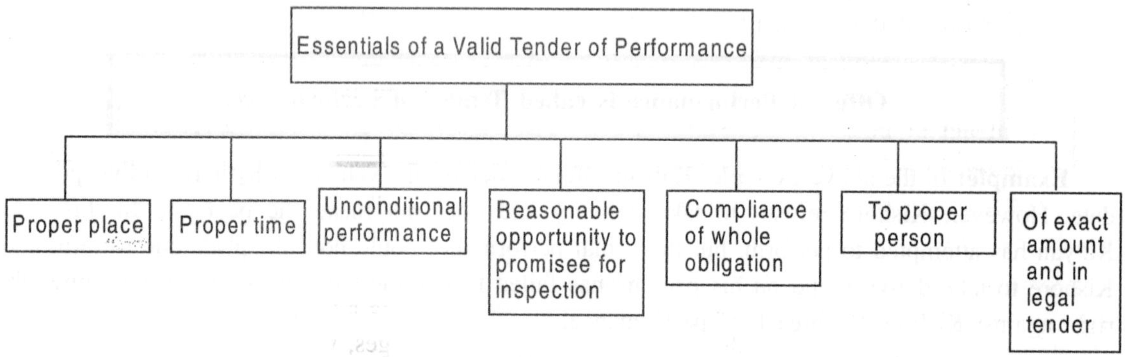

Essentials of Valid Tender of Performance
(Diagram No.11)

The following are the essentials of a valid tender:

(1) Proper Place: Delivery must be made at the proper place. If the place is mentioned in the contract, the promisor must make the performance at the place specified. In case, the place is not specified in the contract, performance has to be made at the promisee's business premises. In case, the promisee does not have separate business premises, performance can be made at the promisee's residence.

(2) Proper Time: Performance or tender to perform must be made at the time specified in the contract. Proper time means during the working hours of business. If the date of performance is stipulated in the contract, tender to perform before the due date is not a valid tender.

Time is essence of contract: If time is essence of the contract, an intention that the time is the essence of contract must be specifically mentioned. A party who is bound to perform the promise fails to perform on the due date specified in the contract, the contract is voidable at the option of the other party. Mere mention of delivery on a specified date does not make time as an important essence of the contract. However, in mercantile transactions, stipulation for time for delivery of goods is deemed to be essence of the contract. **(Mahabir Prasad Vs Dutta – AIR 1961 SC 990)**

It is well settled that unless a different intention appears from the terms of the contract, ordinarily, in commercial transactions, time is the essence of the contract as there are great chances of rapid market fluctuations.

Where a contract does not specify the time of performance, the promisor must perform within a reasonable time. What is reasonable time, it depends on the circumstances of the case.

It has been held time is the essence of the contract in the following three cases:

(i) Where parties have expressly agreed and incorporated time as the important element in the contract

(ii) Where delay operates as an injury

(iii) Nature and necessity is construed from the terms of the contract.

One has to look at the construction of the contract and the intention of the parties in order to decide to ascertain whether time is the essence of the contract or not.

In a contract of sale of immovable property, generally, time is not essence of contract, unless there is a contract to the contrary.

Example: There was an agreement with the railway administration for the transportation of oranges. The railways have specifically stated that they are running a fast train for transportation of such type of goods. The railways have failed to deliver the oranges, within the stipulated period.

Held Railway was liable for damages as time was the essence of the contract. **(Dominion of India Vs Gaya Prashad. A.I.R. 1957 ALL .193)**

Time is not essence of contract: When time is not essence of contract and the promisor fails to perform the obligation within the specified period, the promisee is not entitled to avoid the contract. The promisee is entitled to compensation from the promisor.

Acceptance of performance, out of time: Where the promisee accepts performance from the promisor after the due date, promisee cannot claim compensation, unless he has stated his intention to do so at the time of acceptance of out of time performance.

(3) Unconditional Performance: When performance is tendered, the performance should be unconditional, in terms of the conditions of the contract. The tender must be for whole and not part. Tender in part is no tender. A tender in part is invalid unless the contract so provides.

Example: An agreement is made between Vasu and Suresh for supply of 200 pieces of toys. There is no specific clause about the supply of toys in installments. Vasu offers to supply only 50 pieces to Suresh.

Suresh is within his right not to accept the supply.

(4) Reasonable Opportunity to Promisee for Inspection: Promisor should give reasonable opportunity to the promisee for inspection that the goods, proposed to be supplied, are in accordance of the terms of the contract. Promisee may take time for inspecting the goods to satisfy that the goods offered are in accordance with the terms of the contract.

Example: Sandeep agrees to supply 50 cotton bales to Sumedh on a specified date. It is the duty of Sandeep to bring 50 cotton bales to the warehouse of Sumedh during the business hours on the appointed date and provide adequate time to Sumedh for inspection and acceptance of the goods. If goods are not brought to the warehouse, but only a telephone call is made whether Sumedh would be willing to accept the supply of cotton bales, it is not a valid tender and the performance is not complete.

Sandeep has not complied with the obligation of supply of goods. A telephonic call does not provide the opportunity to inspect the goods. Description of goods may not be as per the terms of the contract. In the absence of opportunity to inspect and decide about the compliance of the terms of the contract, a valid attempt of performance is not deemed to have been made.

(5) Compliance of Whole Obligation: When the promisor disables from performing the promise in its entirety, the promisee may put an end to the contract. By words or conduct, the promisee may agree to waive the total compliance of the obligation.

Example: Radha, a singer, enters into a contract with the theatre manager to sing for 30 days in the month of December, 2006. After singing for 5 days continuously, she has discontinued from singing. After a gap of two days, she has resumed her singing and the manager of the theatre has permitted for continuation of singing.

The manager of the theatre has the right to discontinue her when she has failed to turn up for singing on the sixth day. The singer, by her behaviour, displayed her intention not to complete the whole assignment. The manager is entitled for compensation for the breach of performance.

Here, the manager has permitted her to resume her performance, even after a gap of two days. The manager, by his conduct, permitted her to continue singing even after a gap of two days. So, she is allowed to continue the contract. For her absence of two days, the manager is entitled for compensation for the loss sustained by him.

4.5 PERSONS WHO CAN DEMAND PERFORMANCE

The persons who can demand performance in a contract are as under:

(A) Promisee: It is only the promisee or his agent can demand performance of the promise under a contract. Even though the benefit of the contract is for the benefit of third party, it is only the promisee that can sue the promissor for non-performance.

Example: Rao promises Krishna to sell the vehicle to Radhi. Rao does not keep up the promise. In case of his non-performance, Radhi, who is the beneficiary of the contract, cannot sue Rao. It is the promisee Krishna who can sue Rao.

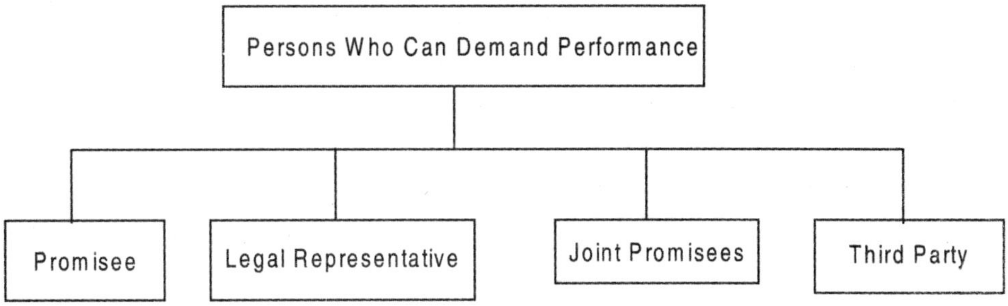

Persons who can Demand Performance
(Diagram No.12)

The general rule is that " a person cannot acquire rights under a contract to which he is not a party." **(T. G. Venkataramana Vs State of Madras) A.I.R. (1970) S.C. 508.**

(B) Legal Representatives: In case of the death of the promisee, his legal representatives can only sue the promisor for non-performance.

Example: Venkat promises to marry Puja. Venkat dies. Puja cannot insist on Venkat's legal representative, his son Pratap to marry her. Nor Pratap can get the benefit of the contract and ask Puja to marry him. Performance is not possible as the contract is of personal nature.

(C) Joint Promisees: All the joint promisees must join together to claim the performance of the promise. In case of the death of any of the promisees, the other promisees and the legal representative of the deceased have to join together to claim performance of the promise.

If some of the parties do not join and all of them do not claim together, the suit is liable to be dismissed under Section 45 of the Act.

Example: A and B jointly lend money to Z and Z promises to repay to them, jointly. B dies. A cannot recover the amount from Z, individually. A and the legal representatives of B can recover the amount from Z. In case A also dies, the legal representatives of A and B, jointly, only can claim the amount from Z.

(D) Third Party: Normally, a third party cannot demand the performance. However, there are some exceptions. A beneficiary for whose benefit the trust is made, though not a party to the contract, can demand the performance.

4.6 WHO HAS TO PERFORM

The persons who are liable for performance are as under:

(A) By the Promisor: From the terms of the contract, if it appears that the intention of the parties is that the concerned person has to perform, the promisor has to perform.

Example: Hussain agrees to paint the picture of Hema. Hussain cannot allow any other person to paint the picture. In case of death of Hussain, the legal representatives cannot be allowed or compelled to paint the picture of Hema. In this case, the personal skill is important and based on the skill of the person, the contract has been entered into. Once this is not possible, the contract comes to an end, due to impossibility of performance.

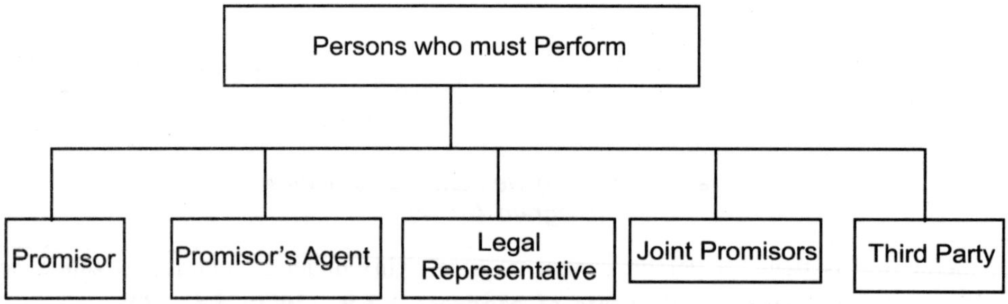

Persons who must Perform
(Diagram No.13)

Joint Promisors: Where two or more persons make a joint promise, the promisee is entitled, in the absence of any agreement to the contrary, to demand performance from any one of the promisors. In other words, the liability of the promisors is joint and several.

Example: X, Y and Z jointly promise to pay Rs. 10,000 to Satya. Satya can compel repayment of the whole amount from any one of the promisors X, or Y, or Z or all together.

(B) **By the Agent:** Where personal skill is not necessary and the work could be done by any one, the promisor may employ any other person as his agent to perform. Thus, a contract to sell or buy the goods can be assigned by the promisor to any other person to do that act on his behalf.

(C) **By the Representatives:** In the event of the death of the promisor, before the performance, his representatives are bound to perform unless personal conditions are involved. On the death of a person, the benefits and burdens of the contract pass on to the legal representatives as a part of his estate.

Where the personal representatives are made liable, they are liable to the extent of the assets of the deceased only.

In other words, the personal representatives are not personally liable. In the event of the inadequacy of the assets of the deceased to repay his liabilities, the personal representatives are not, personally, liable for those debts. Their liability is limited to the assets inherited by them. A deceased cannot bequeath his debts to his children!

Third Party: A third party can also demand performance of the contract. In case of a Trust, the beneficiary of a trust can demand performance. Similarly, the person for whose benefit provision has been made in family arrangements can demand performance. Though, these members are not the contracting parties, still, they have the right to demand the performance in a contract.

4.7 RULES FOR APPROPRIATION OF PAYMENTS BY DEBTOR

When a creditor receives payment from a debtor and a debtor has several debts from the creditor and the remittance amount does not cover all debts, totally, to which debt the amount is to be adjusted? This is called "Appropriation". Appropriation means 'application of payment'.

Appropriation is the primary right given to the debtor.

In other words, the debtor can direct the creditor to which debt the amount is to be adjusted. In case, the debtor advises the creditor, the creditor is bound to comply with the instructions of the debtor. **In case, the debtor is silent while remitting the amount, the creditor can appropriate the amount, in the way he deems fit.**

If the creditor is unable to comply with the instructions of the debtor, creditor should not accept or retain the remittance.

The principles relating to appropriation have been decided in the leading case of English Law **"Clayton's case"**. The principles are embodied in Section 59 to 61 of the Indian Contract Act and they are as follows:

(A) **Debtor's express instructions must be followed:** The first right of appropriation lies with the debtor. While remitting the amount, the debtor can advise the creditor about the manner of application of the remittance. This is the privilege of the debtor, when the debts are more than one.

(B) **Debtor's implied instructions must be followed:** If there are no express intentions, then the debtor's implied intentions are to be followed. The implied instructions can be gathered or understood from the circumstances attending the payment or conduct of the debtor.

Example: Ram has several debts with Srinivas. Srinivas demands payment of Rs. 500, which is one of the debts Ram owes him. When Ram sends Rs. 500, it is the duty of Srinivas to adjust the amount against the debt of Rs. 500 only and cannot adjust the amount against the other debts.

(C) **When principal and interest both are due:** When the principal and interest are due, the debtor can stipulate that the remittance may be adjusted against the principal, while keeping the interest amount outstanding. If creditor accepts the amount, he is bound to follow the instructions of the debtor.

If the debtor does not stipulate anything, the remittance is to be first applied first towards payment of interest by the creditor. **(Srinivasulu Vs. Kondappa -1960 A.P. 174)**

(D) **Appropriation by creditor:** When the debtor has omitted to advise the method of adjustment of remittance and there are no other circumstances that indicate the manner of adjustment, the creditor is totally free to adjust the amount to any lawful debt. The only important requirement is that the debt has to be lawful. In other words, **the creditor has the right to adjust the amount against any debt, which is even time-barred, provided the original debt is lawful. (Punjab National Bank Vs. Surendra Prasad Sinha –AIR 1992 SC 1815)**

However, creditor cannot adjust the remittance to a debt, which is disputed or illegal. Once appropriation is made by the creditor, he cannot alter the appropriation, subsequently.

Example: Sandhya owes two debts Rs. 10,000 and Rs. 20,000 to Kumari. The first debt is time-barred by limitation and cannot be recovered through legal means, even after filing case in a court of law. Sandhya remits Rs. 5,000 and does not give any instructions to Kumari for adjustment of remittance. Kumari adjusts the remittance towards the first debt which is time-barred, as part remittance.

In the absence of express or implied instructions from the debtor, the creditor is entitled to adjust the amount even towards time-barred debt, provided the debt is lawful. In the above circumstances, the action of Kumari is justified.

(E) Appropriation by Law: When neither debtor nor creditor has made any appropriation, the remittance shall be applied in the order of time. In other words, the debt which is outstanding for a longer period has to be adjusted, first. In case, there are more debts and some of them are outstanding from the same date, they have to be adjusted, proportionately. In other words, the amount received is to be distributed between the senior debts, proportionately. Even if the debt is barred by limitation, the adjustment would be made.

To summarise, the debtor has the first right to appropriate. In case, the debtor fails to exercise the right, the creditor has the right to appropriate, even to a time-barred debt. In case, both parties fail to appropriate, the law provides that the appropriation is to be made, in the order of time.

4.8 CONTRACTS WHICH NEED NOT BE PERFORMED

The circumstances under which contracts need not be performed are as follows:

1. **Novation:** At times, the parties may agree to substitute another contract in place of the contract entered into. The original contract need not be performed. Then the new contract comes into force and the old contract ceases to exist. This is called "Novation".
2. **Remission:** If parties to a contract agree to dispense with or remit performance of promise either wholly or in part, the original contract stands discharged. This is technically called as 'Remission.' (Sec. 63)

   In other words, when the original contract is totally dropped, it is Novation.

   Remission occurs when the original contract is amended.
3. **Rescission:** When a person at whose option a contract is voidable rescinds it, the other party thereto need not perform his promise. This is called rescission. (Sec.64)
4. **Refusal to provide required conditions:** If any promisee neglects or refuses to provide the promisor reasonable facilities for the performance of his promise, the promisor is excused for the non-performance of the contract (Sec. 67). For instance, Rahul contracts with Shyam to get his house repaired. Rahul does not allow access to Shyam to undertake the repairs. Shyam is excused for the non-performance of the contract, as it is caused by the refusal.

Check Your Understanding

State whether the following Statements are True or False

1. Offer of Performance is also known as tender of performance in a contract.
2. When promisor offers to repay debt and promisee refuses to accept the payment, promisor is discharged from debt as promisor has tendered the payment of money.
3. When promisee has refused to take delivery of goods and services from the promisor on the stipulated date specified in the contract, he can demand for delivery, again, at his convenience.
4. When the time of performance is stipulated in the contract, tender to perform before the due date is not a valid tender.
5. Where time is the essence of the contract and the promisor fails to perform on the due date specified in the contract, the contract is not voidable at the option of the other party.
6. When time is not the essence of the contract and the promisor does not perform on the specified date mentioned in the contract, the promisee can avoid the contract.
7. In mercantile transactions, timely delivery of goods is deemed to be essence and presumption of the contract.
8. Tender of performance is a valid performance.
9. In case of joint promisors, the liability of the promisors is joint and several.
10. All the joint promisees need not join together to claim the performance from the promisee.
11. Appropriation of remittance is a right given to the debtor when more than one debt is outstanding to the creditor.
12. In the absence of instructions of appropriation from the debtor, the creditor cannot adjust the remittance received in respect of different debts the debtor has with him.
13. Appropriation means 'application of payment received from the debtor by the creditor'.
14. When the principal and interest are due, the debtor can stipulate that the remittance may be adjusted against the principal, while keeping the interest amount outstanding.
15. When the debtor has omitted to advise the method of adjustment of remittance and there are no other circumstances that indicate the manner of adjustment, the creditor has the right to adjust the amount against any debt, which is even time-barred, provided the original debt is lawful.
16. Creditor can appropriate the remittance towards a disputed debt in the absence of express or implied instructions from the debtor.
17. In case, both debtor and creditor fail to appropriate, the law provides that the remittance is to be appropriated in the order of time.
18. Novation means a new contract comes into force in place of the existing contract.
19. Both delivery and payment in a contract are concurrent, unless otherwise agreed.
20. In the event of the death of the promisor, the personal representatives are personally liable for the debts of the deceased.

21. After due date, promisee can accept delivery of goods from the promisor, without any reservation, and is entitled to claim compensation, subsequently, for delayed delivery.
22. When debtor and creditor fail to appropriate the remittance towards any debt, when several debts are pending, the remittance has to be kept pending for legal decision.

Answers:

1.	True	2.	False	3.	False	4.	True	5.	False
6.	False	7.	True	8.	True	9.	True	10.	False
11.	True	12.	False	13.	True	14.	True	15.	True
16.	False	17.	True	18.	True	19.	True	20.	False
21.	False	22.	False						

Discuss Legal Implications

1. **Question:** A, B and C jointly have borrowed Rs. 20,000 from D. B and C are not traceable. A is known to be a man of means. D wants to recover the total debt from A. Is it possible?

   Answer: Yes. In case of joint promisors, their liability is joint and several. All the three parties A, B and C are individually as well as jointly liable. So, D has the option and right to recover the total debt from A, totally. **So, D can recover the total debt Rs. 20,000 from A alone.**

2. **Question:** Ram owes a sum of Rs. 10,000 to Rahim. Sandesh, a third party pays the whole amount. Will the payment by a third party discharge Ram from the whole debt?

   Answer: Yes. The payment by a third party, Sandesh discharges the whole debt due by Ram.

3. **Question:** X borrows Rs. One lakh from A , B and C. When the debt becomes due, X pays the whole amount to A. Is X discharged from the liability?

   Answer: No. X is not discharged from the debt. As per Section 45 of the Contract Act, a payment to one of several joint promisees does not operate as a complete discharge of debt.

4. **Question:** Manmeet has taken two loans from a bank, one of the debts is guaranteed and the other is not guaranteed. First, debt without guarantee has been taken. Later, the guaranteed debt has been taken. Manmeet remits the amount to the bank, without specifying to which debt the amount is to be appropriated. Bank appropriates the amount towards the debt which is not guaranteed as chances of recovery are better with the guaranteed debt. Manmeet sues the bank that the appropriation of remittance is not proper on the ground that the debt which is not guaranteed has been taken subsequently and so the remittance is to be appropriated towards the first debt, which is not guaranteed. Her reasoning is that the appropriation is to be made in the order of time. Can she succeed? Give reasoning.

   Answer: No. Manmeet cannot succeed. In the absence of any express or implied communication of appropriation from the debtor, the creditor is entitled to appropriate the remittance in any manner towards any of the debts outstanding. Bank has the right even to appropriate the remittance towards a debt, even if it is time barred provided it is a lawful debt. So, the appropriation of the remittance towards a debt which is not guaranteed is perfectly valid. Her reasoning that the appropriation is to be made in the order of time is valid only when both the debtor and creditor fail to appropriate, then as per the law, the remittance is to be appropriated in the order of time. This is not the case here, as the creditor, bank, has exercised its right in the absence of any communication from the debtor.

Pick up the Right Answer

(1) Creditor can appropriate remittance received from the debtor for the following:
- (A) Illegal debt
- (B) Time-barred debt
- (C) Disputed debt
- (D) Unacceptable debt

2. The following has the first right to appropriate the remittance:
- (A) Debtor
- (B) Creditor
- (C) Law
- (D) None

3. Debtor can advise creditor for adjustment of remittance for the following:
- (A) Principal
- (B) Interest
- (C) After clearance of Principal, balance towards Interest
- (D) Any way debtor wishes

Answers:

1. (B) 2. (A) 3. (D)

Descriptive Questions

1. What is meant by Performance of Contract? Describe the essential elements of Valid Tender. **(4.2 to 4.4)**
2. Describe the different types of performance. What is the effect of refusal to accept delivery of goods and money on Promisor and Promisee? **(4.3)**
3. State the provisions relating to the time and place of performance of contracts. **(4.4)**
4. Write the essentials of a Valid Tender of Performance. **(4.4)**

5. What do you understand by the term "Performance of Contract"? State who can demand performance and by whom contracts must be performed. **(4.2, 4.5 and 4.6)**
6. Write a brief on "Time is the essence of the contract". **(4.4)**
7. Summarize the rules relating to the Appropriation of Payments by debtor to the creditor. **(4.7)**
8. Discuss the circumstances under which contracts need not be performed. **(4.8)**

5

BREACH OF CONTRACT AND REMEDIES FOR BREACH

5.1 BREACH OF CONTRACT– MEANING

Parties to a contract are bound to perform their respective obligations.

When both the parties perform their respective obligations, there is performance of the contract. Nothing further remains to be done. However, one of the parties performs his obligation and other party to the contract refuses to perform his own obligation, there is said to be **'Breach of Contract'**. So, breach of contract occurs when one of the parties does not perform his obligations, under the contract.

A breach occurs, where a party repudiates or, fails to perform, one or more of the obligations, imposed upon him by the contract.

5.2 OCCURRENCE OF BREACH OF CONTRACT

A contract comes to an end by breach of contract. Breach of contract may arise in two ways:

1. **Actual Breach:** Where a party fails to perform his obligation on the date fixed for performance of the contract.

Example: A buyer, wrongfully, refuses to accept goods and pay the price on the date specified in the contract.

2. **Anticipatory Breach:** Where a party expressly or impliedly repudiates the contract before the due date of performance.

Example: Party to the contract states, expressly, that he will not perform his promise.

Another instance is when a party does some act which disables him from performing his obligation.

Example: A buyer does not secure a license for exporting the goods in an export transaction, where export license is needed.

A singer after entering into an agreement for singing on a specified date enters into another agreement for singing on the same date.

The first form of breach occurs, only, when the performance is due. The second and third forms of breaches have occurred before the performance is due.

Remedies against Anticipatory Breach

The promisee has two options in case of anticipatory breach:

(i) Without waiting for the date of performance, the promisee can treat the anticipatory breach as actual breach.

In this case, the damages are assessed as the difference between the prices on the date of breach and contract price.

(ii) Wait till the due date of performance and avail the legal remedies for breach of contract, against the defaulting party.

Here, the damages would be equal to the difference between the contract price and the ruling price on the date fixed for performance in the contract.

Both the parties are legally entitled to take advantage of the situation as the circumstances may change during the intervening period. After conveying refusal, before the due date of contract, the promisor may change his mind and may perform the contract on the due date fixed in the contract.

5.3 REMEDIES FOR BREACH OF CONTRACT

As soon as either party in the contract commits the breach, the other party is entitled to any of the following reliefs. The party who suffers is called the aggrieved party. The aggrieved party has the following remedies:

A. Cancellation or Rescission
B. Restitution
C. Suit for Specific Performance.
D. Suit for Injunction.
E. Suit for damages, for the loss sustained.
F. *Quantum Meruit*

5.4 CANCELLATION OR RESCISSION

Cancellation of contract is called **'Rescission of Contract'**. It is the way by which the contract can be discharged.

> **When one of the parties commits breach of contract, the other party who is aggrieved can cancel the contract.**

When a contract is broken by one party, the other party may sue for rescission and refuse further performance. In such a case, the aggrieved party is freed from all his obligations under the contract. In a voidable contract, if a party has received any benefit and later cancels the contract, he has to restore the benefit to the person who has paid the amount. In other words, the aggrieved cannot retain the benefit in a voidable contract and at the same time cancel the contract. The party who rescinds the contract is entitled for damages towards compensation of the loss sustained by him.

Example: A singer contracts with a theatre manager to sing every Sunday in the whole month. After singing the first Sunday, the singer abstains from singing from the second Sunday. The theatre manager can cancel the contract and claim compensation from the singer for the loss sustained by non-performance.

Example: Preeti induces Tushar to enter into a contract with her for supply of garments, at a reduced rate, by undue influence. She makes advance payment too to bind him for supply. To execute the order, Tushar, in turn, places the order with Ranadheer & Co for purchase, agreeing for forfeiture of advance paid by him, in case order placed for supply of goods is cancelled, later.

Here, the first contract between Preeti and Tushar is voidable as the contract has been entered under undue influence. When Tushar cancels the contract, he has to refund the advance received from her. It is not open to Tushar to cancel the contract, while retaining the advance. However, Tushar is entitled to claim damages he would sustain in consequence of the cancellation of contract with Ranadheer & Co as garments are no longer needed.

When rescission is granted?

The court may grant rescission in the following two cases:

(A) When the contract is voidable at the option of the aggrieved party, the court grants rescission of the contract to the plaintiff.

Example: A sells his piece of land to B. A, the seller, is aware that there is the right of passage (people can move through the land). At the time of sale, the seller does not inform the factual position of the right of sale to the buyer and so buyer is not aware of it.

Here, the contract is voidable at the option of the buyer. The buyer is entitled to cancel the contract. In case, buyer has given any advance, he can get back the advance paid.

(B) Where the contract is unlawful for causes not apparent on the face of contract and the defendant is more to blame than the plaintiff, the court may grant rescission.

Example: An attorney induces his client, a widow, to transfer her property in the name of attorney to defraud the creditors.

Here, the parties are not at equal standing. The attorney is in a superior position and the client, a widow, is at a disadvantageous position. The intention of the contract is unlawful as it has been entered with the sole purpose of defrauding the creditors. So, the widow is entitled to have the instrument of transfer rescinded.

When rescission may be refused?

The court may refuse to cancel the contract in the following circumstances:

(A) Where the plaintiff has expressly or impliedly ratified the contract, or

(B) Where there is change of circumstances and not possible to restore the original position, or

(C) During the subsistence of the contract, the third parties have acquired the rights in good faith and for value, or

(D) Where a part of the contract is sought to be cancelled and that part is not severable (separated) from the rest of the contract.

The party who wants to rescind the contract has to restore the benefit received under the contract. In other words, he cannot retain the benefit and seek for cancellation of the contract. But, the rescinding party is entitled to receive damages.

5.5 RESTITUTION

'Restitution' means return of benefit received. In a void contract, parties need not perform the contract.

In a void agreement, restitution is not possible as it is void from the beginning.

In case, any benefit has been received by one of the parties, the person who has received the benefit is not required to return the money received.

Example: When A and B enter into an agreement, under which B has to beat C. A gives advance to B for beating. This agreement is void from the beginning hence advance received by B is not required to be refunded.

There is no void contract. A contract can become void. Alternatively, a contract can be discovered to be void. In other words, when the contract was formed, originally, it was valid as the parties were not aware of the defect in the contract. Later, the parties may discover the defect, which makes the contract void.

Example: A promises B to marry the latter's daughter, Z. In consideration of the marriage, B has given Rs. 10,000 to A. At the time of entering into the contract, unknown to both the parties A and B, Z has died in an accident.

When an agreement is discovered to be void, restitution has to be made by the parties to a contract. Here, at the time of entering into the contract, the contract was valid. However, the contract has become void when both A and B discovered that Z was not alive at the time of formation of the contract. So, A cannot retain the benefit and has to refund the amount to B.

5.6 SUIT FOR SPECIFIC PERFORMANCE

The aggrieved person can approach the court for specific performance. The court directs the person responsible for breach of performance, under certain circumstances, to perform the promise as per the terms of the contract. Under the following circumstances only, the court directs for specific performance:

A. Where monetary consideration is not an adequate remedy for breach of performance.

B. When there is no standard for measuring the damages.

Example: A specific painting has been agreed for sale. The party who is to sell the painting has refused to deliver though the painting is in his possession. Here, monetary compensation is not an adequate compensation. It is highly difficult to measure the damages for non-performance. More so, the party concerned is in a position to perform his obligation. The court would direct for specific performance.

In the following cases, specific performance shall not be granted:

A. When the contract is of a personal nature e.g. a contract to marry.

B. Where the damages are an adequate remedy.

Example: Lata agreed to sing a song on a specified date for an agreed sum. Later, Lata refused to sing for her own reasons. The aggrieved cannot seek the specific performance but can request the court for damages sustained. The court cannot grant specific performance as it cannot compel Lata to sing, but can award damages, looking to the loss sustained.

5.7 SUIT FOR INJUNCTION

Injunction is a preventive relief.

An injunction is an order from the court directing the person to perform or refrain from doing some act.

Injunctions are granted only when damages is not an adequate compensation for the loss sustained. It is particularly appropriate in case of anticipatory breach of performance. Here, court intervenes before the actual breach of performance of the contract and directs the concerned to forbid from performing, which may go against the interests of the aggrieved.

Example: N, a film actress agreed to do an exclusive act for Warner Brothers for one year. During the year when she is supposed to perform to Warner Brothers, exclusively, she has entered into a contract to perform with a third party, X.

Warner Brothers has sought an injunction from the court. The court has restrained her performance for X. The court cannot compel the performance to Warner Brothers, but could compel the actress not to perform to a third party. **(Warner Bros. Vs Nelson (1937, I.K.B. 209)**

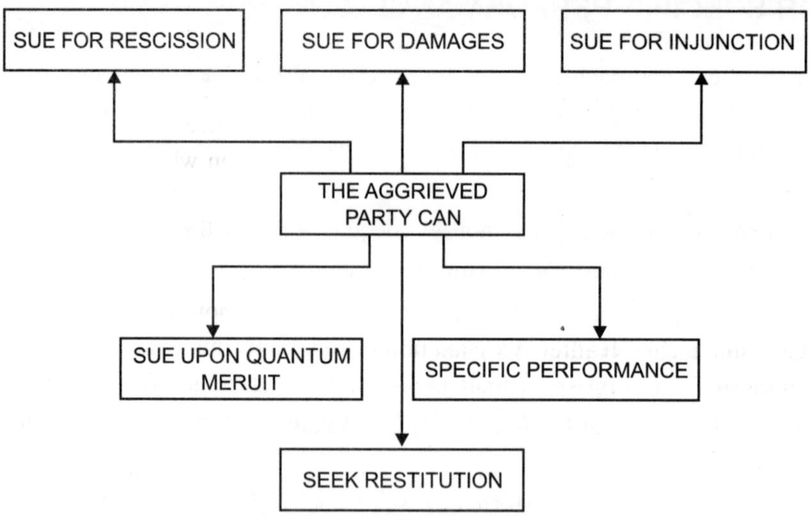

Remedies – Breach of Contract
(Diagram No.14)

5.8 SUIT FOR DAMAGES, FOR THE LOSS SUSTAINED

Damages are monetary compensation allowed to the injured for the loss or injury suffered as a result of the breach of contract.

'Damages' means compensation in terms of money for the loss sustained.

As a general rule, "Compensation must be commensurate with the injury of loss sustained, arising naturally from the breach". The party who is aggrieved may bring an action for damages. If actual loss is not proved, no damages are awarded.

The object of awarding the damages is to put the injured party in the same position as far as money can do it. In other words, the aim is to place him in the same position, in terms of money, as if there is no breach of performance.

Remoteness of Damages: Every breach of contract upsets the expectations of the injured party. It is difficult to estimate the amount of damages the aggrieved party may sustain. The aggrieved may feel the consequences for a long time and in a variety of ways.

Example: For example, a person may agree to supply pure ghee to a ghee dealer. Instead of supplying pure ghee, he may supply impure stuff, instead. The ghee is seized by the food inspector and destroyed on finding that the ghee is adulterated and not fit for consumption.

In consequence, the ghee dealer is arrested, prosecuted and convicted.

Additionally, the ghee dealer suffers loss of ghee, loss of profit, loss of personal prestige and reputation of business. Money, time and energy are wasted on defence, mental agony and torture of the prosecution. Now, a suit is filed by the ghee dealer on the person who has supplied impure stuff. The breach of contract may be endless, but there must be an end to liability. The defendant cannot be held liable for all that follow from the breach. There must be a limit to the liability and beyond this, the damage is said to be remote.

To estimate the amount of damages, the principle of "Remoteness of Damages" has been established in the historic case **Hadley Vs Baxendale (1854).** In this case, a mill was stopped due to breakage of crankshaft. The broken crankshaft was given to the carriers for transporting to the place, where the repair could take place. At the time of handing over the crankshaft, it was conveyed to the transporters that the mill has stopped working due to breaking of the crankshaft, which is given for transporting it for repairs. There has been abnormal delay in transportation. During the interval, the mill has remained idle and there has been loss of profit. Estimating the loss of profit £ 300, the plaintiff has sought to recover the loss from the defendants, the transporters.

In the judgement, it has been observed "When two parties have made a contract which one of them has broken, the damages which the other ought to receive in respect of such breach of contract should be such as may fairly and reasonably be considered either arising naturally, i.e. according to the usual course of things, from such breach of contract itself, or such as may reasonably be supposed to have been in the contemplation of both parties, at the time they made the contract, as the probable result of the breach of it."

On the basis of the judgement, the defendants were not held liable for loss of profits due to delayed delivery. The circumstances communicated to the carriers did not show that the delay in delivery of shaft would result in loss of profits to mill. It was held that the compensation was not to be given for any remote and indirect loss or damage sustained by reason of breach.

5.9 TYPES OF DAMAGES

Damages, generally, are of five kinds:

A. Ordinary Damages
B. Special Damages
C. Vindictive, or Punitive or Exemplary Damages
D. Nominal Damages, and
E. Liquidated Damages

(A) **Ordinary Damages:** Ordinary or General Damages are those which arise, naturally, and directly in the usual course of things from the breach. The defendant is liable for the reasonable and foreseeable consequences of the breach. It means that the damages must be the nearest consequences of the breach. In commercial transactions, the ordinary damages are calculated based on the difference between the contract price and market price of the goods, on the scheduled date of delivery of the contract.

Example: A agreed to supply the goods to B on a specified date @ Rs. 2,000 per rice bag. A failed to supply as the market rate soared to 2,500 on that date. The amount of ordinary damages is Rs.500 per rice bag, which is the difference between the contract rate and prevailing market rate on the specified date of delivery of the contract.

Example: A railway passenger's wife caught cold and fell sick as the railways have asked the passenger to get down at a place, where there is no railway station.

Held, Railways are liable for payment of damages for the personal inconvenience to the passenger, but not for the sickness caused. Sickness is considered as a remote consequence.

(B) **Special Damages:** Special damages are those which arise on account of the unusual circumstances affecting the plaintiff. Special damages are claimed for loss of profits etc.

Special damages are payable only when the special circumstances are brought to the knowledge of the party so that the possibility of the special loss was in the contemplation of the parties.

Example: A, a builder agrees to construct a house before a specified date to B. Based on this agreement, B has let out his house to Z. B has specifically advised A about the lease he has entered into. Before the specified date, the building, built by the builder collapses.

Held that the builder is liable for the cost of rebuilding and also for the loss of rent as the lease matter has been specifically brought to his attention and the consequential loss is known to the builder at the time of entering into the contract.

(C) **Vindictive, or Punitive or Exemplary Damages:** The basic objective of damages is to compensate the aggrieved for the loss sustained. However, here, the objective of vindictive damages is to punish the defendant more than the intention of awarding compensation to the plaintiff.

They are awarded in the following circumstances:

A. Breach of Promise to marry.

B. Wrongful dishonour cheque by the bank, even though sufficient balance is available in the customer's account.

In the first case, the damages are awarded dependent upon the severity of the shock to the sentiments of the promisee. In the second case, smaller the amount of cheque, greater the insult and heavier is the amount of damages.

(D) **Nominal Damages:** Where the plaintiff suffers no loss, still, the court may award the damages in recognition of the right of the plaintiff. The nominal damages are, generally, a token amount just to establish the right of the plaintiff and recognition of the breach of contract by the defendant.

(E) **Liquidated Damages:** It is somewhat usual for the contracting parties to specify the sum payable as damages, in the event of breach of contract. The amount of damages may be liquidated damages or penalty. What is the test of distinction between the two? The liquidated damages are a genuine pre-estimate of the loss, in case of breach. Penalty is the sum fixed to make the party to perform and avoid committing the breach. The English law allows the payment of liquidated damages, but not penalty. In our country, no such distinction is made. The injured party is allowed only reasonable compensation in the event of breach of performance.

Amount of Damages: The courts allow a reasonable compensation for the loss sustained by the aggrieved party. **The named sum in the contract as damages for failure of performance sets the maximum amount.** The amount is only the maximum liability, in the case of breach of contract.

The court will award to the party aggrieved only reasonable compensation, not exceeding the amount named in the contract either as penalty or damages.

The courts allow reasonable compensation to cover the actual loss occasioned due to breach of contract. **"If a contract is broken, the law will endeavour, so far as the money can do it, to place the injured party in the same position as the contract has been performed."** The intention of the law is not to give any benefit to any party.

5.10 MITIGATION OF DAMAGES- DUTY OF INJURED

It is the duty of the injured party to mitigate the damages by taking prompt action. He has to make all reasonable efforts to avoid the losses resulting from the breach so that his loss is kept at minimum level. This rule is frequently applied in sale and purchase of goods.

Example: A and B enter into an agreement where under B aggrees to supply standard 100 cotton bales at a price of Rs.1,000 per bale on a specified date. Before the specified date, B conveys to A that he would not deliver the goods. On the date of refusal to supply the goods, the market price is Rs. 1,100 per bale.

It is the duty of A to buy the cotton bales at the prevailing market price Rs. 1,100. So, A incurs a total loss of Rs. 10,000. A can recover this loss amount as this is a direct loss, caused due to non-performance of the contract. If A postpones to purchase till the market rate further rises to Rs. 1,200 and then wants to recover the loss of 20,000, it is not possible as he has not made reasonable efforts to minimize the loss.

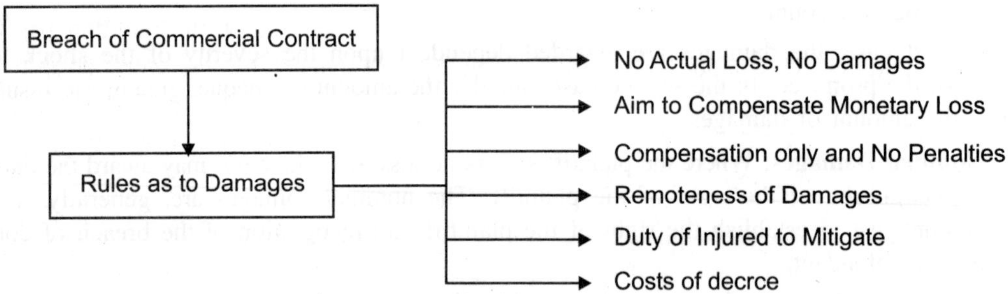

Rules for Payment of Damages
(Diagram No.15)

5.11 QUANTUM MERUIT

The doctrine *Quantum Meruit* literally means **'as much as is earned or deserved' or 'in proportion to the work done'**. Normally, a person who fails to perform the contract is not entitled for any payment.

These are the circumstances when the aggrieved can claim for breach of contract under the principle of 'quantum meruit':

1. Where the work has been done in pursuance of contract, which has been discharged by the default of the defendant. Here, there is no default on the part of the person who has performed his obligation as per the terms of the contract. The other person has terminated the contract in the middle that has resulted in breach of contract.

Example: An author has been engaged to prepare a manuscript by the publishers for a specified sum. The publishers discontinued their business, soon after the author completed a part of the work assigned to him.

Held, the author was entitled for a reasonable remuneration for the trouble he had undertaken. **(Plinche Vs Colburn) (1831)**

The party who has performed the contract is entitled for reasonable payment, when he is prevented from completing the whole contractual obligation, for no fault of the concerned. Here, the important point is the other party has received the benefit and the contract is divisible. The aggrieved party is compensated for the part he has performed.

2. Where the work has been done in pursuance of a contract, which is 'discovered void' or 'become void' provided the contract is divisible.

Example: A person has rendered services to a company under a contract of employment, which has been duly approved by the Board of Directors. Later, it has been found that the composition of the Board to be illegal and so the contract of employment has become void. Here, the employee has rendered the services and so can claim remuneration on the principle of *quantum meruit.* **(Craven Ellis Vs Cannons Ltd. (1936) 2 Kb 403.**

Example: Pratap enters into a contract with a builder 'Rahim & Co.' for construction of two storey building on a piece rate basis. After the completion of one storey, the building has been destroyed by lightning. The builder is entitled to claim the payment for the work done on the principle of *quantum meruit.* In case, the contract is entered into for a lump sum amount for the whole construction of two storey building, the builder cannot claim on the above principle as no money is due till the whole job is done.

Principle of *quantum meruit* is applicable when the contract is entered into on divisible basis.

It is important to check the terms of the contract. If the contract is on divisible basis, the principle '*quantum meruit*' is applicable. If the contract is on a whole term basis, the amount does not fall due, unless the whole job is completed.

5.12 SUMMARY OF RULES REGARDING THE MEASURE OF DAMAGES

The principles governing the payment of damages are summarized hereunder:

1. **Right to recover damages arising naturally:** The aggrieved party can claim compensation only for the actual loss sustained by him, arising naturally in the usual course of things from the breach itself.
2. **Primary aim of damages:** The injured party is placed in the same position, in terms of money, as if the contract has been performed.
3. **Compensation of loss:** Damages are awarded to compensate the loss sustained by the party but not to punish for failure of performance.
4. **Special damages in the contemplation of the parties:** Special damages i.e. damages which are not the natural and probable consequence of the breach are awarded only when the loss is in the knowledge of both the parties, while entering into contract.
5. **Remote damages:** No damages are allowed for remote causes. In other words, the cause for damage should be related and direct consequence of breach of contract. Compensation is not granted for any indirect or remote damage. Loss of profit is not to be taken into account in estimating damages, unless otherwise agreed.

6. **Difficulty of assessment:** The fact that assessment of damages is difficult, it does not prevent the party from recovering the damages. The courts must do its best to determine the amount of damages.
7. **Nominal damages:** When no real loss occurs, only nominal damages are allowed. It is recognition of the right of the aggrieved.
8. **Only compensation, no penalties:** If the parties fix up in advance the sum payable as damages, in the contract, in the event of breach of contract, the court allows only reasonable compensation to cover the actual loss sustained, not exceeding the amount so named in the contract.
9. **Exemplary damages:** Exemplary damages cannot be awarded except in the case of breach of contract of marriage and wrongful refusal by the bank to honour customer's cheque.
10. **Duty to mitigate the loss:** It is the duty of the injured party to make all reasonable efforts to minimize the damage. He cannot seek damages for loss which are not due to the breach but due to his own neglect to mitigate the loss.
11. **Cost of decree:** The injured party is entitled for the costs of the court in getting the decree for damages from the defaulting party.
12. **No compensation for mental agony:** Normally, no damages in commercial contract are awarded for mental agony. The mental agony or injury may relate to the plaintiff's feelings or his mental distress, anguish, annoyance, loss of reputation or social discredit caused in an ordinary commercial contract. In other words, there is no compensation for mental agony, due to breach of contract.

Check Your Understanding

State whether the following statements are True or False

1. Suit for specific performance is a possible remedy when damages are not an adequate relief for the breach of contract.
2. Where the contract is of a personal nature, specific performance has to be awarded to the aggrieved party for breach of performance.
3. Injunction is a preventive relief as a remedy for breach of contract.
4. Cancellation of contract is called 'Rescission'.
5. The party who wants to rescind the contract can retain the benefit received under the contract.
6. When an agreement is discovered to be void, restitution has to be made by the parties to a contract.
7. A breach of contract occurs, where a party repudiates or, fails to perform, one or more of the obligations, imposed upon him by the contract.
8. 'Damages' means compensation in terms of money for the loss sustained.
9. Damages are a form of compensation to be given to the plaintiff for any remote and indirect loss or damage sustained by reason of breach, caused by the defendant.
10. Ordinary or general damages are those which arise naturally in the ordinary and usual course of things.

11. Special damages, in the form of profits, are payable only when the special circumstances are brought to the knowledge of the other party so that the possibility of the special loss is in the contemplation of the parties.
12. Vindictive or punitive or exemplary damages are awarded with a view to punish the plaintiff.
13. Nominal damages are awarded when the plaintiff suffers no loss, but the court awards it as recognition of the right of the plaintiff.
14. It is the duty of the injured party to make all reasonable efforts to mitigate the damages, resulting from the breach, by taking prompt action.
15. When the contract specifies payment of liquidated damages, a sum very much on a higher side, for breach of performance, court does not interfere in estimating the amount of damages.
16. Under the doctrine of '*Quantum Meriut*', a person is allowed reasonable remuneration for the services rendered by him, when he is not allowed to complete the balance contractual obligation for no fault of the concerned.
17. In case of anticipatory breach, the promisee has the option to initiate action for claiming damages on the date of anticipatory breach or wait till the actual date of performance of the contract.
18. Restitution is possible in both void agreement and void contract.
19. Loss of profit is normally taken into account by the courts in estimating the amount of damages.
20. Remote loss is not considered, while awarding damages for breach of performance.
21. Normally, no compensation is allowed in the form of damages for mental agony, due to breach of a commercial contract.

Answers:

1. True	2. False	3. True	4. True	5. False
6. True	7. True	8. True	9. False	10. True
11. True	12. False	13. True	14. True	15. False
16. True	17. True	18. False	19. False	20. True
21. True				

Pick up the Right Answer

1. A customer has adequate balance in his account. Despite the balance covering the cheque, the concerned bank has dishonoured the customer's cheque. The cheque is drawn for a small amount Rs.100. The court would allow the following type of damages for dishonour of the cheque to the customer:
   (A) Nominal damages
   (B) Punitive damages
   (C) Liquidated damages
   (D) Special damages

2. A contract specifies the amount of damages payable. in the event of breach of contract. The court finds the damages fixed are very much on a higher side. In such an event, the court awards the following damages to the injured party:
   (A) General damages
   (B) Punitive damages
   (C) Liquidated damages
   (D) Reasonable damages covering the loss
3. Anticipatory Breach of Contract means
   (A) Performance of contract on due date
   (B) Performance of contract before due date
   (C) Advising before due date, expressly or impliedly of inability to perform contract on due date
   (D) Performing contract after due date
4. Plaintiff means
   (A) Aggrieved person
   (B) Advocate who pleads on behalf of injured person
   (C) Advocate who pleads against injured person
   (D) Person who has created injury
5. The principle in respect of award of damages, in case of breach of contract is
   (A) Compensation must be commensurate for the loss or injury sustained
   (B) Damages are always allowed
   (C) Nominal damages are allowed
   (D) Liquidated damages are allowed, without further question

Answers:

1. (B) 2. (D) 3. (C) 4. (A) 5. (A)

Discuss Legal Implications

1. **Question:** A merchant dealing in crackers, doing business in Sivakasi (Tamil Nadu) entrusts the crackers to Railways to reach a particular destination, before diwali. Due to the negligence of Railway authorities, the crackers reach the specified destination, after diwali season is over. The merchant claims compensation for loss of profit from Railways. Would the action succeed? Discuss.

   Answer: No. This is a case for payment of damages for delayed performance. The merchant is not entitled for payment of damages for loss of profit.

   This case is similar to the case law of Madras High Court in **Madras Railway Co. Vs V. Govinda Rao (1898)**. Here, the plaintiff, a tailor delivered a sewing machine and cloth to the defendant railway company to be sent to a specified place so that he could go there and do business to earn lump sum profit, in view of the forthcoming season. The delivery of goods was delayed and in the meanwhile the season is over. The tailor claimed for the expenses incurred by him in staying at that place and loss of profit, which he would have earned. The court held that the railways were not liable for payment of loss of profit as the special purpose was not known to the railway company.

To estimate the amount of damages, the principle of "Remoteness of Damages" has been established in the historic case **Hadley Vs Baxendale (1854).** In this case, the plaintiff was not held liable for loss of profits during the period of delay in delivery. (Discussed in detail in Para No. 5.8)

2. **Question:** A captain of a ship was engaged for a lump sum to be paid on the completion of the voyage. The captain dies after completing half of the voyage. His legal representatives claim half of the amount agreed to be paid with reasoning that the death of an individual is beyond the control of any one and payment is to be made for the part of the services rendered on the basis of *quantum meruit*. Decide.

   Answer: No. The legal representatives of the captain cannot recover any thing as the doctrine of *quantum meruit* is inapplicable in the current circumstances. The principle of 'Quantum Meruit' is applicable only in the case of divisible contract. Here, the contract is indivisible and the lump sum is to be paid for the whole job as a whole. No money is due till the job is completed.

3. **Question:** Sam has taken up a contract from Amit to complete erection of a factory within a period of four months. It has been further agreed in the contract that damages would be paid @ one lakh per month, beyond the period agreed upon. There has been a delay of two months. Amit has claimed payment of damages of Rs. 2 lakhs as a result of the delay. Sam pleads that damages to that extent have not occurred. The actual damages are Rs. 10,000. There is no dispute about the assessment of the damages. What damages would be awarded? Why?

   Answer: Amit is entitled to recover the actual amount of loss in the form of damages which is Rs. 10,000. When a sum is mentioned in the contract, in the event of breach of performance, that amount would be the maximum amount of damages. The court would allow only reasonable compensation as to cover the actual loss sustained, within the limit stated in the contract. Here, the principle is that the aggrieved party has to be placed in such circumstances, in terms of money, as if there is no breach of performance.

Descriptive Questions

1. Explain the term 'Breach of Contract'. Mention the different types of occurrences of Breach of Contract. **(5.1 and 5.2)**
2. What is meant by Breach of Contract? State the remedies available for breach of contract? **(5.1, 5.3 to 5.8 and 5.11)**
3. Write a note on anticipatory breach of contract. **(5.1 and 5.2)**
4. What is meant by 'rescission of contract'? State the circumstances when court can grant and refuse rescission of contract. **(5.4)**

5. What is meant by 'Damages'? Describe different types of damages. What do you understand by duty of the injured to mitigate loss? **(5.8, 5.9 and 5.10)**
6. What is meant by special damages? **(5.9 –Point B)**
7. "Where there is a right, there is a remedy." Amplify the statement and explain the various remedies available for breach of contract. **(5.1, 5.3 to 5.8 and 5.11)**
8. Explain the principles governing payment of damages for breach of contract. **(5.1, 5.9 and 5.12)**
9. "If a contract is broken, the law will endeavour, so far as the money can do it, to place the injured party in the same position as the contract has been performed." Discuss this statement indicating the rules which guide the court in the assessment of damages.**(5.8, 5.9 and 5.12)**
10. What do you understand by *Quantum meruit*? Give two examples to explain under what circumstances a claim for *Quantum meruit* arises. **(5.11)**
11. What is meant by the term 'Damages, Summarise the rules regarding the measure of damages. **(5.8, 5.9 and 5.12)**

6

CONSUMER PROTECTION LAWS – RIGHTS OF CONSUMERS

- Introduction
- Consumerism – Need for Consumer Protection
- Acts for Protecting Consumers' Interests
- Objectives of Consumers' Protection Act
- Mechanism Available for Redressal of Grievances
- Who is a Consumer?
- Who is NOT a Consumer?
- Some Definitions
- Rights – Protection Available to Consumers under Consumer Protection Act
- Amendments to Act – To Make it More Effective and Customer-friendly
- Procedure for Redressal of Customer Grievances
- On whom Complaints can be Lodged for Deficiency of Service
- Check Your Understanding
- Pick up the Right Answer
- Discuss Legal Implications
- Descriptive Questions

6.1 INTRODUCTION

Consumer is a king. The consumer movement in India is as old as trade and commerce itself. In Kautilya's *Arthashastra,* there are references to the concept of consumer protection against exploitation by the trade and service industry and punishment for those offences.

One of the most important milestones in the consumer movement in the country has been the enactment of Consumer Protection Act, 1986 to protect the interests of the 100 crore odd consumers.

Union Finance Minister P. Chidambaram has stated "This is the age of consumer. It is possible for the consumer today to claim and win compensation for the lost baggage from an airlines company, which was not possible, a few years ago. Policies framed by the Government and those of manufacturers will have to keep in mind the importance of a consumer."

India is a country of population, with vast amount of illiteracy, in particular, in rural areas. Population has been increasing but supply of goods and services are not, proportionately, increasing. Above all, the consumers are poor, helpless and disorganized. The market in India is a sellers' market and it is very easy to dupe the innocent consumer. The consumer needs support and protection from the unscrupulous seller.

6.2 CONSUMERISM – NEED FOR CONSUMER PROTECTION

Consumerism - Meaning: The dictionary meaning of 'Consumerism' is a movement seeking to protect and inform consumers by requiring such practices as honest packaging and advertising, product guarantees, and improved safety standards.

The fundamental cause for consumer movement in any country has been the consumer dissonance. 'Dissonance' means after-purchase doubts, disillusionment, disappointment and dissatisfaction. There is no scope of consumerism if marketing practices are adopted in the real sense because true marketing is 'consumer oriented'.

Unfortunately, in the present life, marketing is meant for sale, not satisfaction of the consumer.

The real need for consumer protection arises as the consumer needs

- Physical protection against goods and services that are spurious, unsafe and endanger health and property.
- Protection against deceptive and unfair trade practices.
- Protection against the abuse of monopoly and restrictive trade practices.
- Protection against sellers.
- Protection against all kinds of pollution.

Now, a separate Department of Consumer Affairs has also been created in the Central and State Governments to exclusively focus on ensuring the protection of rights of consumers.

6.3 ACTS FOR PROTECTING CONSUMERS' INTERESTS

Several Acts have been passed by the Government of India to protect the interests of the consumers, some of them are:

- The Essential Commodities Act
- Prevention of Food Adulteration Act
- Standards of Weights and Measures Act
- Drugs (Control) Act
- Monopolies and Restrictive Trade Practices Act

A common consumer is not in a position to approach the civil court for getting relief of his grievance. An individual consumer does not find his complaint worth pursuing due to disproportionate costs involved in redressal, unduly long-time consuming court process and lack of worthwhile support from any quarter to support his cause.

In this background **to protect the interests of the consumers, the Central Government has enacted a law in the year 1986 for protection of consumers, known as 'The Consumer Protection Act, 1986'.**

The Consumer Protection Act, 1986' marks the real beginning of the growth of consumer protection movement in our country.

The Consumer Protection Act aims at simple, speedy and inexpensive redressal for consumers' grievances, particularly against unfair trade practices and unscrupulous exploitation of consumers by the organized trade circles.

The Act has been primarily enacted in order to protect customers from below standard goods and deficient services offered by unscrupulous traders and service providers.

6.4 OBJECTIVES OF CONSUMERS PROTECTION ACT

The trading community is well organized while the consumers are scattered and unorganized. The rampant problems of illiteracy, ignorance, poverty and backwardness continue to exist and, in consequence, the consumers are always exploited. Some voluntary organisations have come forward to help the consumer movement, but their efforts are limited due to paucity of funds and lack of whole-hearted support of Government officials to the helping hand of the voluntary organizations. **The Consumer Protection Act, 1986 seeks to provide protection to the interests of consumers, in general.**

Basic Objectives of Consumer Protection Act: The basic objectives of Consumer Protection Act are

- To provide for better protection of consumers' interests.
- To establish consumer councils and authorities for protection of the interests of consumers.
- To empower consumer councils and authorities to settle consumers' disputes and matters connected therewith.

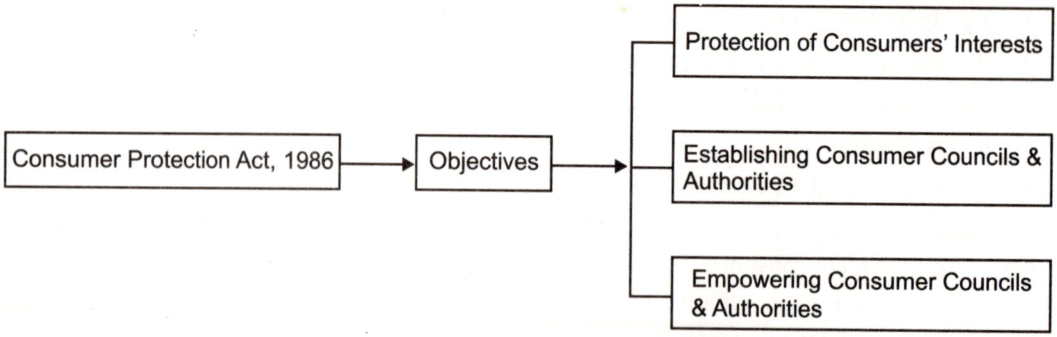

Objectives of Consumer Protection Act
(Diagram No.16)

6.5 MECHANISM AVAILABLE FOR REDRESSAL OF GRIEVANCES

To provide simple, speedy and inexpensive redressal of consumer grievances, the Act has formulated three-tier quasi-judicial machinery at the district, state and national levels.

6.6 WHO IS A CONSUMER?

All of us are consumers of goods and services. Even producers of some goods and services are also consumers of those goods and services, produced by others. **In the Consumer Protection Act, the term 'Consumer' has been defined, separately, for the purpose of goods and services.**

Only consumer is eligible for filing the case in the consumer protection court.

So, the definition of consumer is important. Any person, other than consumer, is not eligible for filing the case in the consumer protection court.

Definition of 'Consumer' for Goods

For the purpose of goods, a consumer means a person belonging to the following categories:

(1) **BUYS** any goods for consideration, which has been paid fully or partly paid or under any deferred system of payment for **PERSONAL USE.**

(2) Any **USER** of such goods with the **PERMISSION** of buyer of goods.

(3) One who obtains goods on **HIRE PURCHASE OR LEASE.**

The expression 'Consumer' *does not include* a person who obtains such goods for re-sale or for any commercial purpose.

The hirer of the goods is not a consumer.

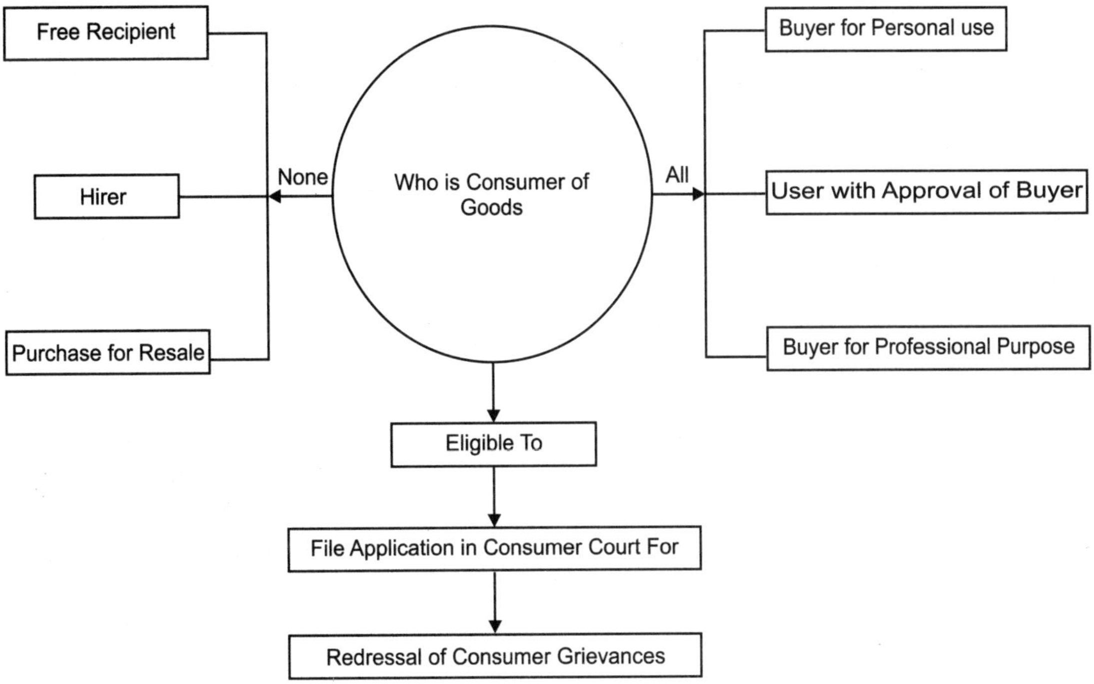

Who is a Consumer?
(Diagram No.17)

Definition of 'Consumer' for Services

For the purpose of services, a consumer means a person belonging to the following categories:

(1) **HIRES** any services for consideration, which has been paid fully or partly paid or under any deferred system of payment.

(2) Any Beneficiary of such services with the **PERMISSION** of buyer of services.

A person has to be a consumer within the definition of the 'Consumer' under the Consumer Protection Act to get remedy.

If any one is a consumer, he is competent to file a case with consumer protection court. So, the definition of the 'Consumer' is very important. The definition of 'Consumer' is wide. It includes not only the actual buyer of goods and services, but also any user of goods or any beneficiary of services who has taken with the consent of the actual buyer. So, both the actual buyer and person who use the goods, with approval of the original owner, are competent to file the case with consumer protection court.

A person who buys goods for the purpose of resale is not a consumer. Purchaser of a cooler, installed at bus stand for public use, is also a consumer.

A person who buys goods and uses them himself, exclusively, for the purpose of earning his livelihood, by means of self-employment, is within the definition of 'Consumer' **[Laxmi Engineering Works Vs P.G.S. Industrial Institute –AIR 1995 SC 1428]**

An owner cum driver of the vehicle, used as a taxi, is also a consumer.

Example: A complainant engaged in medical profession and running a nursing home has purchased equipment for his clinic. When the equipment has started giving problems, he has sought relief under the Consumer Protection Act.

Held, the doctor is entitled for relief as the equipment has been purchased, personally, for earning his livelihood. **(Kody Elcot Ltd. Vs Dr. C. P. Gupta (1996) NCDRC -4CTJ 48)**

A purchase is said to be commercial if there is a 'nexus' or 'connection' between purchase of goods and profit making activity.

Purchase of photocopier by a lady for earning her livelihood has been held to be not for commercial purpose. In other words, the lady has been held as a 'Consumer'. **(Secretary, Consumer Guidance and Research Society of India Vs. B.P.L. India Ltd. 1992 (1) CPC 140 MC).**

Purchase of a computer by a large commercial firm has been held to be for commercial purpose. **(HCL Ltd Vs. Krishna Nanu Naik and Sons & Another 1993 CPJ 11 1174 NC)**

Whether the purchase is for a commercial activity or not is to be decided depending on the individual facts of the case.

Even where the goods are purchased for commercial purpose, if there is a warranty for its maintenance, the purchaser becomes a 'consumer' in respect of the services rendered or to be rendered by the manufacturer, during the warranty period.

6.7 WHO IS NOT A CONSUMER?

A person is not a consumer, if the person

(i) Obtains goods for 'resale' or for any 'commercial purpose'; or

(ii) Buys goods without consideration; or

(iii) Hires or avails of any services, without consideration; or

(iv) Uses the goods, without the approval of the person who has bought the goods for consideration; or

(v) Is beneficiary of the services, without the consent of the person who has hired the services for consideration; or

(vi) Obtains service under a contract of personal service.

If the goods bought are for producing the goods for re-sale or commercial purpose, the person is not a consumer.

Some instances of persons who are held as consumers

(i) Bank customer

(ii) Consumer of electricity

(iii) Nominee of person insured, under LIC
(iv) Subscribers of telephone
(v) Student of MBA institution, who pays fees is also a consumer
(vi) A passenger traveling by train
(vii) A patient receiving medical treatment, after payment

Some instances of persons who are NOT held as consumers

(i) A client hiring services of an advocate
(ii) A patient receiving medical treatment in a Government hospital
(iii) A student hiring services of a private tutor
(iv) Person who obtains goods for 'resale' or 'commercial use'
(v) Tenant is not a consumer
(vi) Purchaser of shares and debentures for resale

6.8 SOME MORE DEFINITIONS

(A) What is Goods?

The meaning of the word 'Goods' under the Consumer Protection Act is the same as defined in the Sale of Goods Act, 1930. Sale of Goods Act, defines 'Goods' as follows:

"Goods mean every kind of movable property, other than actionable claims and money. Goods include stock and shares, growing crops, grass and things attached to or forming part of the land which are agreed to be severed (separated) before sale under the contract of sale."

(B) What is Service?

Service means service of any description, which is made available to potential users. It includes, but not limited to, the provision of facilities in connection with banking, financing, insurance, transport, processing, supply of electrical or other energy, boarding or lodging or both, housing construction, entertainment, amusement or the purveying (providing or supplying) of news or other information. **Service however, does not include the rendering of any service, free of charge, or under a contract of personal service [Sec. 2(o)].**

(C) Deficiency of Service

It is for the complainant to establish that there is deficiency of service. In other words, the onus is on the complainant to establish that there is some deficiency in the service complained against.

> **Deficiency means any fault, imperfection, shortcoming or inadequacy in the quality of service or nature and manner of performance.**

The deficiency is in respect of the service required to be maintained by any law or undertaken to be performed in a contract.

Examples:

1. Lack of facilities promised by the Housing Board is deficiency of service.
2. Failure of insurance company to settle claim is another example.
3. Failure to provide cushioned seats in 1st class is deficiency of service.
4. A trader can be charged for having collected excessive price, in excess of what is displayed on product or fixed by law.

(D) What are Held Not to be Services?

(i) Faulty or medical treatment offered in the Government hospital;

(ii) Services rendered by Municipal Corporation, as payment of direct or indirect taxes by public is not consideration paid for hiring the services;

(iii) Services rendered by a private tutor, as it is a contract of personal service;

(iv) Services rendered by an advocate, as it is a contract of personal service;

(v) Any service which is rendered gratuitously, i.e., for which no consideration is paid;

(vi) Non-allotment of shares in a company;

(vii) Claim for compensation arising out of motor accident in a bus as such a claim cannot be said to be in relation to any service hired of availed by consumer **(Thiruvalluvar Transport Corporation Vs Consumer Protection Council - AIR 1995 SC 1384)**;

(viii) Service rendered by employee to his employer **(Indian Medical Association Vs V.P. Shanta - AIR 1996 SC 550)**;

(ix) Rendering of service by medical practitioner, free of charge to all patients **(Indian Medical Association Vs V.P. Shanta - AIR 1996 SC 550)**.

6.9 RIGHTS – PROTECTION AVAILABLE TO CONSUMERS UNDER CONSUMER PROTECTION ACT

Creation of awareness of different rights to the consumers is the objective of 'The Consumer Protection Act, 1986.'

The Act has recognized the following rights to the consumers:

1. **Right of Protection:** The Act enshrines the right to be protected against the marketing of goods which are hazardous to life and property.
2. **Right of Information:** The consumers enjoy the right to be informed about quality, quantity, potency, purity, standard and price of goods so as to protect against unfair trade practices. This right enables the consumers to take intelligent decisions at the time of purchasing the goods or hiring any services. To meet this objective, it is the duty of the producer to ensure that the goods meet the reasonable standards of durability, utility, reliability and are suited for the purposes for which they are intended.

3. **Right to Choose:** 'Right to Choose' means access to a variety of information for making a final choice. The consumers are provided with the full range of information about availability of different products with their competitive prices. This right enables them to make choice of the product at the lowest price.

   This right does not give any 'guarantee' that the products available are at competitive prices. Right provides 'information' and it is for the customer to decide and make a final decision.

4. **Right to be Heard:** The right to be heard includes the right to be assured that the consumer interest will receive appropriate attention at appropriate consumer forums. Right of representation at various forums to protect consumer welfare is to be made available. The consumer disputes should be resolved, expeditiously, in a fair manner.

5. **Right to Seek Redressal:** This gives the right to seek redressal against unfair trade practices or unscrupulous exploitation of consumers. It also includes the right of fair settlement of the genuine grievances of the customers.

6. **Right to Consumer Education:** The right to consumer education is also an important right available to the consumers. It means the right to acquire the knowledge and skill to be an 'informed customer'.

The objective of the Act is to make the consumers aware of their rights and legal remedies available for protection of their rights.

To achieve this objective, the rights and remedies available are widely explained, advertised and circulated so that public, as a whole, is conscious of their rights.

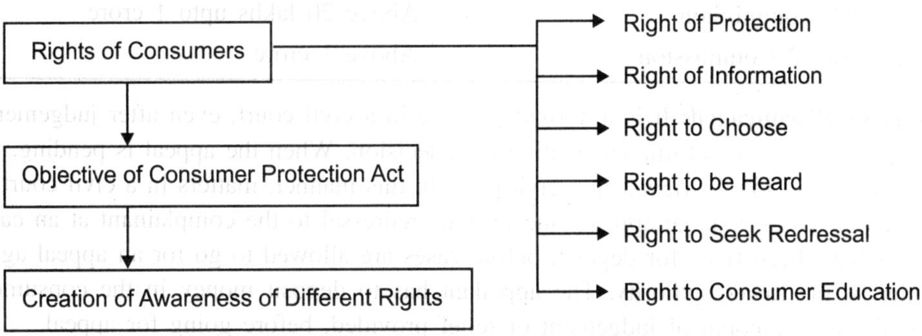

Rights of Consumers under Consumer Protection Act
(Diagram No.18)

6.10 AMENDMENTS TO ACT – TO MAKE IT MORE EFFECTIVE AND CUSTOMER-FRIENDLY

The Consumer Protection Act has been amended in the year 2002, which came into force from 15th March, 2003. The aim of the amendments is two fold:

(A) To simplify, streamline and expedite the dispute resolution process, and

(B) To give consumer courts more powers to deal with wider range of consumer violations in an effective manner.

Accordingly, the following amendments have been made:

1. **Time Frame:** It is usual and customary procedure to drag matters, in an endless manner, in civil courts so that the complainant is vexed and frustrated. A specific Time Frame of 21 days has been fixed for deciding the 'Admissibility of a complaint' under Consumer Protection Act. Similarly, time limits have been fixed for notices to be issued to opposite party, issue of decision and appeals.

Delay is common with civil courts. This delay is sought to be avoided for early redressal to the complainant, with fixation of time frame under the Act.

2. **Enhancement of Monetary Limits:** Earlier, the monetary limits for admissibility of the value of goods or services and compensation for District Forum, State Commission and National Commission were at a low level. **Monetary Limits have been enhanced.** The following are the revised limits, which are intended to provide relief to the consumer at a lower level, as against at a higher level, which was the case, earlier.

Forum	*Revised Limit (in Rs.)*
District Forum	Upto 20 lakhs
State Commission	Above 20 lakhs upto 1 crore
National Commission	Above 1 crore

3. **Appeals Discouraged:** It is a normal practice in a civil court, even after judgement, to go for an appeal to avoid implementation of a decision. When the appeal is pending, no relief is available to the aggrieved in a civil case. In this manner, matters in a civil court drag on for years. To discourage appeals and provide redressal to the complainant at an early date, limits have been fixed for deposit, before cases are allowed to go for an appeal against the order of the lower authority. The appellant has to deposit money in the consumer court, based on the amount of judgement of relief provided, before going for appeal.

The following amount, subject to a minimum of 50% of the amount of compensation, is to be deposited before the admission of appeal.

Forum	*Deposit*
Appeal to State Commission from the order of District Forum	Rs. 25,000
Appeal to National Commission from the order of State Commission	Rs. 35,000
Appeal to Supreme Court from the order of National Commission	Rs. 50,000

Suppose, the District Forum gives judgement directing the opposite party to give a relief of Rs.

1,00,000 to the aggrieved and the opposite party wants to file appeal against the judgement of District Forum. The opposite party has to deposit Rs. 50,000, before he is allowed to go for appeal to the State Commission. This works as a deterrent for appeal to the opposite party and the aggrieved is likely to get early relief.

4. **Spurious goods and Services:** Sale of spurious goods and services have been brought into the purview of the Act.
5. **Issue of Interim Orders:** Redressal agencies have been allowed to issue interim orders for relief, where they consider necessary.
6. **Establishment of Consumer Protection Councils – Necessary Requirement:** Establishment of Consumer Protection Councils at the Central and State levels have been made a necessary requirement. Additionally, establishment of District Consumer Protection Councils at the District level also have been provided.

6.11 PROCEDURE FOR REDRESSAL OF CUSTOMER GRIEVANCES

The following is the redressal mechanism of consumer grievances for goods and services. The Act envisages three tier quasi-judicial machinery at the District, State and National levels.

(A) Complaint

Allegation has to be made by the complainant, in writing. The complaint may relate to

(i) Defect in goods bought or agreed to be bought;

(ii) Deficiency in services hired or agreed to be hired;

(iii) Charging of a higher price by the trader than the price shown on the container or fixed by any law for the time being in force;

(iv) Sale of hazardous goods to life and safety, in contravention of any law for the time being in force in regard to contents, manner and effect of use of such goods;

(v) Any unfair trade practice adopted by the trader.

(B) Who can File Complaint?

Any of the following persons may file a complaint:

(a) Consumer within the definition of the Act (as discussed in Para no.6.6)

(b) Any recognized consumer association, namely any voluntary consumer association registered under the Companies Act or any other law for the time being in force. It is not necessary that the consumer is a member of such an association.

(c) One or more consumers together having same interest, after taking the permission of the District Forum, as a common body for all the consumers, so interested.

(d) Central or State Government

Locus Standi: A person seeking redressal of his complaint, must come within any of the four categories, otherwise he has no *locus standi* to proceed with the case before the Consumer Redressal

Forum. If any person, other than the person falling under any of the above four categories, files any complaint, the same is liable to be dismissed of the ground that he has no *locus standi.* A public cause can be taken up by an association in the form of public interest litigation. Legal heirs/ representative of a deceased consumer, entitled to the estate of the deceased have a *locus standi* and can file a complaint **(Dr. Sr. Louie & Anr. Vs Kannolil Pathumma – 1993 I CPJ 30 NC).** A nominee of a person insured under LIC has a *locus standi.*

(C) Where to file a complaint?

Jurisdiction: The jurisdiction is based on the value of goods or services and the compensation, if any claimed. It is necessary that the claim has to be filed in the appropriate jurisdiction; otherwise the case may be dismissed on the ground that the jurisdiction is not relevant.

The revised monetary limits for different forums are as under:

Forum	***Revised Limit (In Rs.)***
District Forum	Upto 20 lakhs
State Commission	Above 20 lakhs upto 1 crore
National Commission	Above 1 crore

Example: Value of goods is Rs. 20 lakhs and, the aggrieved customer has filed a claim for a relief amount of Rs. 20 lakhs. So, the case can be filed in District forum as the jurisdiction is based on the amount of relief claimed, and value of goods.

The determining point for jurisdiction is the value of the claim / relief sought, and value of the subject matter i.e. goods or services.

However, if the matter is subjudice before any other court, under any other law, the Consumer Forum shall not exercise jurisdiction over such complaints.

There is no need to engage the services of an advocate for filing the case in the consumer forum. The consumer can file the case, without the assistance of advocate. However, it is difficult to avoid the assistance of an advocate for filing case under Consumer Protection Act as draft of complaint is to be made properly. Otherwise, the complaint may be rejected by the consumer forum. It is a sad fact that the level of awareness is not as high as it should be.

For lodging a complaint against a bank, in 'Banking Ombudsman', the aggrieved customer can do directly. In fact, advocate is not allowed in 'Banking Ombudsman'. This is not so with consumer forum. Procedures are more important in the case of consumer forum. Content has to be given importance. Compliance of procedures is to be eliminated, if the purpose is to be served. Unless, an advocate is engaged, the poor consumer cannot get the relief as procedural compliance is still given importance.

This is one more area where the Act has to undergo change, avoiding the presence of an advocate, all together, similar to 'Banking Ombudsman'. Surprisingly, a client cannot file a case against an advocate for deficiency of service while he is allowed for filing a case against a private doctor.

(D) How to File a Complaint?

A complaint should contain the following information:

(a) Name, description and address of the complainant as well as opposite party or parties.

(b) Facts of the complaint and when it arose.

(c) Documents, in support of the allegations contained in the complaint.

(d) Relief sought.

(E) Procedure on Receipt of Complaints

(a) Complaint copy is to be sent within 21 days of date of admission to the opposite party.

(b) Opposite party has to submit the reply within 30 days or such extended period not exceeding 15 days, as may be granted.

(c) Where the alleged defect in the goods require laboratory analysis, the forum should obtain the sample of the goods from the complainant. The said sample is to be sealed and sent for the report of appropriate laboratory. A copy of the laboratory report is to be sent to the opposite party.

(d) The forum should offer opportunity to both the parties to present their views on the laboratory report.

(F) Relief Available to Consumers– Nature and Scope of Remedies under the Act

The consumer forum may direct the opposite party to provide the following remedies to the consumer-complainant to give relief:

(a) Removal of defect as complained in the complaint.

(b) Replace the goods with the new goods.

(c) Refund of price paid by the complainant.

(d) Award of appropriate and reasonable compensation to the complainant.

(e) Removal of defects or deficiencies in the services provided to the complainant.

(f) Order to abandon or discontinue the unfair trade practices etc.

(g) Order to restrain or withdraw from selling the hazardous goods.

(h) Award of reasonable costs to the injured party, apart from compensation.

(G) Time Limit for Speedy Disposal of Case

The complaints shall be decided by the consumer forums, as far as possible, within a period of three months from the date of notice received by the opposite party, where testing of goods is not required. If testing of goods and analysis of sample is required, the time period is five months from the date of receipt of notice by the opposite party.

(H) Appeals

The State Commission shall have the jurisdiction to entertain appeals against the orders of the District forum. The National Commission shall entertain the appeals against the orders of State Commission.

(I) Limitation Period

The limitation period is two years from the date of cause of action for filing the case under the Consumer Protection Act. However, a complaint may be admitted after the period of limitation, provided the delay is condoned.

(J) Fees: Every complaint filed has to be accompanied by a fee, as specified in the table given below:

S. No.	*Value of goods or services and the compensation claimed*	*Amount of fee payable*
(i)	Upto Rs one lake	100
(ii)	Rs. One lakh and above but less than Rs five lakhs	200
(iii)	Rs. Five lakhs and above but less than Rs. 10 lakhs	400
(iv)	Rs. Ten lakh and above but not exceeding Rs. 20 lakhs	500

6.12 ON WHOM COMPLAINTS CAN BE LODGED FOR DEFICIENCY OF SERVICE

Any person who has to provide the service, but fails to provide the required standard of service is a defaulter. What is the required standard depends on case to case basis. Normally, it is the level of service that a prudent person expects in the circumstances the service is provided. The level of service that the industry provides is taken into account in fixing the standard of service.

Now-a-days, complaints are lodged against the following agencies, often, by the public:

- Banks
- Insurance companies
- Telecom companies
- Railways
- Airlines
- Consumer durable companies
- Property builders

6.13 EXAMPLES OF 'DEFICIENCY OF SERVICE'

Example: Chitra has been receiving telemarketing calls, often, at odd hours, followed by frequent SMSs. She has conveyed them that she was not interested in their products and curtly told them not to make calls, again. Despite her warning, the calls did not end and are persisting. Suggest whether she can sue the private telecom operator for the nuisance that is created to her. Advice.

Answer: Chitra is a 'Consumer' and is entitled for the assured quality of service. Telemarketing would be indeed a nuisance, if one is not interested. How irritating one would feel when he is disturbed, while he has been concentrating on an important job? How disgusting it would be, when one is woken up from sleep, without any justified reason, simply, for the sake of marketing products on phone, when one is not interested? Every individual has a right of peace and privacy and intrusion is neither decent nor to be permitted.

There is a landmark judgement on this type of matter by Delhi State Commission. The judgement has fined a private telecom operator and Cellular Operator's Association of India (COAI) for Rs. 50 lakh and directed the two banks to pay a penalty of Rs.25 lakh "for committing nuisance" by calling and sending SMSs at odd hours as a part of telemarketing.

As Chitra has been facing similar circumstances, she can file case in consumer forum for redressal.

Example: Rahim has taken a loan from a bank. For some time, he has paid the installments regularly and of late, has not been paying the installments to bank. Bank has sent reminders too. Even then, he has not paid the installments. Of late, Rahim has been receiving threatening calls and personal visits from 'musclemen' to repay the loan installments, otherwise, he has been warned that physical harm would cause to him and his family. Rahim is very much worried. He seeks advice for steps that may be taken to stop the threats of 'musclemen'. Suggest.

Answer: In the event of default of payment by the borrower, the way for recovery to a bank is filing a case in a civil court. That is the appropriate legal means available to the bank. However, it is a known fact that litigation, filing a case in civil court, is a long-drawn process and results are slow and expensive too. Some banks have been adopting the short-cut method of engaging musclemen as recovery agents. Every one is afraid of physical assault on self and family. So, the deliberate defaulting borrowers, otherwise capable of repaying but delaying deliberately, immediately repay the loans. All said and done, this is not an ethical practice. On the legal side, it amounts to deficiency of service as the bank in this concerned case has left the legal way of recovering and resorted to undesirable practices. So, the customer, Rahim is entitled to file a case in consumer court for redressal of grievance.

In similar circumstances, a district forum has levied a penalty of Rs. 10 lakhs on a foreign bank for 'using musclemen to threaten" a customer to recover the alleged dues.

Check Your Understanding

State whether the following statements are True or False

1. To protect the interests of consumers, the Government of India has enacted a law in the year 1986 for the protection of consumers, known as 'The Consumer Protection Act, 1986'.
2. Consumer need not engage an advocate for filing his complaint in consumer forum and can do himself.
3. 'The Consumer Protection Act, 1986' aims at simple, speedy and inexpensive redressal to consumers' grievances, particularly against unfair trade practices and unscrupulous exploitation of consumers by the organized trade circles.
4. To provide simple, speedy and inexpensive redressal of consumer grievances , 'The Consumer Protection Act, 1986' has formulated a three-tier quasi-judicial machinery at the National, State and District levels.

5. 'Right to Choose' under the Consumer Protection Act guarantees availability of different products to consumers at competitive prices.
6. Creation of awareness of different rights to the consumers is the objective of 'The Consumer Protection Act, 1986'.
7. There are different rights and remedies available to consumers under 'The Consumer Protection Act, 1986'.
8. Any person can file case in consumer protection court for redressal of grievance.
9. A person is not a consumer, if the person obtains goods for 'resale' or any 'commercial purpose' under the Consumer Protection Act.
10. If the goods bought are for producing the goods for re-sale or commercial purpose, the person is also a consumer under the Consumer Protection Act.
11. Purchaser of a cooler, installed at bus stand for public use, is also a consumer.
12. A person has to be a consumer within the definition of the 'Consumer' under the Consumer Protection Act to get remedy.
13. A owner cum driver of a vehicle is not a consumer.
14. If the amount of consumer dispute exceeds rupees one crore, the case is to be filed in State Commission forum.
15. The user of goods, with the consent of the actual buyer, is not competent to file the case with consumer protection court for securing remedy of the grievance.
16. Deficiency of service is not a valid ground for lodging complaint under 'The Consumer Protection Act, 1986' for redressal of consumer grievance.
17. The consumer needs support and protection from the unscrupulous sellers, hence 'The Consumer Protection Act, 1986' has been framed.
18. Bank customer is not a 'Consumer' under 'The Consumer Protection Act, 1986'.
19. The onus is on the complainant to establish that there is some deficiency of service complained against, under 'The Consumer Protection Act, 1986'.
20. The Consumer Protection Act has been amended in the year 2002 to give consumer courts more powers to deal with wider range of consumer violations in an effective manner.
21. There is no fixed time limit for the consumer forums to dispose off the complaints filed by the aggrieved for redressal of consumer grievances.
22. The limitation period is three years from the date of cause of action for filing the case under the Consumer Protection Act.
23. Both the actual buyer and person who use the goods, with approval of the original owner, are competent to file the case with consumer protection court.
24. Even if the dispute related to customer's complaint is subjudice before any other court, under any other law, still, the consumer forum can exercise jurisdiction over such complaints.
25. A client cannot file a case against an advocate for deficiency of service, while he is allowed for filing a case against a private doctor.

Answers:

1. True	2. True	3. True	4. True	5. False
6. True	7. True.	8. False	9. True	10. False
11. True	12. True	13. False	14. False	15. False
16. False	17. True	18. False	19. True	20. True
21. False	22. False	23. True	24. False	25. True

Pick up the Right Answer

1. The monetary jurisdiction of District Forum is enhanced in 2002 amending Consumer Protection Act, 1986 to :
   (A) Rupees 5 lakh
   (B) Rupees 10 lakh
   (C) Rupees 15 lakh
   (D) Rupees 20 lakh
2. This Act provides the mechanism for seeking redressal related to consumer grievances
   (A) The Essential Commodities Act
   (B) Prevention of Food Adulteration Act
   (C) Standards of Weights and Measures Act
   (D) Drugs (Control) Act
   (E) Consumer Protection Act
3. Filing case in consumer protection court is
   (A) More expensive than filing case in civil court
   (B) Less expensive than filing case in civil court
   (C) Free
   (D) Equally expensive as filing a case in civil court
4. Consumer Protection Act protects the interests of
   (A) Consumers
   (B) Suppliers
   (C) Consumers and Suppliers
   (D) Government
5. For the following person, protection is not available for filing case in consumer protection court.
   (A) Consumer
   (B) Self-employed person
   (C) Commercial user
   (D) User with the approval of buyer of goods

6. Consumer Protection Act has been formed in the year
   (A) 1986
   (B) 2002
   (C) 1947
   (D) 1956
7. The following is the normal time frame for deciding the admissibility of the case under the Consumer Protection Act.
   (A) 21 days
   (B) 31 days
   (C) 60 days
   (D) No time frame
8. The monetary jurisdiction for fixing the claim is based on
   (A) value of goods /services and compensation amount claimed
   (B) Value of relief claimed
   (C) Value of relief granted
   (D) None

Answers:

1. (D)	2. (E)	3. (B)	4. (A)	5. (C)
6. (A)	7. (A)	8. (A)		

Discuss Legal Implications

Case No. 1: A customer's cheque was dishonoured by his bank, though the customer has adequate balance in his account. Can the customer approach the consumer protection court for relief?

Answer: Yes. Customer of a bank falls within the definition of 'Consumer' under the Consumer Protection Act. There is deficiency of service on the part of the bank as cheque has been dishonoured though there has been adequate balance in the customer's account. So, customer can file the case under Consumer Protection Act.

Case No. 2: Ram is a taxi driver, plying his own taxi. He has purchased the taxi with bank loan. The taxi has a manufacturing defect and the automobile company has not agreed to remove the defect. He wants to file the case under Consumer Protection Act. Advise the admissibility of filing the case.

Answer: Yes. Ram is plying the taxi for his livelihood as a self-employed person. So, he is a consumer and so eligible for relief under Consumer Protection Act.

Case No. 3: Dheera has bought a refrigerator from a dealer, with bank loan. At the time of purchase, lucky-draw has been announced by the dealer on every purchase of refrigerator. A few days later, she has received the phone call, followed by written communication from the dealer that she has been a lucky winner and her coupon has received a fabulous gift of first prize - Maruti 800. Immediately, she has to oblige a party too for her friends who have not allowed her till a treat is given to them. When she has approached the dealer for claiming the gift of Maruti 800, the dealer has refused to honour the gift coupon she has. She wants to approach consumer forum for claiming the gift. She has the invoice for buying the refrigerator and receipt for full payment. She has no problem with the refrigerator, which has been working well. Advise her in respect of filing the case under Consumer Protection Act for claiming the gift.

Answer: No. Dheera is a 'consumer' for refrigerator under Consumer Protection Act as she has paid consideration at the time of purchase. The Act gives protection to the consumer in respect of the 'goods' purchased to seek remedy for any consumer grievance. The refrigerator, purchased by her, is covered under the Consumer Protection Act. However, she has no complaint or problem with the refrigerator. Her problem is with the gift coupon she has won - gift of Maruti 800, not given to her. This is a gift, announced by the dealer for which she has not paid any consideration, separately. **In other words, there is no consideration for the item for which she wants to stake her claim under Consumer Protection Act.** Unless consideration is paid, goods are not covered under Consumer Protection Act.

Lucky draw is an additional attraction attached to the sale of refrigerator. Lucky draw is not an intrinsic part of the part of contract deal. A similar case with the same type of facts was decided in **Byford Vs S.S. Srivasthava (1993).** In this case, the complainant's argument that this would fall under unfair trade practice in MRTP Act, 1969 was also not accepted.

The gift coupon does not fall within the purview of Consumer Protection Act. For this reason, Dheera cannot file any case under Consumer Protection Act for any relief.

Case No. 4: At the time of sale of a printing machine, a warranty of free service for one year is given. After the sale of machine to Sudhir by the dealer, the machine has developed some defect. The supplier of machine has refused for replacement of defect part since he has been rendering free service for maintenance of the machine for one year. Decide whether Sudhir is a consumer under Consumer Protection Act for relief?

Answer: Yes. Held, in similar facts of the case in **Vishwa Jyoti Printers Vs Moklins of India,** that warranty was a part of the composite contract for supply of printing machine along with its maintenance for a period of one year. The consideration for service to be rendered under the contract was obviously included in the sale price of the machine. It was wrong to maintain that warranty obligations were being rendered free of charge.

So, Sudhir is a consumer under Consumer Protection Act.

Case No. 5: Discuss whether student of MBA institution who pays fees is a consumer?

Answer: Yes. Student of MBA institution who pays fees is also a consumer. The requirement to be a 'consumer' is payment of consideration while availing the services. Fee is the consideration, which is paid to the college. Services are provided by the faculty in the form of teaching and acquiring new skills. If there is deficiency in the services advertised, the student has a right to file the case with consumer protection court for redressal, which can be in the form of refund of fee, even.

Case No. 6: Shyam has taken a locker from a bank. He has been paying the locker rent regularly. A robbery has occurred in the bank which resulted in the loss of valuable ornaments deposited in the locker. He wants to approach consumer forum on the ground that there has been deficiency of service from the bank. Can Shyam plead that he is a consumer under Consumer Protection Act? What are the chances of his success?

Answer: Yes. In the case of **Bank of Maharashtra Vs Mrs. Jyoti Satya 2001 CIJ 352 (NCD2RC)** it has been held by the National Commission that the locker facility provided by the bank is not the relationship of landlord and tenant. In the event of loss of contents of lockers as a result of burglary, the bank has been held liable for deficiency in its services. So, Shyam is a consumer under Consumer Protection Act. His chances of success are bright.

Objective Questions

1. Mention any four Acts meant for Protecting Consumers' interests and explain the need for enacting Consumers Protection Act, 1986. **(6.2 and 6.3)**
2. What was the need for enacting Consumer Protection Act, 1986 and explain its objectives? **(6.2 and 6.4)**
3. Who is a consumer? What protection is available to a consumer under Consumer Protection Act, 1986? Indicate the monetary limits and jurisdiction for filing cases for getting the relief. **(6.6, 6.9 and 6.10 – Point No. 2)**
4. Describe who is not a consumer for whom protection is not available for filing case in consumer protection court? Write four instances of a 'Consumer' and 'Not Consumer.' **(6.7)**
5. What is meant by 'Deficiency of Service'? Give some examples. **(6.8 –Point C)**
6. Describe the rights and protection available to consumers under Consumer Protection Act. **(6.9)**
7. What amendments have been made to "Consumers Protection Act, 1986 to make it more effective and customer-friendly? **(6.10)**
8. Describe the procedure for redressal of customer grievance under Consumers Protection Act, 1986. **(6.11)**
9. Define 'Consumer'. Explain his rights under Consumers Protection Act, 1986. Describe the mechanism available for redressal of grievances. **(6.6, 6.9 and 6.5)**
10. What is meant by 'Deficiency of Service'? State a few agencies against which complaints can be filed for redressal of deficiency of service. Substantiate with two examples. **(6.8 – Point C, 6.12 and 6.13)**
11. What is meant by 'Complaint'? On whom complaints can be lodged for deficiency of service under Consumers Protection Act, 1986. **(6.11 (Points – A & B) and 6.12)**

7

POLLUTION CONTROL AND ENVIRONMENT PROTECTION

7.1 INTRODUCTION

God has introduced first Earth, Sun, Moon, Stars and other planets. Later, God has created man. However, Man has, slowly, started making entry into other species and, if possible, wants to take control of other creations of God. In this bargain of conquer, the natural resources are exploited. **Pollution in the environment is the creation of man.** This pollution has become more due to fury of God – visible in the form of storms, earthquakes, and unnatural incidents of nature – floods and cyclones and many more, not anticipated by human kind.

State, Citizens and Courts are the three agencies, which have to shoulder the responsibility to identify the causes of pollution, cure the same, be extra protective from the recurrence of causes to avoid further aggravation and safeguard the environment, not yet polluted.

Self conscious efforts and discipline of individuals in the daily behaviour, legislative efforts of the State and alertness of courts to punish those responsible for deterioration of environment are the greatest need of the hour.

Pollution and global warming are on increase. The greenery of India may perish and Thar desert may expand its limits. Removing pollution, all together, is not possible. Retaining pollution at controlled levels should be the aim of the agencies involved.

Rapid industrialization and economic development have given us better products, increased comforts and, of course, a better style of living. But, the development has brought in its blazing trail the problem of environmental pollution. **Development and environment do not go together.** More development results in more pollution. "As societies grow richer, their environments grow poorer." 'Mere breathing in Mumbai is equivalent to smoking ten cigarettes a day'- according to a report of Central Health Education Bureau reported in Economic Times, dated 5th June, 1996.

The Environment (Protection) Act, 1986, commonly known as EPA, owes its origin to Bhopal Gas Tragedy. The Bhopal Gas Tragedy would be remembered so long as the humanity continues to remain. **It has been recognized development should not be at the cost of environment.**

To safeguard the future, the natural basics of life must be protected. Every individual must contribute to maintain our habitat (planet) for future generations.

The Environment (Protection) Act, 1986 has been enacted to provide for prevention of Bhopal Gas Tragedy incidents, protection and improvement in environment and for the matters connected therewith.

7.2 POLLUTION – CAUSES

Pollution means any adulteration to the natural environmental surroundings. Unregulated industrial development is the main cause for pollution.

(A) Industrial Air Pollution

In factories and industrial plants, the main culprit is the process adopted to manufacture chemicals etc. Manufacturing an item is required, but equally necessary is the necessity to control the pollutants created, during this manufacturing process as byproducts.

If a system is well designed to produce, chances of pollution are remote. However, many of the plant designers do not have the concept of pollution control in their minds, while designing plants. They, normally, have the objective to design to manufacture the right product, at low capital and costs. Reducing costs and improving profitability is their main concern. Pollution control is considered as secondary or even optional. Due to this approach, most of the industrial plants generate large quantities of pollutants in air, mostly in the form of gases.

Another reason of this is the dearth of pollution control consultants.

The main products polluting air are acid vapors, sulphur-dioxide, chlorine, carbon monoxide, hydrogen sulphide, ammonia, particulates, benzene byproducts etc. These products are not supposed to be released in the atmosphere.

Faulty pipes and duct joint openings are the main source from which these products escape. In other words, the main cause of air pollution is the release of those gases, which are not supposed to be released into the environment.

To exercise effective check and control, it is necessary that each and every unit has to be doubly checked, with in-house consultants to ensure that problems do not arise, later.

(B) Water Pollution

Water is the wonderful gift of nature. The common water pollutants are the industrial effluents and municipal waste.

> **It is estimated more than 60% of the diseases are water borne diseases in India.**

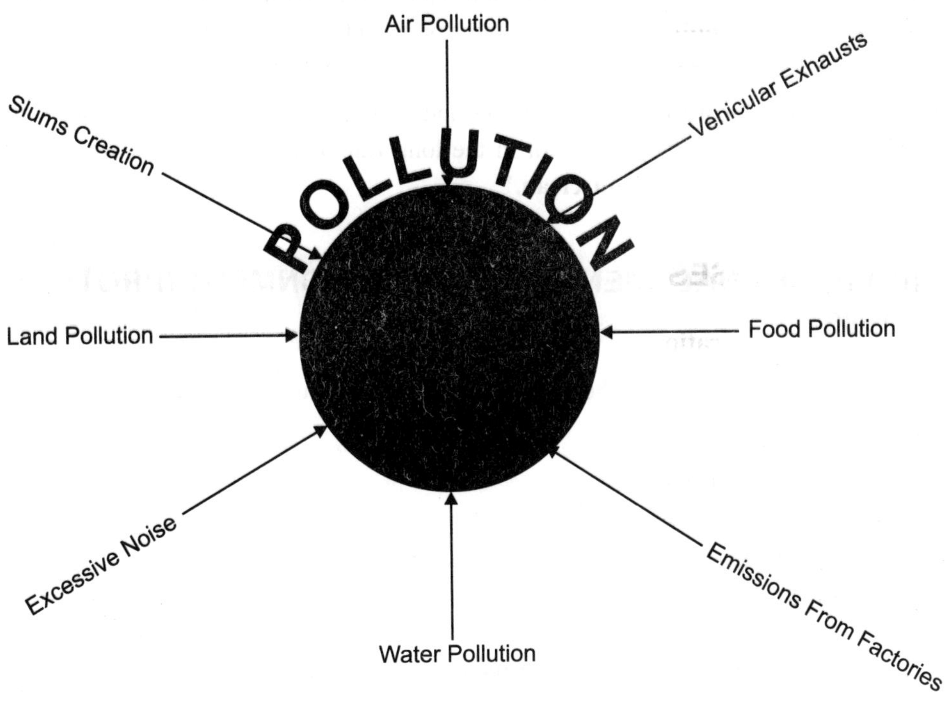

Causes of Pollution
(Diagram No.19)

7.3 NEED OF POLLUTION CONTROL

Pollution control is necessary due to two reasons:

- Polluted air and water are harmful to life. Air pollution creates problems for healthy living beings and plants. Water pollution also creates problems for all living beings, agriculture, water bodies, all plants and animals living in water, land fertility etc.

  Thus, one's consciousness should always be to attempt to generate means to control pollution of any type.

- Most of the governments all over the world have laws by which no one is supposed to exceed creating pollution in air or water, beyond prescribed limits.

  Law breakers often face punishments to the tune of heavy fines and even stoppage of work.

> **Self realization in the human beings is the only real key that prevents further deterioration in the environment.**

Bhopal gas tragedy is the best example to explain the necessity to take adequate measures to control pollution. Thousands of people have been affected due to lack of adequate measures.

Another example is the BSES plant at Dahanu, India. While preparing feasibility report, plant designers have not considered the low sulphonation plant, while starting the unit. With more than 10 years of litigation, it has surfaced now and the court had to order stoppage of work or take necessary steps.

The above examples are enough to make one understand the need to take measures to control pollution. Steps taken, initially, would benefit in the long run. This is the reason we say **'Pollution Control Pays Back – Earn while you clean.'**

7.4 PURPOSE OF ENACTMENT OF THE ENVIRONMENT (PROTECTION) ACT, 1986

The Environment (Protection) Act, 1986 is enacted with three purposes and they are three fold:

(i) Protection of environment

(ii) Improvement of environment

(iii) Prevention of hazards to

  (A) human beings

  (B) other living creatures

  (C) plants, and

  (D) property

Central Government has been given the powers to take measures and protect the environment.

To provide for the prevention and control of water pollution, the Water (Prevention and Control of Pollution) Act, 1974 has been enacted with the rules there under. For the preservation of quality of Air and control of air pollution, Air (Prevention and Control of Pollution) Act, 1981 has been enacted, with the rules made there under.

7.5 OBJECTIVES OF THE ENVIRONMENT (PROTECTION) ACT, 1986

The objectives of the Act are as under:

(A) **Coordination of activities of the various agencies**, already in existence.

(B) **Creation of Authority or Authorities with adequate powers** for environmental protection.

(C) **Regulation of discharge** of environmental pollutants and handling of hazardous substances.

(D) **Speedy response in the event of accidents** threatening environment.

(E) **Provision of deterrent punishment** to those who endanger human environment, safety and health.

7.6 EXPLANATION OF TERMS

Some of the terms in the context of pollution and environment protection are explained:

(A) Pollution

Pollution means any adulteration to the environmental surroundings. Adulteration may be in solid, liquid or gaseous substance. It causes harm and hazards to life, either to human beings, animals, plants or nature. Even smells and noise may cause harm and injury to health, both mental and physical.

(B) Environment

Environment includes water, air and land. There is an inter-relationship among water, air and land. Additionally, it shows the relationship between water, air, land on one side and human beings, other living creatures, plants, micro-organism and property on the other side.

(C) Environmental Pollution

Environmental pollution means presence of environment pollutants in the environment.

Environment pollutants may be solid, liquid or gaseous substance present in such concentration in environment, which may be injurious to health.

(D) Hazardous Substance

Hazardous substance means any substance or preparation of it which causes harm to human beings, other living creatures, plants, micro-organisms, property or any environment.

The harm could be caused due to chemical or physi-chemical properties or handling of hazardous substances.

(E) Occupier

Occupier in relation to a factory or premises means a person who is in control over the affairs of the factory or the premises. It also includes any person who is in possession of the hazardous substance.

(F) Stream

Stream includes

(i) river;

(ii) water course (wheather flowing or for the time being dry)

(iii) inland water (wheather natural or artificial)

(iv) sub-terranean waters;

(v) sea or tidal waters to such extent or, as the case may be, to such a point as the State Government may, by notification in the official gazette specify in this behalf.

(G) Trade Effluent

Trade effluent includes any liquid, gaseous or solid substance which is discharged from any premises used for carrying on any industry, operation or treatment and disposal system. **Trade effluent does not include domestic sewage.**

(H) Emission

Emission means any solid liquid or gaseous substance coming out of any chimney, duct or flue or any other outlet.

7.7 WHAT CAUSES ENVIRONMENTAL POLLUTION?

Pollution is either natural or man made pollution.

Natural Pollution: Natural pollution includes earthquake, flood, cyclone, famine, drought etc.

Artificial Pollution: Artificial pollution is man made. It is created due to various activities like water pollution, air pollution, land pollution or food pollution.

Environmental Pollution: Environmental pollution is basically due to lack of controls and safeguards. Exploitation of natural resources, beyond the permissible level, is also a basic cause for environmental pollution.

One of the primary reasons for environmental pollution in undeveloped and under-developing countries is population growth.

Fundamental cause for environmental pollution is rapid population growth, without matching availability of food, shelter, health facilities and sanitation.

Vehicular exhausts, uncontrolled emissions from industries, excessive noise, radiations and rural migration to urban areas causing slums play a vital role in causing environmental pollution. Heavy vehicles, buses, trucks and vehicles used in defence contribute, significantly, for pollution strides.

The Supreme Court has held that the courts are competent to issue necessary directions even if such noise is the direct result connected with religious and social activities. **(Church of God (Full Gospel) in India Vs. K.K. of Majestic colony Welfare Association 2000 (7).** The intention of apex court is clear. Religious and social activities should not create environmental pollution. In our country, religious and social activities have become a guise for some to exploit others and create public inconvenience. In such circumstances, the only saver is court.

7.8 POWERS OF THE CENTRAL GOVERNMENT TO PROTECT AND IMPROVE ENVIRONMENT

The following are the powers of the Central Government under The Environment (Protection) Act, 1986 to protect and improve environment.

(A) **Power to take Measures to Protect and Improve Environment (Sec. 3):** The Central Government has been given the powers to take all measures to protect and improve the quality of environment. It can take all steps, as may be necessary, to prevent, control and abate environmental pollution. Government is empowered to take the following measures:

(i) **Coordination of actions** by State Governments and its officials.

(ii) **Planning and execution** of nationwide programmes.

(iii) **Laying down standards for quality of environment** in various aspects.

(iv) **Laying down standards for emission** or discharge of environmental pollutants.

(v) **Restriction of areas** in which any industries, operations or processes shall not be carried out and safeguards, if allowed to be carried out.

(vi) **Laying down procedures and standards** for handling hazardous substances.

(vii) **Carrying out or sponsoring research** relating to problems of environmental pollution.

(viii) **Inspection** of any premises, process, plant, equipment, machinery, manufacturing or other processes and issuing directions in the form of orders for prevention, control and abatement of environmental pollution.

(ix) **Establishment and recognition of laboratories and institutes** to carry out the functions under the Act.

(x) **Collection and dissemination of information** relating to environmental pollution.

(xi) **Preparation of manuals and codes** for prevention, control and abatement of environmental pollution.

(xii) **Any other matters** as the Central Government may deem necessary for securing effective implementation of the Act.

(B) Power to Appoint Officers and their Powers and Functions (Sec. 4): The Central Government may appoint officers with such designations as it thinks fit and entrust the necessary powers for performing the functions under this Act.

(C) Powers of Central Government to give Directions (Sec. 5): The Central Government has the powers to direct

(i) **Closure, Prohibition and Regulation** of any industry, operation or process.

(ii) **Stoppage** of electricity, water or any other service.

However, no direction can be given without giving the opportunity of being heard.

(D) Power to Make Rules to Regulate Environmental Pollution (Sec. 6): The rules may relate to any of the following matters:

(i) Standards of quality of air, water and soil for various areas and purposes.

(ii) Maximum allowable limit for various environmental pollutants.

(iii) Procedures and safeguards for handling of hazardous goods.

(iv) Prohibitions and restrictions on the handling of hazardous goods.

(v) Prohibitions and restrictions on the location of industries, carrying on processes and operations in different areas.

(vi) Procedures and safeguards for prevention of accidents which may cause environmental pollution.

(E) Furnishing of Information to Authorities and Agencies in Certain Cases (Sec. 9): Where the discharge of environmental pollutant is in excess of the prescribed standards, the person responsible for such discharge has to intimate the fact of such occurrence or apprehension of such occurrence to the prescribed authorities. Further, he is bound to prevent or mitigate the environmental pollution and render all such assistance as the authorities may require.

(F) Powers of Entry and Inspection (Sec. 10): Any authority empowered by the Central Government has a right to enter into any place, at all reasonable times, for performing the functions entrusted to him. The authority has the right of examining and testing any equipment, industrial plant, document or record. In case, the authority believes that any offence has been committed or is being committed, he has the power for seizing the equipment, industrial plant, document or record.

(G) Power to Take Sample (Sec. 11): The Central Government or any officer empowered by it has the power to take any sample of air, water, soil or other substances from any factory, premises or any other place. During check, if the concerned authority wants to take any sample for laboratory analysis, the authority has to give notice of his intention to take sample for further analysis. Notice is to be served to the occupier of the premises in Form 1. Two samples are to be taken and one is to be sealed, under the signature of the occupier and authority, for analysis. The second sample is to be given to the occupier and acknowledgment is to be obtained. In the absence of notice, sample would not be admissible in legal proceedings. **Notice can be served then and there too.**

While taking the sample, the stipulated procedure under the Act has to be followed.

The sample has to be collected in the presence of the occupier or his agent.

For the purpose of taking the sample, notice has to be served on the occupier or agent, in charge of the place where from the sample has to be taken.

(H) **Power to Establish Environmental Laboratories (Sec. 12):** After issuing a notification in the official gazette, the Central Government has the power to establish environmental laboratories or recognize any one of the existing laboratories as environmental laboratories.

(I) **Penalty for Contravention of Act, Rules and Directions (Sec. 15):** Penalty for contravention is five years' imprisonment or fine which may extend to rupees one lakh or both.

(J) **Offences by Companies:** Where any offence is committed by the company, every person who is in charge of and responsible for the conduct of the business of the company, as well as company, shall be deemed to be guilty of the offence and prosecuted.

Protection of Action Taken in Good Faith: No suit, prosecution or other legal proceedings shall lie against Government or any officer or employee of the Government for any act done, in good faith, in pursuance of the provisions of the Act.

7.9 EVALUATION - IMPACT OF THE ENVIRONMENT (PROTECTION) ACT, 1986

Positive Side: The Act has empowered the Central Government to take steps to prevent and control pollution.

The Act is a comprehensive piece of legislation, which provides the needed powers to prevent and control the growing menace –Pollution.

Water (Prevention and Control of Pollution) Act seeks control of water pollution. Air (Prevention and Control of Pollution) Act controls air pollution. But, The Environment (Protection) Act, 1986, popularly known as EPA, is more comprehensive in its scope and powers.

The Act provides stringent punishment for contravention.

The Act applies to Government departments too.

Negative Side: The full impact of the real implementation of the Act is, yet, to be felt by the public. We see the vehicles emitting the pollution and noise. Mikes would be blaring through out the night, causing inconvenience to students who may be appearing for the examinations and disturbing sleep of the general public.

Medak in Andhra Pradesh is a classical example of development, accompanied by the decay of environment. Late Smt. Indira Gandhi has won the Lok Sabha seat in 1980 from that constituency.

In recognition, after becoming the Prime Minister of the country, she has developed Medak, an undeveloped area. Due to her efforts, several industries have come up due to rapid industrialization. With the growth of industries, development has occurred, but at the cost of environment. Several people have died due to epilepsy -a disease.

Unless adequate safeguards are introduced to check pollution, development would occur only at the cost of environment. Only proper implementation of the Act, in its true spirit, makes possible development and environment, undisturbed, go hand in hand.

7.10 PRESENT ENVIRONMENTAL POLICY OF GOVERNMENT OF INDIA

Pollution and destruction of natural resources have reached such dimensions in India that in some regions they pose an imminent risk to human health. Reasons lie in poverty, uncontrolled industrialisation and urbanization.

Some Facts on Environment in India

- *India is the world's sixth largest and second fastest growing producer of greenhouse gases.*
- *Delhi, Mumbai and Chennai are three of the world's ten most polluted cities.*
- *Two-thirds of city dwellers lack sewerage; one-third lack potable water.*
- *Indian urban population grows equivalent of another New York City every year. This equals to a projected urban population of over 500 million in 20 years.*

Environmental Issues in India

Environmental issues in India include various natural hazards, particularly, *cyclones* and annual *monsoon* floods, and various combinations of *poverty*, population growth, increasing individual consumption, industrialization, infrastructural development, poor agricultural practices, and resource maldistribution have led to substantial human transformation of India's natural environment.

Soil Erosion: An estimated 60% of cultivated land suffers from *soil erosion,* water logging, and salinity. It is also estimated that between 4.7 and 12 billion tons of topsoil are lost, annually, from soil erosion.

Decline of Water Levels: From 1947 to 2002, average annual per capita water availability declined by almost 70% to 1,822 cubic meters, and overexploitation of ground water is problematic in the states of *Haryana, Punjab,* and *Uttar Pradesh.* Forest area covers 19.4% of India's geographic area (637000 km). Nearly half of the country's forest cover is found in the state of *Madhya Pradesh* (20.7%) and the seven states of the north-east (25.7%); the latter is experiencing net forest loss.

Reduction of Forest Area: Forest cover is declining because of harvesting for fuel wood and the expansion of agricultural land. These trends, combined with increasing industrial and motor vehicle pollution output, have led to atmospheric temperature increases, shifting precipitation patterns, and declining intervals of drought recurrence, in many areas.

Administration of Environmental Pollution: Till the enactment of EPA, pollution control has been the administrative responsibility of State Pollution Control Boards and the Central Board. Because of the multiplicity of agencies, need for an authority has been felt, which would assume the lead role. The main reason for passing EPA has been to overcome the coordination problems. The EPA has vested broad powers in Central Government for studying, planning, coordinating and implementing long term requirements of environmental safety and to meet emergency situations threatening environment.

While the standards fixed by EPA for the emission or discharge of the environment pollutants are not adequate, more stringent standards can be provided by Water (Prevention and Control of Water Pollution) Act, 1974 and Air (Prevention and Control of Air Pollution) Act, 1981 for any specific industry, operation or process.

The primary objective is to preserve environment, without allowing it to be polluted. Pollution has been increasing, significantly for various reasons, already, discussed in detail. What has been polluted is highly difficult to restore it to the original level of purification. In this process, several rivers are under purification schemes of Central Government.

Check Your Understanding

State whether the following statements are True or False

1. Environment includes water, air and land.
2. Pollution means any adulteration to the natural environmental surroundings.
3. Environmental pollution means absence of environment pollutants in the environment.
4. Trade effluent includes domestic sewage.
5. Emission means any solid, liquid or gaseous substance coming out of any chimney.
6. Pollution is only natural.
7. One of the primary reasons for environmental pollution in undeveloped and under-developing countries is population growth.
8. The Central Government or any officer empowered under the Act have the power to take any sample of air, water, soil or other substances from any factory, premises or any other place, without serving any notice to the occupier of the premises.
9. Where any offence is committed by the company, every person who is in charge of and responsible for the conduct of the business of the company, as well as company shall be deemed to be guilty of the offence and shall be prosecuted.
10. Legal proceedings can be made by the aggrieved of the order against any officer or employee of the Government for any act done, in good faith, in pursuance of the provisions of the Act.

11. The Environment (Protection) Act, 1986 does not apply to Government departments.
12. Generally, development would occur only at the cost of environment.
13. Any sample collected from the factory is to be kept in a container and is to be sealed, under the signature of the authority and occupier or his agent, for admissibility of evidence in a court.
14. Exploitation of natural resources, beyond the permissible level, is also a basic cause for environmental pollution.
15. Religious and social activities are beyond the purview for controlling environmental pollution.
16. The Environment (Protection) Act, 1986 has been passed earlier to the enactment of Water (Prevention and Control of Pollution) Act and Air (Prevention and Control of Pollution) Act.
17. Even smells and noise may cause harm and so they are also included in the causes of pollution.
18. The Environment (Protection) Act, 1986 is more comprehensive in its scope and powers compared to Water (Prevention and Control of Pollution) Act and Air (Prevention and Control of Pollution) Act.

Answers:

1. True	2. True	3. False	4. False	5. True
6. False	7. True	8. False	9. True	10. False
11. False	12. True	13. True	14. True	15. False
16. False	17. True	18. True		

Pick up the Right Answer

1. Stream includes:
   (A) River.
   (B) Water course
   (C) Sub-terranean water
   (D) All of the above
2. Environment and development:
   (A) Go together
   (B) Are opposed to one another
   (C) One operates in the absence of other
   (D) Cancel one another
3. The purpose of enactment of Environment (Protection) Act, 1986 is
   (A) Protection of environment
   (B) Improvement of environment

(C) Protection and improvement of environment

(D) Deterioration of environment

4. Environment includes

(A) Water

(B) Air

(C) Land

(D) Water, air and land

Answers:

1. (D) 2. (B) 3. (C) 4. (D)

Objective Questions

1. Discuss the background for the formation of The Environment (Protection) Act, 1986. **(7.1)**
2. Development should not be at the cost of environment. Comment. **(7.1 and 7.9)**
3. Development and environment do not go together – Discuss. What legislative steps has been taken to ensure their combination, together? **(7.1 and 7.9)**
4. What is meant by 'Pollution'? What are the causes of pollution control? **(7.2)**
5. Explain the need of pollution control? **(7.3)**
6. Write the different purposes to be achieved for Enactment of The Environment (Protection) Act, 1986. **(7.4)**
7. State the objectives of The Environment (Protection) Act, 1986? **(7.5)**
8. Explain the following terms: **(7.6)**

   (A) Pollution

   (B) Stream

   (C) Trade effluent

   (D) Occupier

   (E) Emission

   (F) Environment

   (G) Environmental pollution

   (H) Hazardous substance
9. Define the terms 'Environment' and 'Pollution'? What are the causes of pollution. **(7.6 – B, A and 7.2)**
10. What are the causes for environmental pollution? **(7.2 and 7.7)**
11. Bring out the powers of the Central Government under The Environment (Protection) Act, 1986 to protect and improve the environment. **(7.8)**

12. Explain in brief the provisions of The Environment (Protection) Act, 1986 related to the powers of Government to protect and improve environment: **(7.8)**
13. Detail environmental issues in India and bring out an explanatory note on the present Environmental Policy of the Government of India? **(7.7 and 7.10)**

8

INTELLECTUAL PROPERTY RIGHTS

8.1 INTRODUCTION

Basically, human beings make efforts for personal gain. Every individual wants to reap benefits of the efforts he makes. Some think even beyond. Even after their death, they want their progeny, family members, to enjoy the fruits of their efforts. If there is no guarantee that the concerned individual or his family members only would enjoy the results of their efforts, there would be no incentive for them to work hard. This would be more the case, when their efforts are time consuming and results not guaranteed.

8.2 MEANING OF INTELLECTUAL PROPERTY RIGHTS

Intellectual property is the creation of human intellect. The Intellectual Property Rights guarantees the right to the concerned and their family the results of their efforts for exclusive possession and enjoyment.

An intellectual property right (IPR) is, according to Black's Law Dictionary, an intangible right "protecting commercially valuable products of the human intellect." It may comprise patents, copyrights, trademarks and other similar rights. An IPR includes the right to exclude others from exploiting the non-corporeal asset.

The term 'intellectual property' reflects the idea that this subject matter is the product of the mind or intellect.

8.3 BASIC OBJECTIVE AND SCOPE - LAW WITH INTELLECTUAL PROPERTY RIGHTS

The basic objective of intellectual property rights is to protect the interests of inventors and encourage further efforts towards innovation, whereby social welfare would be achieved in the process of development to the public, in general.

The main reason why an IPR is granted is to give an incentive for innovation, research and investment. In the absence of IPR protection, other firms would be able to take a free ride on the R&D investment made by the inventor firm.

To achieve this objective, the law provides the rights in such intellectual pursuits, which is termed as intellectual rights. **Intellectual property basically lies in the concept, ideas, thought, initially, and later turns into actual product when it becomes registered, under the relevant law.**

In law, intellectual property (IP) is an umbrella term for various legal entitlements which attach to certain names, written and recorded media, and inventions.

Scope: The law dealing with the intellectual property rights has changed, substantially, in the last decade. India has become a signatory to General Agreement on Trade and Tariff (GATT) and secured membership of World Trade Organisation (WTO). Consequent on these developments, changes in intellectual property rights have taken place and the related laws too have undergone amendments to suit the changed circumstances.

8.4 TYPES OF INTELLECTUAL PROPERTY RIGHTS

There are different laws on intellectual property rights. Reason is the Intellectual Property Rights are more than one. For each type of intellectual property, the law is different.

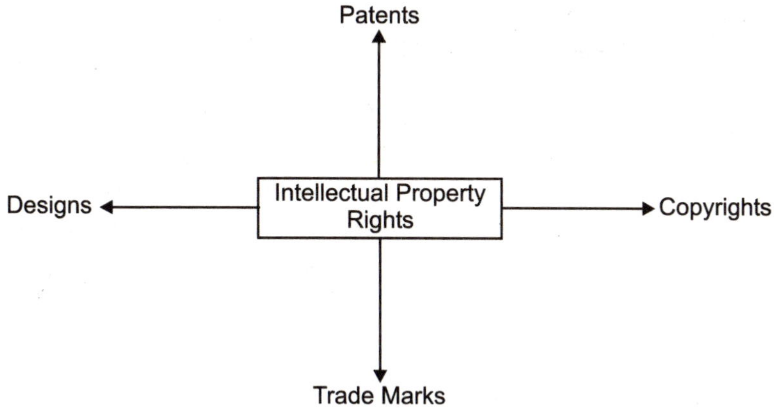

Types of Intellectual Property Rights
(Diagram No. 20)

(A) Patents

One kind of intellectual pursuit may lead to the creation of new substances, products, technologies, devices, methods or processes, which are of value. These are protected as 'Patents' under Patents Act, 1970.

(B) Copyrights

Human intellect may express in the form of art, literature, music, films or broadcasts. These are protected as copyrights under the Copyrights Act.

(C) Trade Marks

A trademark is a distinctive sign. It is used to distinguish the products or services of different businesses.

Trade marks can be words, symbols, names and devices or combinations of all. The Trade Marks Law grants manufacturer or trader an exclusive right to use the mark for identifying his goods, which distinguishes them from other goods. There is no intrinsic value about a trade mark. However, on hearing the trade mark, the consumer recalls some product, which becomes the very identity of the firm. For example, the name 'Xerox' has no meaning. However, when we hear the name of 'Xerox' we recall photocopier. If the trademark is not protected, the goodwill that is earned, after several years of efforts in image building, would be lost. Any one who appropriates that name is consuming the goodwill of that firm, earned through by providing the quality product.

(D) Designs

A design refers to features of shape, configuration or pattern. A design is necessarily part and parcel of the article manufactured. A trademark need not be so. This is the difference between the trademark and design.

An industrial design right protects the form of appearance, style or design of an industrial object (e.g. spare parts, furniture, or textiles).

8.5 HISTORY OF PATENT LAW IN INDIA

Prior to passing of Indian Patents Act, 1970, drugs and pharmaceuticals have been covered by Product Patents. All most all the allopathic drugs have been developed by the companies in industrialized nations. So, availability of any life-saving medicines has been dependent upon their whims and fancies of the foreign companies. Indian consumers have been at the mercy of the foreign companies for availability and the price fixed by them has no control. Foreign drug companies, operating in India, have been fleecing Indian consumers. Any consumer who is in need of those medicines either has to shell out the required price, fixed by them, or go without the drug.

It is quite literally a dead end when we see how access to medicines is denied to those who need it as prices are locked in a high way, beyond the reach of many. To correct the situation, the Government had no option other than bringing a distinction between a product patent and process patent by passing the Patents Act, 1970.

> **The Indian Patents Act, 1970 has made a distinction between a product patent and process patent.**

The Indian law has not permitted product patents to be given to certain products. Medicines and drugs have been included in the list of non-patentable products. This is an intentional move of Government of India to take advantage of the drugs, developed outside the country.

In other words, even if a person has been able to produce a new and useful medicine or chemical product, after 1970, patent has not been given. However, if a person comes up with a new process or method, whether it is for existing or new product, he could claim patent for the process patent.

Reverse Engineering: In the field of medicines and drugs, only Process Patenting has been permitted, but not Product Patenting in our country. The Indian industry has been able to examine the drug, find out the chemical composition and find a new different process for making the product. The Indian industry could innovate and come out with a new process for manufacturing to cure the diseases. This has been called as **"Reverse Engineering"** of a medicine. This has helped the nascent Indian industry to develop new process and manufacture products, required by the nation. This strategy has given time for the Indian industry to stabilize, develop and compete with the outside market.

> **'A low level of Patent Protection' has been a deliberate move in our country to boost industrial development to catch with the rest of the world.**

Under-developed and undeveloped countries can copy the developed nations, till they acquire the level of matured development. It cannot be said as unethical practice as all the nations have to be at the same level in business for fair play. Our country has not matured in development at that stage. To make medicines available at affordable prices, the Government has adopted that type of policy, at that time, in the interests of the general public, in particular, the common man who has not been able to afford the unreasonable prices of medicines of foreign products.

No difference between Product Patent and Process Patent

With the protection policy adopted by the Government, the pharmaceutical industry in the world has been aggrieved. Their contention has been that they have spent huge amounts for research and clinical research for product development, before the product could become commercially successful. Our country has been taking the benefit, without any investment and pains involved in the process of development of a new drug. Their grouse has been that their interests are not protected as the Indian pharmaceutical industry has been, freely, using their efforts and money. To overcome the situation, GATT has required the distinction between product patent and process patent be eliminated. GATT has wanted a product patent be allowed on all new products. GATT has fixed a ten year period for India to bring in product patent regime, fully. In the meanwhile, intermediate targets have been fixed. This ten year period has ended by 31st December, 2004. Now, the Indian industry has matured enough to compete with the outside world. The Government of India has promulgated an ordinance in December, 2004 to bring this into effect. **Now, there is no difference between product patent and process patent under Patent Act.**

Application of Patents Act to Seeds and Organisms

Farmers in India have been using the developed seeds and organisms of the west, without paying any royalty as they have not been patented. This has been a matter of concern to the west for loss of their profits. A new law has been passed, in line with the commitments made by India, as a signatory to the Trade Related Intellectual Property (TRIPS). **Now, a separate Act titled "Biological Diversity Act, 2002" has been passed to protect the interests of the rights of breeders and innovators of new forms of seeds and plants.**

Period of Patent Right

Earlier, the life of the patent right has been 14 years. Now, the life of patent right for all categories of inventions has been increased to 20 years.

8.6 MEANING OF PATENT AND ITS ADVANTAGES

A patent gives monopoly right to the inventor for using it. **A patent, generally speaking, is a grant of right conferred by Government on the grantee for a limited period of time.** Patent is an exclusive privilege of making, selling and using the invention for which the patent has been granted.

8.7 WHAT CAN BE PATENTED?

Patent can be granted for inventions. In simple words, invention is something new which did not exist, before. It is the creative work of some one. To be patentable, an innovation must be new, involve an innovative step (i.e. non-obvious) and be capable of industrial application.

8.8 WHAT CANNOT BE PATENTED?

The following are a few examples, not inventions, within the meaning of this Act, and so cannot be patented registered:

(A) Invention which could go against public morality or prejudice health to human, animal or plant life, including environment.

(B) A method of agriculture or horticulture.

(C) Any medicinal, surgical, curative or diagnostic process or other treatment of human beings that may render them free of disease or a similar treatment for animals.

(D) A presentation of information.

Examples: Using a sprinkler is a method of farming. The person who invented the idea is not given the right to patent it.

Similarly, a doctor who has come up with a new technique of doing open heart surgery cannot patent the process of surgery. Laser surgery cannot be patented.

8.9 PROCEDURE FOR REGISTRATION OF PATENTS

The first Patent Act has been passed in the year 1856. This has given an exclusive privilege rights to the patentees for a period of 14 years, now, increased to 20 years.

The Patent Act prescribes the procedure for grant of patent.

(A) Eligibility for Application

Any person claiming to be true and first inventor of the invention is eligible to apply.

(B) Requisites of Invention

For an idea to qualify as an invention, the following requisites are to be fulfilled:

- Novelty or inventiveness
- Non-obviousness
- Usefulness

If the invention does not meet the above criterion, the application for registration of patents may be denied under Section 3 of Patents Act.

(C) Authority to Apply

Application should be filed at the appropriate office of the Patent Office. The residence or principal place of business determines the jurisdiction for making the application. In the case of a company, the registered office of the company is accepted as the principal place of business.

(D) Method of Application

The principle is one application, for one invention. The application should be made in the proper form, prescribed under the Act. Every application has to state that the applicant is the true and first inventor and is in possession of the invention. Provisional or complete specifications should be stated in the application.

Grant of patent would be given from the date of submission of the application.

So, the person who has made full divulgence of complete specifications is protected, provided the application is accepted for grant of patent. The necessary fee has to accompany the application. The application has to be submitted to the Controller.

Where the application is made by virtue of assignment of the right for a patent, the proof of the right is to be enclosed with the application or to be submitted, within three months of its filing.

(E) Verification by Patent Office

The application of the inventor is referred by the controller to the examiner. The examiner checks whether the application complies with the requirements of the Act. The examiner also checks whether the invention has been claimed by some other person or already published. A register is maintained by the patent officer for the patents, already granted. The examiner searches the register to satisfy the eligibility for registration. After examination, the patent office communicates any objections, it may have. If the applicant is unable to remove the objections, the application is rejected.

(F) Publication in Official Gazette

If the applicant is successful in removing the objections, the controller advertises the application in the official gazette. The publication in official gazette is to provide an opportunity to the public to raise objections, if any.

(G) Grant of Patent

After successful removal of the objections, a patent is granted.

(H) Date of Patent

Every patent shall be patented as of the date on which the complete specification was filed. The date of patenting is entered in the Register of Patents.

8.10 RIGHTS OR ADVANTAGES IN OBTAINING PATENTS

The person in whose favour a patent is granted is called a **Patentee**. It is in the interests of the inventor to get his invention or any improvement patented.

There are certain advantages in obtaining patents:

(A) Exclusive Right

Once patent is registered, patentee would have the exclusive right to use his invention. By grant of patent, protection by way of monopoly is made available for a limited period. Patent is allowed for invention, not for discovery. It would not make any difference if the patent is known to others from the date of patent. **The date of patent is the date when the complete specifications are filed with the registering authority.**

(B) Right to Sell

Once the patent is registered, the patentee can sell the patent for commercial use, in case he does not have the means to develop. The person who acquires license rights can exploit the patent and earn money. The 'Right of Registration' makes it possible to secure fruits of efforts of invention to the patentee. The Act confers the right on the patentee to assign fully or partly in favour of any third party. In case the patent is assigned, the licensee, equally, enjoys the right to manufacture and develop for further gains. Both the patentee and licensee are benefited.

(C) Suit for Infringement

When any person makes or supplies that substance, commercially, for use by others, knowingly or unknowingly, the rights of the patentee are affected, which is called infringement. Both the patentee and licensee can file a suit for infringement, in case of contravention of their rights by any third party. They can pray for an injunction and also can claim damages for loss of profits against the person who infringes their rights.

The burden lies on the defendant to prove that the process used by him is different from the patented process. **There is no need for the plaintiff to establish that he has sustained commercial loss.** In other words, even if there is no loss, still the plaintiff can file case against the defendant.

It would be the onus or burden of the plaintiff to prove that the defendants have made, sold or used the invention, without his license or counterfeited or imitated.

(D) Patent of Addition

A patentee can make developments or modifications to the original patent and obtain the grant of patent for the improvement or modification in the form of 'Patent of Addition'.

(E) Period of Patent

By an amendment to the Act, the period of a patent right for all inventions has been raised to 20 years from the earlier period of 14 years.

8.11 MEANING AND PURPOSE OF COPYRIGHT

Artists, musicians and writers spend their life-time to create a master piece. Earlier, these creative persons used to work for fame and recognition. Now, it has become a commercial activity. Copyright Act, 1957 has been framed to give protection to this intellectual property.

What can be copyrighted?

Copyright is available for a very wide range of expressions. This includes literary, musical, artistical and dramatic works.

> **Copyright gives the owner of work an exclusive right in respect of reproduction, publication, performance, communication to the public to enable him to derive financial benefit by exercising such right.**

Terms of Copyright

The term of protection for copyright, under the Copyright (Amendment) Act 1999, has been made 60 years, after the death of the author. In other words, literary, dramatic, musical or artistic works enjoy copyright protection for life term of the author plus 60 years. In case of joint authorship, the term of the copyright is to be calculated from the death of the author who dies last.

The period prescribed under TRIPs is only 50 years.

Two masters of English literature – Charles Dickens in England and Mark Twain in America – have suffered much unhappiness from the piracy of their works.

The primary function of the copyright law is to protect the original creator from piracy. Only work is protected, not the idea. In other words, the same idea can be taken by others and new work can be developed.

8.12 PROCEDURE FOR REGISTRATION OF COPYRIGHT

A person becomes the owner of a creative work, once he produces it. There is no need to register the ownership. Registration is, totally, voluntary and optional. If a dispute arises about the ownership, registration would be a useful prima facie evidence for ownership.

The provisions for registration of copyright are as follows:

(1) Register of Copyrights

Copyright subsists in literary work, music, film, artistic work, record, computer software and radio and television broadcast work. A register of copyright is kept at the Registrar of Copyrights. Details of names or titles of works along with names and addresses of authors are entered in the register.

(2) Registration of Copyrights

Registration of Copyrights is optional. It is reiterated that registration is not compulsory. A copyright can exist even without registration and an action can be brought, even without registration. However, registration provides prima facie evidence of title in favour of the person, claiming the copyright. The Act does not deprive the right, merely, on account of non-registration. Certificate of Registration becomes useful evidence before a court of law, if a dispute arises in relation to the infringement of the copyright.

(3) Entries in Register of Copyrights

The author or publisher may approach the Registrar of Copyrights with an application in the prescribed form, with required fee, for entering the particulars of the work in the Register of Copyrights. After holding such enquiry as he may deem fit, the Registrar enters the particulars of the work in the Register of Copyrights.

Once the Registrar of Copyrights certifies the documents to be copies, they would be admissible in the court of law, without further proof of production of original.

(4) Effect of Registration

A copyright holder has the exclusive right to reproduce the work. Without copyholder's permission, others are prohibited from using the work.

(5) Inspection of Register

Any person can inspect, at all reasonable times, the Register of Copyrights. Any person is entitled to take copies or make extracts of the register, after payment of the necessary fee, as may be prescribed.

(6) Register of Copyrights

Register of Copyrights is a prima facie evidence of the particulars entered therein.

(7) Correction of entries in the Register of Copyrights

The Registrar of Copyrights can make necessary corrections in respect of the errors in any name, address or particulars, subject to the compliance of prescribed conditions.

(8) Publication in Official Gazette

Every entry made in the Register of Copyrights or corrections of any entry entered therein would be published by the Registrar of Copyrights in the official gazette or in such manner as he may deem fit.

(9) Certificate of Registration

Once Registrar of Copyrights is satisfied with the correctness of the information submitted, he issues Certificate of Registration to the applicant.

8.13 ASSIGNMENT OF COPYRIGHTS

Copyright is a personal movable property, capable of being transferred by assignment.

Assignment must be done, in writing, and must be stamped, according to the provisions of the Act.

Copyright is a beneficial interest. However, it need not be registered. **[(Gramophone Co. India Ltd. Vs Shanti Films Corp, AIR 1997 Calcutta (63)]**

Patentee can assign the right, fully, partially or conditionally to another or others.

Example: A producer has assigned all rights of negatives of a film to another person in 1961. It was held that the producer could assign TV and Video rights to others.

8.14 RIGHT OF OWNER OF COPYRIGHTS

A copyright is, essentially, a right to prohibit others from copying a work.

No one can reproduce the work, in any material form. Neither translation nor adoption by others is allowed.

8.15 ACTIVITIES WHICH ARE NOT COPYRIGHT VIOLATIONS

Freedom of every individual is subject to certain constraints, in particular, when it relates to property of others. We find, at times, some authors copy the work of others, even without a formal acknowledgment. To what extent, this is permitted? Reading or reiteration in public of any reasonable extract from any published literary work is permissible. Similarly, publication of short passages from others' publications does not fall within the purview of the violation of copyrights. The relevant point is the extent should be 'reasonable'.

8.16 AN OVERVIEW OF EXISTING COPYRIGHTS

Copyright is a set of exclusive rights regulating the use of particular expression of an idea or information. It is the most important type of Intellectual Property Right. The copyright policies are different from one country to another. It protects skill, labour, talent of an author who are responsible for publication of a document, a piece of music, photograph, TV serials and other creative works.

According to the copyright, the owner has a right to prevent others from copying, selling, hiring out, performing, broadcasting or amending the work/innovations, publications developed by them.

The copyright law is subject to international treaties. The important international treaties are Berne convention and Universal copyright convention. Berne convention allows following minimum basic copyright laws and allowing for reciprocal protection for Nationals of different countries. For example, a UK author can enjoy the US copyright laws and as well as USA author enjoys UK copyright laws. But, different countries follow different copyright laws. As a result, it is very difficult to have uniform laws among them. And many authors have advocated that infringement of laws is worse in the networked environment. Many have opined that the establishment of single uniform law throughout the World for networked environment will minimize copyright laws. But, it is not easy to establish such laws.

8.17 ISBN AND PURPOSE

ISBN

As and when author enters into an agreement with the publisher, the publisher acquires the rights of publication, in terms of the agreement entered into. The publisher acquires ISBN numbers, in bulk, from ISBN agencies and assigns them to the publications, it makes.

ISBN stands for International Standard Book Number.

The International Standard Book Number (ISBN) is a 10-digit number that uniquely identifies books and book-like products, published internationally.

Purpose of ISBN

The purpose of the ISBN is to establish and identify one title or edition of a title from one specific publisher. It is unique to that edition, allowing for more efficient marketing of products by booksellers, libraries, universities, wholesalers and distributors.

Check Your Understanding

State whether the following statements are True or False

1. Intellectual property is the creation of human intellect.
2. The Intellectual Property Rights guarantees the right to the concerned and their family the fruits of their efforts for exclusive possession and enjoyment.
3. There is only one law on intellectual property rights.
4. One kind of intellectual pursuit may lead to the creation of new substances, products, technologies, devices, methods or processes, which are of considerable value, known as patents.
5. Human intellect expressed in the form of art, literature, music, films or broadcasts is not protected in any form.
6. The basic objective of intellectual property rights is to protect the interests of inventors and encourage further efforts towards innovation whereby social welfare would be achieved in the process of development to the public, in general.
7. The Trade Marks Law grants manufacturer or trader an exclusive right to use the mark for identifying his goods, which distinguishes them from other goods.
8. A patent does not give monopoly right to the inventor for using it.
9. All inventions cannot be patented.
10. Patent is allowed both for invention and discovery.
11. A method of agriculture or horticulture cannot be patented.
12. Farming through sprinkling can be patented.

13. There is difference, presently, between Product Patent and Process Patent under Patents Act.
14. The life of patent right for all inventions has been increased from 14 years to 20 years.
15. Rights of breeders and innovators for new forms of seeds and plants are protected under the "Biological Diversity Act, 2002".
16. The life term of protection for copyright under the Copyright (Amendment) Act, 1999 has been 60 years, after the death of the author.
17. Registration of Copyrights is compulsory.
18. Copyright is a personal movable property, capable of being transferred by assignment.
19. The burden lies on the defendant to prove that the process used by him is different from the patented process.
20. It is necessary for the plaintiff to prove that there has been commercial loss for claiming damages, in case of use by an unauthorized person of a registered patent.
21. Certificate of Registration is useful prima-facie evidence before a court of law, if a dispute arises in relation to the infringement of the copyright.
22. Every invention can be registered under Patents Act, 1970.
23. No approval is needed for material reproduction of the work of an author.
24. Every patent shall be patented as of the date on which the complete specification was filed.
25. The patentee is not allowed to file a suit for infringement, in case of contravention of rights by any third party, when the patent is sold as the law considers it is the right of the licensee only to file a case for infringement.
26. An author cannot assign the Copyrights of his book partially or conditionally to any publisher for publication.

Answers:

1. True	2. True	3. False	4. True	5. False
6. True	7. True	8. False	9. True	10. False
11. True	12. False	13. False	14. True	15. True
16. True	17. False	18. True	19. True	20. False
21. True	22. False	23. False	24. True	25. False
26. False				

Pick up Right Answer

1. Intellectual Property Rights includes
   (A) Patents
   (B) Copyrights
   (C) Designs

(D) Trade Marks

(E) All the above

2. Present life of a patent right for all categories of inventions is

(A) 5 years

(B) 10 years

(C) 15 years

(D) 20 years

3. The term of protection for copyright, after the death of the author, under the Copyright Act is

(A) 50 years

(B) 60 years

(C) 5 years

(D) 20 years

4. Trade marks are

(A) Words

(B) Symbols

(C) Names

(D) Devices

(E) Combinations of above all

Answers:

1. (E) 2. (D) 3. (B) 4. (E)

Descriptive Questions

1. What is meant by 'Intellectual Property Rights' and discuss the object and scope of Intellectual Property Act? **(8.1 to 8.3)**
2. Explain the meaning of 'Intellectual Property Rights'. Describe the different types of such rights. **(8.2 and 8.4)**
3. Explain the meaning of Patent and its advantages. What can be patented? Name the patents that cannot be registered. Give two examples of inventions that can not be registered as patents. **(8.4 (A), 8.6 to 8.8)**
4. What is meant by 'Patent'? Bring out the procedure for obtaining Patent Rights in India. **(8.4(A) and 8.9)**
5. "The Patent Act has been hailed as the saviour of the developing countries like India and

has been copied by other developing countries too," Elucidate. **(8.1 and 8.5)**

6. Describe History of Patent Law in India and bring out the recent changes that have been brought in drugs and pharmaceuticals to comply with the requirements of GATT. **(8.1 and 8.5)**
7. 'A low level of Patent Protection' has been a deliberate move in our country to boost industrial development to catch with the rest of the world' discuss. **(8.1 and 8.5)**
8. Bring out the difference between Product Patent and Process Patent. Comment on the latest position under the Patents Act. **(8.1 and 8.5)**
9. Detail the Rights or Advantages in obtaining Patents. **(8.4 (A) and 8.10)**
10. What is the meaning and purpose of a copyright? Explain the procedure for registration and assignment of copyrights? **(8.4(B), 8.11 to 8.13)**
11. Write short notes on: **(8.5)**

    (A) Reverse Engineering

    (B) Product Patent and Process Patent

    (C) Biological Diversity Act, 2002

9

MERGERS AND ACQUISITIONS
—Includes the Competition Bill, 2007

- Introduction
- Alternative Ways of Growth
- Forms of Expansion – Business Combination
- New Trends in Mergers
- Forms of Business Combinations
- Merger or Amalgamation
  - Absorption
  - Consolidation
- Acquisition
- Holding Companies
- Types of Mergers
  - Horizontal Merger
  - Vertical Merger
  - Conglomerate Merger
- Attractions/Advantages of Mergers-Synergy
- Realities between Merger and Acquisition
- Factors Responsible for M&A
- Multi-National Company or Corporation
- Legal and Procedural Aspects of Mergers & Acquisitions
- Approval of Court – Merger and Amalgamation
- New Opportunities – Big Deals of Lending to Indian Banking
- The competition Act, 2002
  - Amendments in Act –The Competition Bill, 2007
- Check Your Understanding
- Pick up the Right Answer
- Match the Following
- Descriptive Questions

9.1 INTRODUCTION

The concept of Mergers and Acquisitions (M & A) has, of late, become quite popular. It has gained a lot of importance after the 1990s since India has entered into the era of Liberalization, Privatization and Globalization. The winds of LPG are blowing over all the sectors of the Indian economy, but their maximum impact is seen in the industrial sector. The market has thus become hyper competitive and in order to avoid unhealthy competition and compete with international and multinational companies, Indian companies are going for M & A. This area has thrown up immense opportunities of growth to corporate sector in India. One of the opportunities is in the area of corporate restructuring. The last few decades, in India, have witnessed a large number of mergers. The trend is clear, towards consolidation in order to become number one or two in the industry, in the area of manufacture or service, they deal in.

Corporate India has been restructuring and repositioning itself to seize the opportunities and meet the challenges thrown open by globalization. The management strategy is on mergers and acquisitions (M&A) – to achieve an optimum size as a means of survival and growth in the competitive economy. The trend is to acquire profitable competitive structure. The basic objective is to acquire profitable companies, which can contribute for more profit and growth of the group and sell those, which are drain on resources.

Acquisitions and mergers have become strategic devices in the hands of more and more firms, not only to stay in competition but also to extend their dominance.

India has entered the world map of M & A activity, in a big way, with mega acquisition by Tatas and Mittals.

9.2 ALTERNATIVE WAYS OF GROWTH

There are primarily two ways of achieving growth, organic and inorganic for a business organization. A firm focusing on organic growth essentially aims at achieving business growth through enhanced customer base as well as higher sales, both physical and financial, which results in a steady jump in revenue. Essentially, organic growth is aided and induced by progressive and increasing deployment of the four inputs viz., men, money, materials and machines. An inorganic growth opportunity provides the organization with an avenue for attaining accelerated – in a way instantaneous – growth enabling it to skip a few steps on the growth ladder.

Mergers and acquisitions (M&A) constitute one of the most important methods of securing inorganic growth.

9.3 FORMS OF EXPANSION - BUSINESS COMBINATION

'Expansion' is the key word for fast growth. The different forms of Expansion are

- Internal Expansion
- External Expansion

Expansion is possible through the enlargement of existing activities, which is known as internal expansion. However, the mega player position - increased business activity in the form of more sales and profits – cannot be achieved overnight by internal expansion. Internal expansion takes time and a lot of effort is involved in achieving the desired result.

Acquisition of ownership and control of other concerns is the way for external expansion.

External expansion requires more planning and resources. External expansion is otherwise known as 'Business Combination'. Here, two or more business concerns combine and expand their business activities. Combination is the coming together of persons and organizations, with the main motive to achieve maximization of profits and elimination of competition. **The process of business combination can take either the route of 'Merger' or 'Acquisition'.** Companies who are cash rich or flush with funds opt these routes.

The Main Idea

One plus one makes three: One plus one makes three is the special equation behind a merger or an acquisition. **The key principle behind is to create shareholder value over and above that of the sum of the two companies.** Two companies together are more valuable than two separate companies - at least, that's the reasoning behind M&A.

This rationale is, particularly, alluring to companies when times are tough. Strong companies act to buy other companies to create a more competitive, cost-efficient company. The companies come together hoping to gain a greater market share or to achieve higher efficiency. Because of these potential benefits, target companies often agree to be purchased, when they know they cannot survive, alone.

9.4 NEW TRENDS IN MERGERS

The trend in mergers is more visible in the white sector goods or emerging sunrise industries. In the past, foreign companies have acquired Indian companies. Now, a reverse trend has started. With the permission for Indian companies to invest abroad, there is a trend of merger of foreign companies with Indian companies. Tata tea has created a history by acquiring controlling stake in Tetley. A number of software companies have started moving to take over software companies by mergers in U.S.A. and Europe. After software sector, the turn has been for rising industries like media, communication and biotech companies to acquire companies, abroad.

Mergers have great impact on our economies. These mega mergers create what Tofler calls 'Corporate Nations'. However, these mergers cause sleepless nights to many employees, creating uncertainty of their future employment and growth.

9.5 FORMS OF BUSINESS COMBINATIONS

The different forms of business combinations are:

- Absorption
- Consolidation
- Acquisition
- Holding Company

At times, some of these terms are used, interchangeably. However, it is important to note that there is a legal distinction between the different kinds of business framework.

9.6 MERGER OR AMALGAMATION

A merger is a combination of two or more companies to form into one company.

There is some disagreement on the precise meaning of various terms related to the forms of business combinations. Under income-tax the term 'Amalgamation' is used for merger.

> **Both the terms 'Merger' and 'Amalgamation' mean the same, while the term 'Amalgamation' is used under Income-Tax Act.**

According to Section 2(1B) of Income-Tax Act, 1961, the term 'Amalgamation' means a merger of one or more companies with another company or merger of two companies to form one company in such a manner that:

(i) all the property of the amalgamating company or companies, immediately before the amalgamation, becomes the property of the amalgamated company, by virtue of amalgamation.

(ii) all the liabilities of the amalgamating company or companies, immediately before the amalgamation, become the liability of the amalgamated company, by virtue of amalgamation.

(iii) the shareholders holding not less than 75%, in value, of the shares in the amalgamating company or companies become shareholders of the amalgamated company by virtue of amalgamation. However, the value of the shares held by the amalgamated company or by its nominee or by its subsidiary companies should be excluded in computing the above 75% of the value of shares. For example, 'A' company holds 30% of shares in 'B' company. 'B' company wants to merge with 'A' company. Shareholders of 'B' company holding at least 75% of the remaining shares i.e. 52.5% (75 × 70)/100 should become shareholders of 'A' company.

In other words, under Income-Tax Act, amalgamation can be absorption or consolidation. Only one word 'Amalgamation' is used in income-tax.

Merger:

Merger may be taken as an abbreviation, which means:

M	–	Mixing
E	–	Entities
R	–	Resources for
G	–	Growth
E	–	Enrichment and
R	–	Renovation

Merger can be of two types:

- Merger through Absorption
- Merger through Consolidation

(A) Absorption

A combination of two or more companies into an existing company is known as 'Absorption'.

There are two, acquiring company and the company that is acquired. After acquisition, the acquired company is no longer alive.

Definition: When one company takes over another and clearly establishes itself as the new owner, the purchase is called 'absorption'.

From a legal point of view, the target company ceases to exist.

Suppose there are two companies A Ltd. and B Ltd. B Ltd. is merged into A Ltd. In this process, B Ltd. ceases to exist. The assets and liabilities of B Ltd. are acquired by A Ltd. After, absorption, the assets and liabilities of B Ltd. appear in the balance sheet of A Ltd. The name of B Ltd. is struck off from the list of registered companies. A typical case is the absorption of Reliance Polyproplene Ltd. (RPPL) with Reliance Industries Ltd. The shareholders of RRPL were offered the shares of Reliance Industries Ltd. A shareholder of 100 shares (RPPL) has secured 20 shares (RIL).

Another example is A Ltd. and B Ltd. may be acquired by an existing company C Ltd. In this case, both A Ltd. and B Ltd. disappear and only C Ltd. continues with the assets and liabilities of A Ltd. and B Ltd.

(B) Consolidation

A Consolidation is a combination of two or more companies to form a new company.

In this form of merger, all the existing companies go into liquidation. **A new company is formed, with a new identity, which takes over the assets and liabilities of the companies liquidated.** Suppose, there are two companies Radhi Ltd. and Kalyan Ltd. They form into a new company 'Radhi & Kalyan Ltd." or "Cherry Ltd."

Difference between Absorption and Consolidation

Although the terms Absorption and Consolidation are often uttered in the same breath and used as though they were synonymous, both mean different things.

Absorption and Consolidation are different types of merger. There is an important difference between the two. The important feature of 'Absorption' is an existing company takes over the other company. No new company is formed for this purpose. When one company takes over another and clearly establishes itself as the new owner, the purchase is called an acquisition. From a legal point of view, the target company ceases to exist. The buyer "swallows" the business and the buyer's stock continues to be traded. The shares of the swallowed company are not quoted on the stock exchange, after acquisition.

In consolidation, a new company is formed by the union or combination of two or more concerns. A small size company is merged with a big company through absorption. In consolidation, two equal-size companies join together.

Both the terms absorption and consolidation are used, interchangeably. However, the methods and problems of financing between the two are different.

9.7 ACQUISITION

An essential feature of absorption and consolidation is the merger of the companies. The acquiring company takes over the ownership of two or more companies. Their operations are combined. **In Acquisition, there is no combination of companies. The companies concerned continue to remain physically as they are.** Simply, control over management is taken over or acquired. Acquisition and Takeover mean the same result.

Takeover is a business strategy of acquiring control over the management of the target company – either directly or indirectly. The motive of the acquirer is to gain control over the Board of Directors of the target company for synergy in decision-making. The eagle eyes of raiders are always on the look out for cash-rich and high-growth companies, with low equity stake of promoters.

Absorption and Acquisition are different. After Absorption, companies combine together, while they work, separately, as before, even after Acquisition.

Acquisition can be of two types:

- Friendly take-over
- Hostile take-over

In case of 'Friendly take-over', the control and management of another company is acquired, with the consent or cooperation of the other company.

In case of 'Hostile take-over', the control and management of target company is acquired with force, even though opposed by the other company. Here, the control is exercised over an unwilling entity.

Friendly takeovers often have a positive effect on the price of the stock of the company that is acquired. Unfriendly takeovers can have a negative effect on the stock price of the company acquired.

The advantages and disadvantages of takeover, in brief, are as under:

Pros:

1. Increase in sales/revenues (e.g. Procter & Gamble takeover of Gillette).
2. Venture into new businesses and markets.
3. Profitability of target company.
4. Increased market share.
5. Decrease in competition (from the perspective of the acquiring company).
6. Reduction of overcapacity in the industry.
7. Enlarge brand portfolio (e.g. L'Oréal's takeover of Bodyshop).

Cons:

1. Reduced competition and choice for consumers in oligopoly markets.
2. Likelihood of price increases and job cuts.
3. Cultural integration/conflict with new management.
4. Hidden liabilities of target entity.

Reverse Takeover: A reverse takeover is a type of takeover where a public company acquires a private company of a higher value. This is usually done at the instigation of the larger, private company, the purpose being for the private company to effectively float itself while avoiding some of the expense and time involved in a conventional initial public offer (IPO).

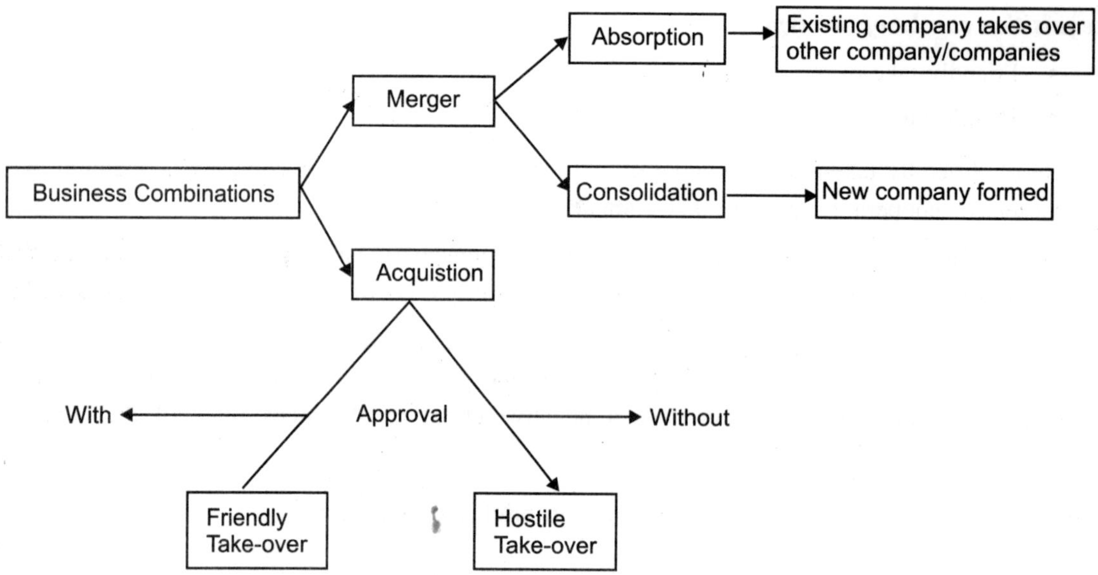

Business Combinations- Merger and Acquisition (Diagram No.21)

Recent Acquisitions

Period	*Company*	*Acquirer*	*Deal Worth US$*
Feb. 2007	Novelis	Hindalco	6.0 billion
Jan. 2007	Corus Group	Tata Steel	12.1 billion
Jan. 2007	Ritz-Cariton Boston	Indian Hotels	170 million
Sept. 2006	Jeco Holding AG	M & M	180 million
July 2006	Arcelor	Mittal Steel	30.0 billion
June 2006	Eight O'Clock Coffee	Tata Tea	220 million
June 2006	Sabah Forest Ind	BILT	261 million
March 2006	Hansen	Suzlon Energy	565 million
March 2006	Terapia	Ranbaxy	324 million
Feb. 2006	Betapharm	Dr. Reddy's	570 million
July 2005	Teleglobe	VSNL	239 million

Source: Chartered Secretary – Special issue (April 2007) on Takeovers, Mergers & Amalgamations.

9.8 HOLDING COMPANIES

The other form of partial consolidation is Holding Company. Legally, a holding company is the one which holds the majority of the amount of share capital and exercises the voting power, directly, or through nominee in the subsidiary company. It can exercise the power to appoint the maximum number of directors. The holding company and subsidiary companies have separate legal existence. However, the subsidiaries are under the effective control of the holding company.

9.9 TYPES OF MERGERS

Various types of mergers have been taking place in India. These are:

(A) Horizontal Merger

When companies of same business merge together, it is called 'Horizontal Merger'. When two or more companies, dealing in similar lines of activity, combine together then horizontal merger takes place.

Advantages

The purpose of Horizontal Merger is

- elimination or reduction in competition,
- putting an end to price cutting,
- achieving economies of sale in production, research and development, marketing and management, etc.

These mergers offer financial, marketing, production and personnel synergies. So, this type of merger is most advantageous to those companies involved in the process of merger.

Disadvantages

However, there are certain disadvantages too. Industry or business risk does not reduce with this type of merger. The impact of recession-business fluctuations-would be more pronounced for the merged companies. In other words, there is no diversification of risk. If growth occurs, they would be highly benefited. Equally, if there is fall in business, they would be worst affected. There may be no advantage in respect of cash flows.

> **Horizontal Merger works as a double-edged sword as both growth and fall would be magnified.**

These mergers are very popular. A large number of mergers take place every year.

(B) Vertical Merger

When supplier company of raw materials and buyer company merge together, or seller company and customer company merge together, it is called 'Vertical Merger'. Think of an ideal example, a cone supplier is merging with an ice cream maker. The object is cost reduction and efficient marketing.

> **Merger not only creates significant shareholder value, but also positions the combined company to compete vigorously with other companies.**

In the case of vertical merger, a company acquires its 'upstream' or 'downstream' units. Upstream are the suppliers of raw material where as down streams are marketing or retail outlets.

The purpose of such merger is to

- reduce buying cost of raw materials,
- lower distribution costs,
- secure assured supplies and market,
- increase or create barriers to entry for potential competitors.

Basically, this type of merger occurs to achieve marketing and financial synergy.

Examples: A railway company may join with the coal mining company. A textile unit may join with a transport company engaged in carrying its products to different places.

The idea behind the Vertical Merger is to take up different stages of work in a combined manner to ensure speedy production or quick service.

Other forms of vertical merger are:

Market-extension Merger: Two companies that sell the same products in different markets.

Product-extension Merger: Two companies selling different but related products in the same market. Example is two companies engaged in manufacturing razor blades and shaving cream combine together. Both the products are needed to complete the simple operation i.e. shaving.

(C) Conglomerate Merger

In this type, two companies that have no common business areas merge.

When companies having different types of business operations merge together, it is called 'Conglomerate merger'. In marked contrast, Conglomerate Merger is a type of combination where a firm established in one industry combines with another firm in another unrelated industry. The rationale for such merger move is

- diversification of risk.

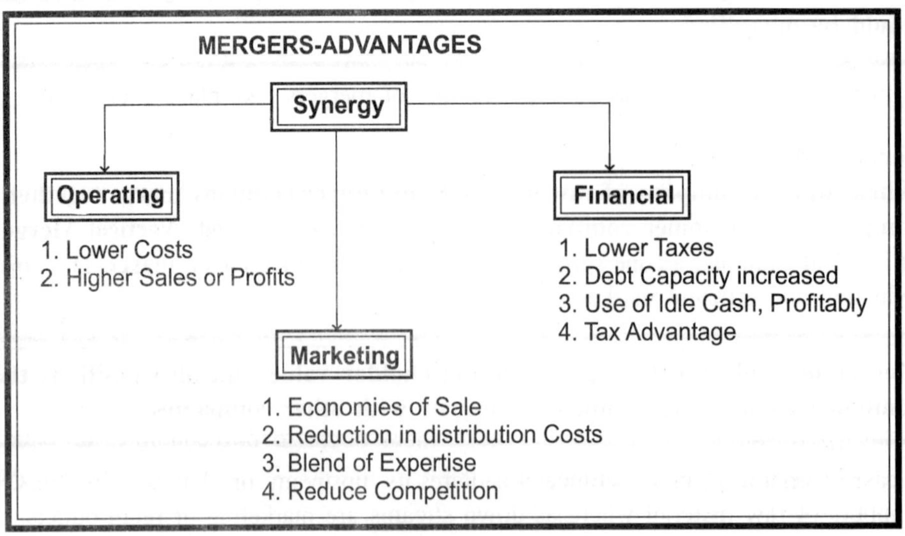

Advantages of Mergers
(Diagram No.22)

9.10 ATTRACTIONS/ADVANTAGES OF MERGERS – SYNERGY

Meaning of Synergy: Synergy means the enhanced result of two or more people, groups or organizations working together. In other words, one and one equals three! It comes from the Greek "synergia," which means joint work and cooperative action. The word is used quite often to mean that combining forces produces a better product.

> **Synergy is the magic force that allows for enhanced cost efficiencies of the new business.**

All mergers and acquisitions have one common goal. They are all meant to create synergy that makes the value of the combined companies greater than the sum of the two parts. The success of a merger or acquisition depends on whether this synergy is achieved.

Synergy takes the form of revenue enhancement and cost savings. There are different types of synergies that can be achieved. By merging, the companies hope to benefit from the following:

(A) Improved Market Reach and Industry Visibility

Companies buy other companies to reach new markets and grow revenues and earnings. A merger may expand two companies' marketing and distribution channels and give them new sales' opportunities. A merger can also improve a company's standing in the investment community. Bigger firms often have an easier time in raising capital than smaller ones.

(B) Economies of Scale

Yes, size matters. Whether it is purchasing stationery or a new corporate IT system, a bigger company placing the orders can save more on costs. Mergers also translate into improved purchasing power to buy equipment or office supplies - when placing larger orders, companies have a greater ability to negotiate prices with their suppliers.

(C) Acquiring New Technology

To stay competitive, companies need to stay on top of technological developments and their business applications. By buying a smaller company with unique technologies, a large company can maintain or develop a competitive edge.

(D) Staff Reductions

As every employee knows, mergers tend to mean job losses. Consider all the money saved from reducing the number of staff members from accounting, marketing and other departments. Job cuts also include the former CEO, who typically leaves with a compensation package.

Negative Side: Achieving synergy is easier said than done. Synergy is not, automatically, realized once two companies merge. Normally, there ought to be economies of scale when two businesses are combined, but sometimes, just, the opposite may happen with a merger. At times, one and one add up to less than two.

Sadly, synergy opportunities may exist only in the minds of the corporate leaders and the deal makers. Where there is no value to be created, the CEO and investment bankers - who have much to gain from a successful M&A deal - will try to create an image of enhanced value. The market, however, eventually sees through this and penalizes the company by assigning it a discounted share price. This may result in the failure of M&A.

9.11 REALITIES BETWEEN MERGER AND ACQUISITION

In the pure sense of the term, a merger happens when two firms, often of about the same size, agree to go forward as a single new company, rather than remain separately owned and operated. This kind of action is more precisely referred to as a "merger of equals." Both companies' stocks are surrendered and new company stock is issued in its place. For example, both Daimler-Benz and Chrysler have ceased to exist when the two firms have merged, and a new company, DaimlerChrysler, has come into existence.

In practice, however, actual mergers of equals do not happen, very often. Usually, one company buys another and, as part of the deal's terms, simply allow the acquired firm to announce that the action is a merger of equals, even if it is, technically, an acquisition. Being bought out often carries negative connotations, therefore, by describing the deal as a merger, deal makers and top managers try to make the takeover more palatable.

Whether a purchase is considered a merger or an acquisition really depends on whether the purchase is friendly or hostile and how it is announced. In other words, the real difference lies in how the purchase is communicated to and received by the target company's board of directors, employees and shareholders.

9.12 FACTORS RESPONSIBLE FOR M&A

Although, it is difficult to draw up a comprehensive list of factors propelling M&A activity, the usual factors are as under:

(a) **Liberalization of government restrictions:** Liberalization of government restrictions, falling trade barriers, easing of cross-border cash flows and advances in technology give scope for securing competitive advantages.

(b) **Possibility of securing strategic benefit:** Possibility of securing strategic benefit such as higher market share, product portfolio expansion, in consequence of mergers, enable the firms to "leap frog" to a higher stage of growth.

(c) **Differential advantages** can be secured from intellectual property assets, held by companies such as patent, trademarks, copyrights and trade secrets.

(d) **Optimization of synergies:** Consolidation of the business of both the companies through optimization of synergies produce higher efficiency, economies of scale and improved profits.

(e) **Alignment of core competencies:** Alignment of core competencies by leveraging respective strengths and saving on brand development, advertisement and sales promotion.

(f) **Pooling:** Pooling of financial, managerial and technical resources, personnel, capabilities, skills, expertise and technologies of the merging companies lead to increased competitive strength, cost reduction, productivity gains and logistic advantages.

(g) **Tax advantage:** Provision of Tax shields where one of the merging firms is having accumulated losses and/ or unabsorbed depreciation which can be gainfully set off against the accumulated revenues of a profit making firm.

9.13 MULTI- NATIONAL COMPANY OR CORPORATION

Multi-national Company or Corporation is one which operates in more than two countries.

Mergers, being a global phenomenon, bring about cross-border taxation issues, namely double taxation issues, with respect to ESOP.

9.14 LEGAL AND PROCEDURAL ASPECTS OF MERGERS & ACQUISITIONS

Mergers and acquisitions are regulated under various laws in India. The objective of the laws is to make these deals transparent and protect the interests of all shareholders.

Mergers & Acquisitions are regulated through the provisions of the Companies Act, 1956.

The Companies Act lays down the legal procedures for mergers or acquisitions. The procedure is long drawn and involves some important legal dimensions.

(1) Analysis of Proposal by the Companies

Whenever a proposal of merger comes for consideration of the management of the companies, the proposal is examined, in depth, from the view point of the efficiencies likely to be achieved in terms of costs, markets, tax implications and, finally, the profitability aspects for the companies concerned. The likely reactions of the shareholders, creditors and others are also assessed. If necessary, external professional help is also sought about the implications of merger. If the proposal is considered beneficial, it would proceed ahead, otherwise, the proposal would be shelved.

(2) Permission for Merger

Two or more companies can amalgamate only when the amalgamation is permitted under Memorandum of Association.

The acquiring company should have the permission in its object clause to carry on the business of the acquired company. In the absence of the provision in the Memorandum of Association, it is necessary to seek the permission of the board of directors, shareholders and the Company Law Board before affecting the merger.

(3) Determining Exchange Ratio

Merger or Amalgamation involves exchange of shares. The shareholders of the amalgamating company get shares in the amalgamated company. Normally, a number of factors such as book value per share, market value per share and potential earning per share are taken into consideration for determining the exchange ratio.

(4) Approval of Board of Directors

The board of directors of the individual companies should approve the draft proposal for amalgamation and authorise the managements of the companies concerned to pursue, further, the proposal of amalgamation.

(5) Shareholders' and Creditors' Meetings

The individual companies should hold separate meetings of their shareholders and creditors for approving the amalgamation scheme. According to Section 391 of Companies Act, at least, 75 percent of shareholders in value and majority in number, voting in person or by proxy, must accord their approval to the scheme.

In a separate meeting of creditors, amalgamation scheme should be approved by majority of creditors, in numbers, and three-fourths in value.

(6) Application in the High Court

An application for approving the draft amalgamation proposal, duly approved, by the individual companies should be made to the High Court.

(7) Sanction by the High Court

After the approval of the shareholders and creditors, on the petitions of the companies, the High Court will pass an order, sanctioning the amalgamation scheme after it is satisfied that the scheme is fair and reasonable. The date of the court's hearing will be published in two newspapers, and also, the regional director of the Company Law Board will be intimated.

The court will consider the viewpoint of all parties appearing, if any, before giving its consent. The court may accept, modify or reject the amalgamation scheme and pass orders, accordingly. However, it is up to the shareholders whether to accept the modified scheme or not.

It is necessary for the Registrar to send a report to the court to the effect that the affairs of the company are not being conducted prejudicial to the interests of the members or the public. Without the report of the Registrar of Companies, the amalgamation cannot be approved by the court.

(8) Filing of the Court Order

After the Court order, its certified true copies will be filed with the Registrar of Companies.

(9) Transfer of Assets and Liabilities

The assets and liabilities of the acquired company will be transferred to the acquiring company, in accordance with the approved scheme, with effect from the specified date.

(10) Payment by Cash or Securities

As per the proposal, the acquiring company will exchange shares and debentures and/or cash for the shares and debentures of the acquired company. These securities will be listed on the stock exchange.

(11) Other Regulations

The other applicable Acts are The Foreign Exchange Management Act, 1999 and the Income Tax Act,1961. Besides, the Securities and Exchange Board of India (SEBI) has issued guidelines to regulate mergers and acquisitions. The SEBI (Substantial Acquisition of Shares and Take-overs) Regulations, 1997 and its subsequent amendments aim at making the take-over process transparent and also protect the interests of minority shareholders.

(12) Approval of Reserve Bank of India

Permission of the RBI is needed for issue of any security to a person, resident outside India. Accordingly, the transferee company has to obtain the permission before issuing shares in exchange of shares held in the transferor company.

(13) Information to the Stock Exchange

The acquiring and the acquired companies should inform the stock exchanges (where they are listed) about the merger.

(14) Regulation through The Competition Act, 2002

The Monopolies and Restrictive Trade Practices (MRTP) Act, 1969 has become obsolete. This Act has been choking the growing Indian economy.

The Competition Act has been enacted in 2002 keeping in the wake of economic developments that resulted in the opening up of the Indian economy, removal of controls and consequent economic liberalization.

The Competition Act, 2002 regulates the various forms of business combinations through Competition Commission of India. Under the Act, no person or enterprise shall enter into a combination, in the form of an acquisition, merger or amalgamation, which causes or is likely to cause an appreciable adverse effect on competition in the relevant market. Such a combination is void.

Prohibition of entering into Anti-competitive Agreements

Now, it is not lawful for any enterprise or association of enterprises to enter into an agreement in respect of production, supply, storage, distribution, acquisition or control of goods or provision of service which causes or is likely to cause an appreciable adverse impact on the competition, within India.

Enterprises intending to enter into a combination may give notice to the Commission, but this notification is voluntary.

It is important to note that notification is not compulsory. The Competition Commission of India, upon knowledge relating to the acquisition, inquires into the appreciable adverse impact on competition in India. However, such inquiry cannot be made, after the expiry of one year from the date on which the combination has taken effect. All combinations do not call for scrutiny unless the resulting combination exceeds the threshold limits in terms of assets or turnover as specified by the Competition Commission of India.

The Commission while regulating a 'combination' shall consider the following factors:

a. actual and potential competition through imports;
b. extent of entry barriers into the market;
c. level of combination in the market;
d. degree of countervailing power in the market;
e. possibility of the combination to significantly and substantially increase prices or profits;
f. extent of effective competition likely to sustain in a market;
g. availability of substitutes before and after the combination;
h. market share of the parties to the combination, individually, and as a combination;
i. possibility of the combination to remove the vigorous and effective competitor or competition in the market;
j. nature and extent of vertical integration in the market;
k. nature and extent of innovation;
l. whether the benefits of the combinations outweigh the adverse impact of the combination.
m. Relative advantage by way of combination to the economic development.

Thus, the Competition Act does not seek to eliminate combinations and only aims to eliminate their harmful effects.

9.15 APPROVAL OF COURT- MERGER AND AMALGAMATION

Approval of court is essential for any scheme of merger or amalgamation.

Under Sections 391 and 394 of Companies Act, the court is concerned to look into that the scheme of Merger is

- Not unfair,
- Not contrary to the public policy,

- Not unconscionable or against the law,
- Procedure set out in the Act is met and complied with, and
- Proposed scheme of compromise or arrangement is not violative of any provision of law.

A company can be brought to an end in several ways:

1. A company can be brought to an end by winding it up. Winding up is a legal process provided for in the Companies Act.
2. A company can cease to exist by merging itself in another company. This is called Absorption.
3. A company can join with another company to form a new company. This is called Consolidation.

The company is free to absorb or consolidate. However, such decisions may be to the detriment of small shareholders and creditors. Thus, the **Companies Act has created protection by requiring approval of the court for every merger.**

While giving approval, what power the court can exercise and what role the court is expected to play in the process of amalgamation?

The legal decisions help us in understanding the powers of the court as well as role of court in the matter of merger.

Power of Court

(A) Merger should not be manifestly unfair

In the case of **Re, Mankam Investments Ltd.** (1995) 4 Comp LJ 330 (Cal.), it has been held:

> **"It is a matter for the shareholders to consider, commercially, whether amalgamation or merger is beneficial or not.** The Court is really not concerned with the commercial decision of the shareholders until and unless the Court feels that the proposed merger is manifestly unfair or is being proposed unfairly and/or to defraud these other shareholders."

"The Court is really not concerned with the exact details of the matter and if the shareholders approve the scheme by the requisite majority, then the Court only looks into the scheme as to find out that it is not manifestly unfair and/ or is not intended to defraud or do injustice to the other shareholders."

(B) Merger is not contrary to Public Interest

In the case of **Hindustan Lever Employees' Union Vs Hindustan Lever Ltd.** 1995 Supp (1) SCC 499: (1994 AIR SCW 4701)

Section 394 casts an obligation on the Court to be satisfied that the scheme for amalgamation or merger was not contrary to public interest. "The basic principle of such satisfaction is none other than the broad and general principles inherent in any compromise or settlement entered between parties that it should not be unfair or contrary to public policy or unconscionable. In amalgamation of companies, the Courts have evolved, the principle "prudent business management test" or that the scheme should not be a device to evade law. But when the Court is concerned with a scheme of merger with a subsidiary of a foreign company, then test is not whether the schemes shall result in maximizing profits of the shareholders or whether the interest of employees was protected but it has to ensure that merger shall not result in impeding promotion of industry or shall obstruct growth of national economy. Liberalized economic policy is to achieve this goal. The merger, therefore, should not be contrary to this objective."

Role of the Court

By virtue of provisions of Section 391 of the Companies Act, a scheme sanctioned by the Court is statutorily binding on all its shareholders and creditors including those who dissented from or were opposed to the scheme being sanctioned. Since by law a procedure has been prescribed by which every shareholder and creditor in the absence of individual agreement, gets bound by the scheme, which would otherwise be necessary to give its validity.

A duty is cast on the Court to satisfy itself that the affairs of the compromise or settlement entered into between the parties is not unfair, contrary to the public policy, unconscionable or against the law.

There is no adjudication as such. **Any modification proposed by the Court in the scheme is also subject to its being accepted by the transferor and the transferee company.** If any one of them objects to the modifications suggested by the Court, then the scheme would not be sanctioned. The scheme would be sanctioned only if there is an acceptance to the modification proposed by the Court to the scheme by the transferor as well as transferee company. On acceptance of the same, it gets incorporated in the compromise or arrangement arrived at between the two companies. Modification in the scheme becomes a part of the compromise or arrangement arrived at between the parties.

The foundation of the court order for amalgamation is the agreement between two or more companies.

While exercising its power in sanctioning a scheme of agreement, the Court has to examine as to whether the provisions of the statute have been complied with. Once the Court finds that the parameters set out in Section 394 of the Companies Act have been met, then the Court would have no further jurisdiction to sit in appeal over the commercial wisdom of the class of persons who with their eyes open give their approval, even if, in the view of the Court better scheme could have been framed. This aspect was examined in detail by this Court in **Miheer H. Mafatlal Vs Mafatlal Industries Ltd.,** 1997 (1) SCC 579...... Two broad principles underlying a scheme of amalgamation which has been brought out in this judgment are:

1. That the **order passed by the court amalgamating the company is based on a compromise or arrangement arrived at** between the parties; and
2. That the jurisdiction of the Court while sanctioning the scheme is supervisory only, i.e., to observe that the procedure set out in the Act is met and complied with and that the proposed scheme of compromise or arrangement is not violative of any provision of law, unconscionable or contrary to public policy. The Court is not to exercise the appellate jurisdiction and examine the commercial wisdom of the compromise or arrangement arrived at between the parties.

The role of the court is that of an umpire in a game to see that the teams play their role as per rules and not overstep the limits.

Subject to that, how best the game is to be played is left to the players and not to the umpire.

Scope and Ambit of Court

The scope and ambit of the court while giving the sanction is summarized as follows:

- Requisite statutory procedure is complied with.
- Concerned meetings of creditors and members have been held.
- Necessary material has been placed at the concerned meetings.
- Proposed scheme of compromise and arrangement is not found to be violative of any provision of law.
- Not contrary to public policy.
- Members or Creditors have acted in good faith and not coerced the minority to promote their interest.
- Scheme, as a whole, is found to be just, fair and reasonable from the view of the prudent men of business taking a commercial decision.
- If all the above requirements are met, the court has no further jurisdiction to sit in appeal over the commercial wisdom of the majority of the class of persons who have taken the decision.

9.16 NEW OPPORTUNITIES – BIG DEALS OF LENDING TO INDIAN BANKING

Mergers and acquisitions provide huge potential for increasing lending portfolio of banks and improving the cake of profitability, with better utilization of resources. When the Indian industries take over the units located overseas, the deals are always big. Some corporate are highly aggressive in their global plans. These deals require huge quantum of funds, demanding funding in a massive manner, quick decisions and strategic pricing of the deal, as a whole, in the highly competitive global environment. Though several deals have been made by the Indian industry, major beneficiaries have been the foreign banks as they have financed the Indian companies in respect of those deals. Most opportunities in the form of larger slice of M&As have been seized by the foreign banks due to their inherent global strength and their competence to handle, smartly. Indian banks have been lagging behind in the race, while competing with foreign banks.

The funding of overseas acquisitions by Indian companies has, hitherto, been a virtual monopoly of foreign banks, operating in India. In this scenario, ICICI Bank, the country's second largest commercial bank, has formed a new strategic business unit (SBU) to cater to the global needs of the top 50 companies in India. The bank has formed this new unit to provide single window for all their business needs. While reporting this initiative, The Financial Express has commented in its daily on 24th, July, 2007 that State Bank of India has also begun aggressive M&A funding. The paper has added in its reporting that the ICICI bank has already run an exposure over $ 1 billion deals involving overseas M&A plans.

The report has further added that in the recent past, ICICI bank has part funded some of the largest overseas deals by India Inc, including the Tata Corus deals, the UB buyout of Whyte & Mackay and the other deals by Tata Chemicals and Tata Tea.

Major Constraint: The Reserve Bank of India guidelines do not permit Indian banks to fund overseas M&As from their local balance sheet. In other words, such overseas funding has to be made from overseas assets. The foreign banks enjoy an edge in this area. To overcome this funds constraint to a certain extent, ICICI Bank has made remittances from overseas to India free to lure NRIs to make their remittance to India through their banking channel.

The smaller balance sheet size is constraining Indian banks' participation in financing overseas acquisition of Indian companies. The balance sheet strength of Indian banking companies is, relatively, low compared to foreign banks. To overcome the picture, State Bank of Saurashtra is merging with State Bank of India. The merger of SBI's associate banks with State Bank of India is considered for the past several years. A beginning has been made with the proposed merger of State Bank of Saurashtra. Merger of several nationalized banks may not be far off to counter the overwhelming strength of foreign banks.

Over a period, foreign exchange reserves position has improved, substantially, and is highly comfortable in our country. Now, it is time for changing the laws, suitably, to enable Indian banks to compete, globally, for availing the opportunities the global scenario is offering.

9.17 THE COMPETITION ACT, 2002

The globalised and liberalized Indian economy has been witnessing cutthroat competition. To provide institutional support to healthy and fair competition, there is a requirement of better regulatory and adjudicatory mechanism. To achieve this effect, India has enacted the new competition law, 2002. This is a shift from curbing monopolies to encouraging competition.

The ambit of the Monopolies & Restrictive Trade Practices Act, 1969 has been found to be inadequate for fostering competition in the market and eliminating anti-competitive practices in the national and international trade.

Accordingly, the Government of India, in tune with international trends and to cope with changing realities, has enacted the Competition Act, 2002.

Aims of The Competition Act

- Eliminate practices adversely affecting competition,
- Promote and sustain competition,
- Protect consumers' interests and
- Ensure freedom of trade carried on by other participants in markets.

The Competition Act has been enacted keeping in the wake of economic developments that resulted in the opening up of the Indian economy, removal of controls and consequent economic liberalization.

One of the important aims of The Competition Act is to provide institutional support to healthy and fair competition.

The Competition Act, amongst other things, has provided for the establishment of

The Competition Commission of India ("CCI").

Amendments in Act —The Competition Bill, 2007

The Competition Bill, 2007 has been passed in the Parliament and is yet to become an Act. The following would be the changes once the Bill becomes the Act.

The Competition Commission of India (CCI) would, eventually, replace the Monopolies and Restrictive Trade Commission.

The CCI would be an expert body, which would function as a market Regulator to prevent and regulate anti-competitive practices in the country.

Major Changes of the Competition (Amendment) Bill, 2007

It has been envisaged that the Bill would pave the way for a powerful competition Regulator for promoting and regulating competition in markets, enhancing efficiency and maximizing consumer welfare.

The Bill has laid down strict norms for disclosures of mergers and acquisitions (M&As) to prevent corporations from building dominant market positions, artificially.

The major changes are:

1. **Statutory Powers:** The Competition Commission of India would enjoy statutory powers and, now, acts as an expert body in an advisory capacity, to prevent and regulate anti-competitive practices.
2. **Formation of Competition Appellate Tribunal:** Earlier, appeals from the orders of the CCI lay before the Supreme Court. Under the Bill, a Competition Appellate Tribunal is empowered to hear and dispose off appeals from any order or decision of the CCI.
3. **Mandatory Notification:** It would be mandatory for all mergers and acquisitions – including between two overseas companies – to notify regulator, if the combined entity meets specified threshold limits. Earlier, this notification to the Regulatory Authority has been voluntary. Now, no longer it is voluntary, but mandatory.

THRESHOLD LIMITS

The merged entity will inform the commission, if its turnover is above Rs. 3,000 crore or has assets of above Rs. 1,000 crore.

In case, a foreign company buys a domestic one, the turnover and asset threshold limits of the merged entity are fixed at Rs. 1,500 crores and Rs.500 crores respectively.

If the merged entity's turnover is less than the threshold limit, it would still have to inform the commission, if the group turnover is above Rs.600 crores or has an asset value of Rs.200 crores.

4. **Violation would be Criminal:** Competition Commission of India has the power to imprison and fine. In case, any agreement between companies results in a cartel, they might have to pay hefty financial penalties up to thrice the value of profits earned. Contravention of the order, in the first instance, will be a civil offence with monetary penalty. In the second instance, violation would be criminal.
5. **Time-Frame:** The CCI would be bound to render its ruling within a stipulated period of 210 days from the date of the intimation.

International Scene Vs. India

Economic Times has compared the international scene with the picture in India on the matter of competition, relevant extract is reproduced hereunder:

Searching New Laws to Promote Competition
20th October, 2007

"Recently, Microsoft lost a judicial appeal against the European Commission's charge of abuse of dominance in bundling its operating software with other add-ons, such as media player.

There are other suppliers, but they get shut out by Microsoft's exclusionary behaviour. This reduces customer choice and increases costs.

So after a nine-year battle, Microsoft has to pay a record fine of e497 million, as hopes of them getting a stay on that at the apex European court is rather dim.

Earlier, the US and UK competition authorities slapped British Airways with record fines of over half a billion dollars for running a trans-Atlantic cartel on passenger and goods fares in partnership with its arch rival Virgin. What do these two incidents have to do with India? Quite a lot!

Firstly, whatever happens in Europe or in the US has a spillover effect on markets and consumers all over the world, including India, where these two businesses operate. In India too they indulge in the same type of anti-competitive practice.

The Monopolies & Restrictive Trade Practices Commission (MRTPC) has tried to deal with Microsoft's exclusionary behaviour in India, and against several cartels, but did not succeed as the MRTP Act is quite weak.

Therefore, after setting in motion the process of adopting a new and modern Competition Act in 1999, we adopted a law in 2002. In 2007, Parliament passed a revised version of the Act. It has taken eight years to do so. Despite the delay, the economy continued to grow at 8-9%.

Had the revised law been in operation, the growth rate would have been higher by at least 2-3%. An effective competition law, along with other market regulatory laws, ensures that markets are orderly and economic democracy prevails.

Cartels and abuse of dominance in the goods and services sectors will be the two major areas for the new competition authority to engage in, with determination and skills". ....

"Finally, the most important role of the new competition agency will be enforcement. It will need to deal with myriad anti-competitive practices, such as the formation of cartels and abuse of dominance pointed out in the beginning. To begin with the agency should tackle winnable cases to build up public acceptance and raise the morale of its staff. It should then move ahead slowly and steadily, as in a marathon".

Check Your Understanding

State whether the following statements are True or False

1. Acquisition of ownership and control of other concerns is the way for external expansion.
2. When companies having different types of business operations merge together, it is called 'Conglomerate merger'.
3. When companies of same business merge together, it is called 'Vertical Merger'.
4. Horizontal mergers, generally, result in financial, marketing, production and personnel synergies.

5. A merger is a combination of two or more companies into one company.
6. Merger can be of through Absorption or Consolidation.
7. Absorption and Consolidation mean the same.
8. Acquisition can either be friendly take-over or hostile take-over.
9. After Acquisition, the target company ceases to exist.
10. The process of business combination can take either the route of 'Merger' or 'Acquisition'.
11. The idea behind vertical merger is to take up different stages of work in a combined manner to ensure speedy production or quick service.
12. While approving the scheme of amalgamation, the role of the court is that of an umpire in a game to see that the teams play their role as per rules and not overstep the limits.
13. Once court accepts or modifies the amalgamation scheme and passes orders, it is compulsory to the shareholders to accept the modified scheme.
14. Multi- national Company or Corporation is one which operates in more than two countries.
15. Two or more companies can amalgamate when the amalgamation is permitted under the Memorandum of Association.
16. While approving the scheme of merger, the court is concerned to look into that the scheme of merger is not unfair, contrary to the public policy and unconscionable or against the law.
17. Friendly take-over and Hostile take- over are not different types of Acquisition.
18. The aim of Competition Act is to prevent the formation of monopolies, which go against the interests of free trade.
19. There is no law to prevent any association of enterprises to enter into an agreement in respect of production of goods which is likely to cause an appreciable adverse impact on the competition, within India.
20. Enterprises intending to enter into a combination such as mergers have to obtain the prior approval of the Commission under The Competition Act, 2002.
21. The Reserve Bank of India guidelines do not permit Indian banks to fund overseas M&As from their local balance sheet.
22. Merger requires approval of the court, which is intended to protect the interests of small shareholders and creditors.
23. Absorption and Acquisition are one and the same.
24. When unrelated industries merge together, the rationale for such merger is diversification of risk.
25. Risk level changes in Horizontal Merger and Conglomerate Merger in the same direction.
26. One of the important aims of The Competition Act is to provide institutional support to healthy and fair competition.

Answers

1. True	2. True	3. False	4. True	5. True
6. True	7. False	8. True	9. False	10. True
11. True	12. True	13. False	14. True	15. True
16. True	17. False	18. True	19. False	20. False
21. True	22. True	23. False	24. True	25. False
26. True				

Match the following:

	Category A	*Category B*
1.	An existing company is brought to an end.	Amalgamation
2.	A company joins with another to form a new company.	Winding up
3.	Companies of same business merge together.	Vertical Merger
4.	Companies of different business merge together.	Horizontal Merger
5.	Seller company and customer company merge together.	Conglomerate Merger
6.	Companies which operate in more than two countries.	Consolidation
7.	In taxation, merger is called as	Multi-national company
8.	Both Absorption and Consolidation are called as	Acquisition
9.	Physically, both the companies continue even after	Amalgamation

Answers

1. Winding up	2. Consolidation	3. Horizontal Merger
4. Conglomerate Merger	5. Vertical Merger	6. Multi-national company
7. Amalgamation	8. Amalgamation	9. Acquisition

Pick up the Right Answer

1. This is a form of Business Combination
   (A) Absorption
   (B) Consolidation
   (C) Acquisition
   (D) Holding Company
   (E) All the above
2. This is the case of Absorption.
   (A) A Ltd. and B Ltd. become C Ltd.
   (B) A Ltd. and B Ltd. become AB Ltd.

(C) A Ltd. and B Ltd. become Z Ltd.

(D) "A Ltd." ceases and "B Ltd." takes over assets and liabilities of "A Ltd."

3. This is a case of Acquisition between X Ltd. and Z Ltd.:
   (A) X Ltd. and Z Ltd. become C Ltd.
   (B) X Ltd. and Z Ltd. become AB Ltd.
   (C) X Ltd. and Z Ltd. continue as they are but control and management of Z Ltd. is taken over by X Ltd.
   (D) X Ltd. ceases and Z Ltd. takes over assets and liabilities of X Ltd.
4. After Acquisition, the following would be the status of target company:
   (A) ceases to exist.
   (B) continues to be as before.
   (C) control over management is taken over.
   (D) B & C is correct.
   (E) B & A is correct.
5. When companies of same business merge together, it is called
   (A) Horizontal Merger
   (B) Vertical Merger
   (C) Conglomerate Merger
   (D) None
6. Under Companies Act, merger requires the approval of the company by way of
   (A) 75 percent of shareholders, in value, in shareholders' meeting
   (B) 51 percent of shareholders, in value, in shareholders' meeting
   (C) Approval of Board of Directors
   (D) A and C
   (E) B and C
7. While approving the scheme of merger with a subsidiary of a foreign company, the Court is, additionally, concerned with that the scheme of merger
   (A) results in maximizing profits of the shareholders.
   (B) protects the interests of employees.
   (C) shall not impede promotion of industry and obstruct growth of national economy.
   (D) is similar to any merger of any Indian company.
8. Which is the law that prevents elimination of total competition in business or services?
   (A) Competition Act, 2002

(B) Monopolies and Restrictive Trade Practices (MRTP) Act

(C) No law exists to prevent such total competition

(D) Consumer Protection Act, 1986

Answers

1. (E)	2. (D)	3. (C)	4. (D)	5. (A)
6. (D)	7. (C)	8. (A)		

Descriptive Questions

1. Explain the different forms of Expansion. What are the different forms of Business Combinations? **(9.3 and 9.5)**
2. What is meant by 'Merger'? Explain different types of mergers. What is the recent new trends in Mergers in India? **(9.6 and 9.4)**
3. What is meant by Acquisition? Explain the different types of acquisition. Narrate the pros and cons of takeover. Write a few recent Acquisitions that have taken place in our corporate history? **(9.7)**
4. Describe different types of Mergers and explain their relative individual merits and demerits. **(9.6) and (9.9)**
5. What is meant by 'Synergy'? Describe the different types of synergies that are achieved through the process of Mergers. **(9.10)**
6. Describe the factors responsible for Mergers and Acquisitions. **(9.6) and (9.12)**
7. Discuss the Legal Provisions and Procedural aspects for Mergers and Acquisitions. **(9.14)**
8. "While approving the scheme of amalgamation, the role of the court is that of an umpire in a game to see that the teams play their role as per rules and not overstep the limits"- Discuss. **(9.15)**
9. Discuss the funding scenario of overseas acquisitions through Mergers and Acquisitions by Indian companies. **(9.16)**
10. Write a note on 'The Competetion Act,' 2002 and amendments proposed. **(9.17)**

10

INFORMATION TECHNOLOGY ACT
—Includes 'Digital Signature—How it Works'?

10.1 CYBER LAWS IN INDIA

The Information Technology Act has been enacted in the year 2000 to give a boost to e-commerce and provide mechanism for e-governance. It is the first Cyber law in India.

Cyber laws aim to provide the legal infrastructure for e-commerce in India.

The cyber laws have a major impact for e-businesses and, in turn, the economic growth in India.

By cyber law we, generally, mean law relating to electronic communication network and virtual reality and this is done through the use of computers and Internet.

Today, computers and Internet touch and influence almost every aspect of our life and we are, greatly, dependent on the computers.

The house we live in, the electricity we use, the transportation by which we commute, the water we drink, the food we eat, the appliances we use, the medicines we consume, our hospital records, our government, our banks, our entertainment - in fact, many without which life seems incomplete - all are dependent, in some way or the other on computers. Technology is integrated with the human life in such an intricate way, apart from the business, which is heavily dependent on the advancement of technology. It is necessary that there are sufficient safeguards in the system to ensure privacy, protection and safeguard intrusion from unauthorized.

Advantages of Cyber Laws

The IT Act 2000 attempts to change outdated laws and provides ways to deal with cyber crimes.

We need such laws so that people can perform purchase transactions over the 'Net' through credit cards without fear of misuse.

The Act offers the much-needed legal framework so that information is not denied legal effect, validity or enforceability, solely on the ground that it is in the form of electronic records.

Meaning of Information Technology

When we use this term, 'Information Technology', we refer to the different activities and technologies associated with the use of computers and communication. Information technology (IT) is "the study, design, development, implementation, support or management of computer-based information systems, particularly software applications and computer hardware."

Information technology deals with the use of electronic computers (hardware) and computer software to convert, store, protect, process, transmit and retrieve information, securely.

IT facilitates the management to receive, store, retrieve the information for decision-making, with limited response time to act that results in speedy decisions and execution to achieve the desired level of profit, by reducing costs and eliminating unproductive records. In short, use of computers is essential for business decision-making to achieve the bottom line targeted.

10.2 RATIONALE AND NEED OF INFORMATION TECHNOLOGY ACT

Formation of contract is the foundation of business. Business has grown from the era of paper to paperless trade. New practices require new laws to protect the interests of the persons concerned. The introduction of Information Technology has created new opportunities as well as challenges.

e-commerce has been the boon of information technology and assumed unimaginable importance, revolutionizing trade.

In electronic commerce (e-commerce), the buying and selling of goods or services is done over the Internet as well as conducting the incidental financial transactions.

Electronic commerce eliminates the need of paper-based transactions. Internet has turned into a new mode of communication due to its fastness and ease in the business world. This changed situation has also raised several new problems to cope up with. When the trade is based on written documents, the documents contain signatures of the parties, which could be verified and are produced in a court of law, in case of a dispute for settlement. How to deal with these matters, in a situation of paperless trade? Electronic commerce has created the following concerns:

- How to identify the authenticity of the parties involved in trade?
- What is the way to verify their signatures?
- Is there legal recognition and support for the trade made?
- In case of dispute, where is the evidence to produce in a court of law?

Although people are aware of the advantages of Information Technology, they have been reluctant to conduct the business in the electronic form due to lack of suitable infrastructure and legal support.

A need has been felt to make suitable amendments in the existing laws to provide legal recognition for electronic records and digital signatures to facilitate e-commerce.

Role of Information Technology in e-Governance

The Information Technology has not left the functioning of the Government, untouched. Government at various levels has initiated e-Governance to run in parallel with the growth of trade.

e-Governance implies Governance employing Information Technology in administration - for collection of information, processing and providing information in prescribed format and using them for decision-making etc.

Highlights of Information Technology Act, 2000

- e-mail would now be a valid and legal form of communication, approved by law.
- Companies shall, now, be able to carry out electronic commerce using the legal infrastructure.
- Digital signatures have been given legal validity and sanction in the Act.
- Doors of entry for corporate companies into the business of Certifying Authorities for issuing Digital Signatures Certificates.
- Allows Government to issue notification on the web thus heralding e-governance.
- Enables the companies to file any form, application or any other document with Government in electronic form.
- Important issues of security have been addressed, critical to the success of electronic transactions.
- A statutory remedy, in case if anyone breaks into computer systems or network and causes damages or copies data. Remedy provided by the Act is in the form of monetary damages, not exceeding Rs. 1 crore.

Need to frame Information Technology Act, 2000

The United Nations Commission on International Trade Law (UNCITRAL) in the year 2001 has adopted the Model Law on Electronic Signatures. The General Assembly of the United Nations, by its resolution no. 56/80, dated 12th December, 2001, has recommended that all States accord favourable consideration to the said Model Law on Electronic Signatures. Since the digital signatures are linked to a specific technology under the existing provisions of the Information Technology Act, it has become necessary to provide for alternate technology of electronic signatures for bringing harmonization with the said Model Law.

To put it simply, a need has been felt to frame a new Act – Information Technology Act, 2000 to protect the interests of trade and functioning of Government.

10.3 OBJECTIVES OF INFORMATION TECHNOLOGY ACT

The act has facilitated electronic filing of documents with the Government agencies as an alternative to paper based methods of communication and storage of information.

The basic objective has been to provide legal recognition to the transactions carried out by means of electronic data interchange and other means of electronic communication, commonly referred as "Electronic Commerce".

The objectives have been to

- Give a fillip to the growth of electronic based transactions,
- Provide legal recognition for e-commerce and e-transactions,
- Accord legal recognition to Digital Signatures for authentication of any information or matter under any law,
- Facilitate electronic filing of documents with Government departments for achieving e-governance,
- Facilitate electronic storage of data,
- Facilitate and give legal recognition to electronic fund transfers between banks and financial institutions,
- Give legal recognition for keeping books of accounts by banks in electronic form,
- Prevent computer based crimes and
- Ensure security practices and procedures, in the context of widest possible use of information technology, worldwide.

Problems and Challenges

Information Technology Act has been passed to alleviate some of the problems that have arisen out of communication over computer network. It has amended the Evidence Act of 1872 and amended Indian Penal Code 1860. Banker's Book Evidence Act, 1891 has been suitably amended in order to facilitate collection and admissibility of evidence in fighting electronic crimes. This has been one of the most significant amendments to the Evidence Act, which has been enacted more than 132 years back.

The definition of evidence has been amended to include electronic record as admissible documentary evidence under section 3 of the Evidence Act.

Thus, by and large, the legislature has performed its role in adopting the emerging technology into the statute book.

With the adoption of Information Technology Act, 2000 business and contract has become faster and easier.

The requirement of written documents are no longer necessary and contract can be executed with electronic record and digital signature duly certified by Certifying Authority constituted by the Act.

The Information Technology Act has assumed greater importance with proliferation of information technology enabled services such as e-governance, e-commerce and e-transactions, protection of personal data and information and implementation of security practices and procedures relating to these applications of electronic communications.

The electronic messages, commonly known as e-mails, are also statutorily recognised as a sufficient communication to the addressee concerned.

A rapid increase in the use of computer and internet has given rise to new forms of crimes like publishing sexually explicit materials in electronic form, video voyeurism and breach of confidentiality and leakage of data by intermediary, e-commerce frauds like personation commonly known as Phishing, identity theft and offensive messages through communication services. So, penal provisions have been included in the Information Technology Act, the Indian Penal Code, the Indian Evidence Act and the Code of Criminal Procedure to prevent such crimes.

10.4 CHANGES IN INFORMATION TECHNOLOGY ACT

Since its promulgation, the IT Act 2000 has undergone some changes. One big change is the recognition of electronic documents as evidence in a court of law. Market players believe this will go a long way in giving encouragement to electronic fund transfers and promoting electronic commerce in the country.

Present Situation

- Electronic documents are now accepted as evidence in a court of law.
- Electronic cheques are now accepted as a valid means of transaction.

In electronic cheques, no physical cheques are drawn. Once authorization to debit the account is given, the recipient service provider goes to the bank and gets the signature of the authorized persons verified and the mandate given in favour of the service provider is noted in bank records.

Working of Electronic Clearance Cheques

The service provider enters into an agreement say, with the electricity department or telephone agency to collect the monthly billing charges from the subscribers, directly. The service provider, initially, approaches the individual subscribers of electricity or telephone to collect their mandate (authorization) to make payment after debiting their accounts with the respective banks. After collecting the mandate, the service provider goes to different banks and gets the signatures of the subscribers verified and gets the mandate noted in the bank records.

In terms of the agreement entered, the service department such as electricity or phone agency sends the consolidated list of subscribers, with monthly charges, to the service provider. Bills are sent to the subscribers, in the normal course, for information. Then, the service provider sends the lists to different banks for debiting the respective subscribers' accounts. Bank debits the respective accounts of subscribers and gives credit or pays the aggregate amount to the corresponding bank that maintains the account of the electricity department or phone agency. The entire process is done through clearing. By this process, the individual subscribers do not have to remit the amount of electricity or phone bill, directly. The service provider sends the e-mail to the individual subscriber too as and when the consolidated bill for payment is received from the service agencies. They send e-mail, once again, after the payment is made. Banks debit the customers' accounts as 'ECS Charges- Electronic Clearing Service Charges' and also collect a nominal amount towards their service charges. The service charges are deregulated and totally discretionary on the part of each individual bank.

This exercise eliminates

- Monthly issue of cheques by the subscribers.
- Long process of waiting to deposit them at the collection centres, monthly.
- Service agency, electricity or phone agency does not have the accounting work of depositing individual cheques (monthly charges), into the bank for collection.

Electronic Clearance Cheques facility and attending conveniences would not have been possible but for the advancement of e-commerce and the significant role of information technology.

10.5 DIGITAL SIGNATURE

The law of Information Technology recognizes the digital signature so that contract formed through Internet secures legal recognition. It is not possible to affix physical signature to the Internet mail, message or contract for authentication.

Digital signature is the electronic equivalent of the handwritten signature.

Digital signature serves the same purpose what a written signature does on documents. Digital signature means authentication of electronic record by means of an electronic method or procedure by a subscriber. In other words, digital signature is an electronic or digital method to authenticate the record. Any subscriber can authenticate electronic record by affixing digital signature. Digital signature certificate is issued to a subscriber by his application to the Certifying Authority and following the prescribed procedure. Only after obtaining the certificate from the competent authority, the electronic signature provided by the subscriber would carry validity or authenticity.

What is a Digital Signature Certificate?

Digital Signature Certificate (DSC) is an electronic file, which contains personal information about its owner, such as the name and e-mail address, as well as this owner's public key. Digital Signature Certificate is the digital equivalent (that is electronic format) of physical or paper certificate.

Examples of physical certificates are drivers' licenses, passports or membership cards. The nature of digital signature certificate is similar to a driving license or PAN card.

Certificate serves as proof of identity of an individual for a certain purpose. For example, a driver's license identifies someone who can, legally, drive in a particular country.

A digital certificate acts as an identity card of the sender for each user. It identifies the sender to all other participants – users of the information, report or e-mail. It also shows the proof of ownership of a public key.

A digital certificate is similar to a driving license in the function of establishing identity of the sender in respect of the mail or message sent, while the former is in electronic form and later in manual form.

A digital certificate can be presented, electronically, to prove identity, access information or services on the Internet or sign certain documents, digitally.

A Certifying Authority (CA) issues certificates. Certifying Authority is responsible for their content. The CA signs the certificates it creates. This enables users to rely on the information, based on the certificate.

Why Digital Signature Certificate is (DSC) required?

Like physical documents are signed manually, electronic documents, for example e-forms are required to be signed digitally, using a Digital Signature Certificate.

Digital signature certificate is a guarantee to the users that the subscriber has complied with the requirements of the law for using digital signature.

Who Issues the Digital Signature Certificate?

A licensed Certifying Authority (CA) issues the digital signature certificate. Certifying Authority (CA) means a person who has been granted a license to issue a digital signature certificate under Section 24 of the Indian IT- Act, 2000.

The list of licensed certifying authorities, along with their contact information is available on the MCA portal (www.mca.gov.in).

What is Public Key Cryptography?

The digital signature certificate is provided to the subscriber who registers himself with the certifying authority. Each subscriber (user) would have a pair of electronic keys, which are linked:

- A private key, which the user must keep secret;
- A public key, which is published and available to all.

Using these keys, two communicating parties can safeguard information they send to each other. The sender encrypts, or scrambles, information before sending it. The receiver decrypts, or unscrambles, the information after receiving it. While in transit, the encrypted information is unintelligible (not readable) to an intruder.

Authentication of Electronic Records

Any subscriber can authenticate an electronic record by affixing his digital signature.

The authentication of the electronic record is effected by the use of 'asymmetric crypto system' and 'hash function'.

Both envelop and transform the initial electronic record into another electronic record. With Digital signature, the initial electronic record is converted into another electronic record.

Verification of Digital Signature

Subscriber gets a public key as well as private key on registration with the competent authority. Any person with the use of public key of the subscriber can verify the electronic record.

The public and private keys are unique to each subscriber and constitute a functioning key pair.

In the case of electronic transmission of business or legal message / document, it is necessary to establish that they are authentic and not tampered by any person during transmission. To achieve this end in view, the authentication of the electronic record is effected by the use of 'asymmetric crypto system' i.e. by using encryption (coding) and 'decryption' (decoding) methodologies and software tools. In other words, encryption stands for coding and decryption for decoding.

An encryption software program takes the normal and readable text message (Plaintext) and scrambles into unreadable coded text. The recipient then uses another software program (the corresponding decryption program) to decode the scrambled message into normal plaintext message.

Any third party who intercepts the message is not able to read or alter the message, unless he has the key.

Public and Private Key

In 'asymmetric crypto system', each person would have two corresponding and matched keys – one called the private and the other called the 'public key'.

The 'private key' is always kept with the subscriber and shares the 'public key' with the required persons.

These two keys, public key and private key, are used to encrypt and decrypt the messages, respectively.

Private key is used to create a digital signature while Public key is used to verify a digital signature, listed in the Digital Signature Certificate.

Method Transmission and Reading of Communication

The sender uses the intended receiver's public key (which he can freely obtain from the receiver or download from the public depository) to encrypt the message. The receiver, on receiving the coded message, uses his corresponding private key (which is available only with him) to decrypt the encrypted message. Important point is the message is sent using the public code of the intended receiver. That person only who has the private key can read the message.

Public key can remain with many, but private key has to remain with only one person to maintain confidentiality and integrity of data.

To put it simply, the person to whom the message is meant can decode and read the message, originally sent. The public key and the private key of any person or entity can be mathematically linked that a message encrypted, using one key, can only be decrypted by using the corresponding other key. Although the two keys are mathematically related, it is computationally not possible to deduce one key from the other. The most commonly used public key cryptography algorithm is **RSA**.

The corresponding private key can only decrypt a message encrypted with a public key. The opposite is also true. If a private key encrypts a message, the corresponding public key can only decrypt it.

Digital Signature —How it Works?

There are two types of Encryption:

- Symmetric-Key Encryption (Secret key cryptography)
- Asymmetric Encryption (Public-key encryption)

Symmetric-Key Encryption (Secret Key Cryptography)

In Symmetric-key encryption, there is only one key. The same key is used for coding (encryption) and decoding (decryption). Information encrypted using one key can only be decrypted using the same key. Symmetric-key encryption provides an effective level of cryptography, only if both the parties keep the symmetric key secret. If a third party discovers the symmetric key, he can decrypt messages as well encrypt new messages. It would appear as if one of the two parties has generated the new message.

Symmetric-key encryption is similar to a house having two keys, original and duplicate key. When father and son are living in the same house, any one can enter the house. If one of them loses the key of the house, then any one who steals or finds it can enter the house. Here, the situation is similar. So long as the key is not lost or shared, till then there is safety or integrity for the data.

Pictorial presentation of Symmetric-key encryption is as under:

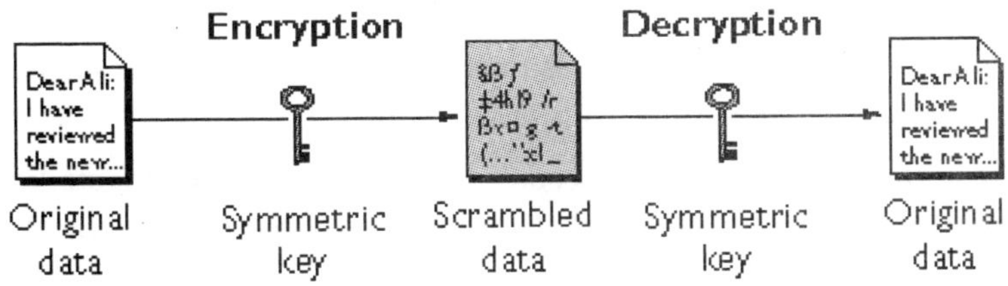

Symmetric-key encryption
(Diagram No.23)

Implementations of Symmetric-key encryption can be highly efficient, so that users do not experience any significant time delay as a result of the encryption and decryption.

> Symmetric-key encryption also provides a degree of authentication, since information encrypted with one symmetric key cannot be decrypted with any other symmetric key.

Thus, as long as the symmetric key is kept secret by the two parties using it to encrypt communications, each party can be sure that it is communicating with the other.

Symmetric-key encryption is effective only if the two parties involved keep the symmetric key secret. If anyone else discovers the key, it affects both confidentiality and authentication. A person with an unauthorized symmetric key not only can decrypt messages sent with that key, but also can encrypt new messages and send them as if they have come from one of the two parties who have been originally using the key, as stated earlier.

> Symmetric-key encryption is similar to a house with original key and duplicate key. Any one who obtains possession of any of the keys can enter the house.

Asymmetric Encryption (Public Key Encryption)

The two main branches of public key cryptography are:

- Public key encryption — a message encrypted with a recipient's public key cannot be decrypted by anyone except the recipient possessing the corresponding private key. This is used to ensure confidentiality.
- Digital signatures — a message signed with a sender's private key can be verified by anyone who has access to the sender's public key, thereby proving that the sender signed it and that the message has not been tampered with. This is used to ensure authenticity.

An entity, using Public-key encryption, can authenticate its identity, electronically, or sign or code the data.

Public-key encryption (also called asymmetric encryption) involves a pair of keys - a public key and a private key. These two keys work together. So, a message scrambled with the private key can only be unscrambled with the public key and vice versa.

Each public key is published, and the corresponding private key is kept secret. Data encrypted with the public key can be decrypted only with private key.

The more digits in these keys, the more secure are the process. The private key is kept secret, while the public key may be widely distributed. The keys are related mathematically, but the private key cannot be practically derived from the public key.

A message sent by a private key can be decoded by a public key. But, a message *encrypted* with the public key can be decoded only with the corresponding private key.

Practical Working

Kalyan & Co. has registered with the certifying authority and obtained the digital signature certificate. So, Kalyan & Co. gets a public key as well as private key. The private key is confidential and retained by them. Public key can be shared with any one. So, they have shared the public key with Radhi and Cherry with whom they deal, often. Kalyan & Co. has sent a message, with digital signature to both Radhi and Cherry asking them to quote their best rate for the goods they want to buy. Kalyan & Co's message would be coded or encrypted. By this process, others, who are not in possession of public key, would not be able to read. Radhi and Cherry can access the message and decode through public key. They can satisfy themselves that the message has been sent by Kalyan & Co only and has not been tampered, during transit, before receipt. They can ensure the correctness of the message on account of the digital certificate, enclosed.

Radhi and Cherry can quote their best rates and send the respective messages, using public key. Kalyan & Co. can read the information, using their private key and take suitable decision for buying. However, neither Radhi can read the message sent by Cherry nor vice versa. So, confidentiality of the rates quoted is ensured.

Confidentiality and Integrity of Data

The persons holding public key can read the information sent by the person with the corresponding private key. However, only person, using the corresponding private key, can access the messages sent by the persons, holding public key.

Person who holds a public key cannot access the message sent by others, holding public key.

In practice, asymmetric key algorithm are typically hundreds to thousands times slower than a symmetric key algorithm.

It is virtually impossible for a third party to decrypt the information without having the correct private key.

Conversely, secret key cryptography, also known as symmetric cryptography uses a single secret key for both encryption and decryption.

> Symmetric cryptography uses a single secret key, while asymmetric cryptography have a pair of fuctional keys – Private key and Public key.

Analogy of Public Key Encryption

An analogy for public-key encryption is that of a locked mailbox with a mail slot. The mail slot is exposed and accessible to the public. Its location (the street address) is in essence the public key. Anyone knowing the street address can go to the door and drop a written message through the slot. However, only the person who possesses the key can open the mailbox and read the message.

An analogy for digital signatures is the sealing of an envelope with a personal wax seal. The presence of the seal authenticates the sender.

The following diagram shows the simplified view of the way public-key encryption works.

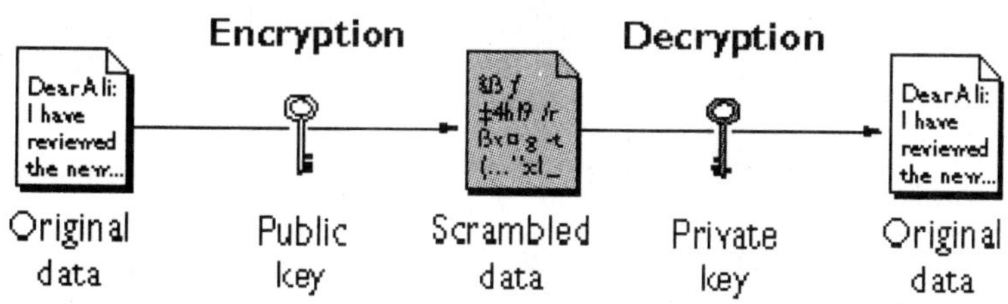

Public-key encryption
(Diagram No.24)

The scheme lets free distribution of a public key, and only the subscriber can read data encrypted using this key. In general, to send encrypted data to someone, the data is encrypted with that person's public key. The person receiving the encrypted data decrypts it with the corresponding private key.

Compared with symmetric-key encryption, public-key encryption requires more computation and is therefore not always appropriate for large amounts of data. However, it's possible to use public-key encryption to send a symmetric key, which can then be used to encrypt additional data.

Client software such as Communicator can then use public key to confirm that the message has been signed with the corresponding private key and that it hasn't been tampered with, since being signed.

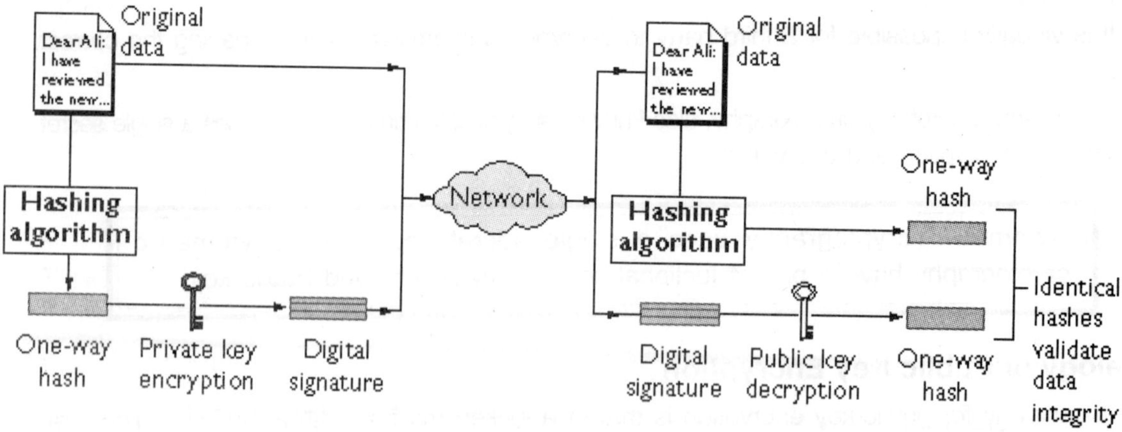

Validation of data integrity, using a digital signature
(Diagram No. 25)

Validation of Data Integrity

The original data and the digital signature, which is basically a one-way hash (of the original data) has been encrypted with the signer's private key. To validate the integrity of the data, the receiving software first uses the signer's public key to decrypt the hash. It then uses the same hashing algorithm that generated the original hash to generate a new one-way hash of the same data.

Finally, the receiving software compares the new hash against the original hash. If the two hashes match, the data has not tampered after sending and before its receipt. If they don't match, the data may have been tampered with since it has been sent.

If the two hashes match, the recipient can be certain that the public key used to decrypt the digital signature corresponds to the private key used to create the digital signature.

The significance of a digital signature is comparable to the significance of a handwritten signature. Once some data is signed, it is difficult to deny later, assuming that the private key has not been compromised or out of the owner's control. This quality of digital signature provides a high degree of non-repudiation.

> The digital signatures make it difficult for the signer to deny having signed the data. A digital signature may be as legally binding as a handwritten signature.

The most obvious application of a public key encryption system is confidentiality. A message which a sender encrypts using the recipient's public key can only be decrypted by the recipient's paired private key.

10.6 LEGAL RECOGNITION OF DIGITAL SIGNATURES

A verbal contract is a valid contract. However, in some cases, law provides that information or any other matter has to be in writing or in other written type form. Notwithstanding anything contained in such law, such requirement shall be deemed to have been satisfied, if such information or matter is authenticated by means of digital signature affixed in such manner as may be prescribed by the Central Government.

Digital signature enjoys the legal recognition, similar to a written document, and constitutes evidence in a court of law.

Recognition of Agreement Entered into through e-mails

"Does a law court recognize an agreement entered into through e-mails?" The answer is, yes.

An agreement, the terms of which have been transmitted through an e-mail or the contents of which are saved in a word file, i.e., in electronic form, is a valid agreement. A court of law will not refuse to admit an agreement solely because it is in electronic form.

The written agreement and electronic agreement stand on the same footing.

10.7 DEFINITIONS

1. "Asymmetric crypto system" means a system of a secure key pair consisting of a private key for creating a digital signature and a public key to verify the digital signature;
2. "Certifying Authority" means a person who has been granted a licence to issue a Digital Signature Certificate under section 24;
3. "Certification practice statement" means a statement issued by a Certifying Authority to specify the practices that the Certifying Authority employs in issuing Digital Signature Certificates;
4. "Computer" means any electronic magnetic, optical or other high-speed data processing device or system which performs logical, arithmetic, and memory functions by manipulations of electronic, magnetic or optical impulses, and includes all input, output, processing, storage, computer software, or communication facilities which are connected or related to the computer in a computer system or computer network;
5. "Computer network" means the interconnection of one or more computers through
   (i) the use of satellite, microwave, terrestrial line or other communication media; and
   (ii) terminals or a complex consisting of two or more interconnected computers whether or not the interconnection is continuously maintained;
6. "Computer resource" means computer, computer system, computer network, data, computer database or software;
7. "Computer system" means a device or collection of devices, including input and output support devices and excluding calculators which are not programmable and capable of being used in conjunction with external files, which contain computer programs, electronic instructions, input data and output data, that performs logic, arithmetic, data storage and retrieval, communication control and other functions;

8. "Controller" means the Controller of Certifying Authorities appointed under sub-section (l) of section 17;
9. "Cyber Appellate Tribunal" means the Cyber Regulations Appellate Tribunal established under sub-section (1) of section 48;
10. "Data" means a representation of information, knowledge, facts, concepts or instructions which are being prepared or have been prepared in a formalised manner, and is intended to be processed, is being processed or has been processed in a computer system or computer network, and may be in any form (including computer printouts magnetic or optical storage media, punched cards, punched tapes) or stored internally in the memory of the computer;
11. "Digital signature" means authentication of any electronic record by a subscriber by means of an electronic method or procedure in accordance with the provisions of section 3;
12. "Digital Signature Certificate" means a Digital Signature Certificate issued under sub-section (4) of section 35;
13. "Electronic form" with reference to information means any information generated, sent, received or stored in media, magnetic, optical, computer memory, microfilm, computer generated microfiche or similar device;
14. "Electronic Gazette" means the Official Gazette published in the electronic form;
15. "Electronic record" means data, record or data generated, image or sound stored, received or sent in an electronic form or microfilm or computer generated microfiche;
16. "Function", in relation to a computer, includes logic, control arithmetical process, deletion, storage and retrieval and communication or telecommunication from or within a computer;
17. "Information" includes data, text, images, sound, voice, codes, computer programs, software and databases or microfilm or computer generated microfiche:
18. "Intermediary" with respect to any particular electronic message means any person who on behalf of another person receives, stores or transmits that message or provides any service with respect to that message;
19. "Key pair", in an asymmetric crypto system, means a private key and its mathematically related public key, which are so related that the public key can verify a digital signature created by the private key;
20. "originator" means a person who sends, generates, stores or transmits any electronic message or causes any electronic message to be sent, generated, stored or transmitted to any other person but does not include an intermediary;
21. "Private key" means the key of a key pair used to **create** a digital signature;
22. "Public key" means the key of a key pair used to **verify** a digital signature and listed in the Digital Signature Certificate;
23. "Secure system" means computer hardware, software, and procedure that-
    (a) are reasonably secure from unauthorised access and misuse;
    (b) provide a reasonable level of reliability and correct operation;
    (c) are reasonably suited to performing the intended functions; and
    (d) adhere to generally accepted security procedures;

24. "Security procedure" means the security procedure prescribed under section 16 by the Central Government;
25. "Subscriber" means a person in whose name the Digital Signature Certificate is issued;
26. "Verify" in relation to a digital signature, electronic record or public key, with its grammatical variations and cognate expressions means to determine whether-
    (a) the initial electronic record was affixed with the digital signature by the use of private key corresponding to the public key of the subscriber;
    (b) the initial electronic record is retained intact or has been altered since such electronic record was so affixed with the digital signature.

10.8 REGULATION OF CERTIFYING AUTHORITIES

The IT Act, 2000 provides the regulations for the appointment of Certifying Authorities, their functions, powers and duties. The Central Government, by notification in the official gazette, appoints a Controller of Certifying Authorities. The controller discharges the functions under the Act, subject to the control and discretion of the Central Government. Deputy Controllers and Assistant Controllers would support the Controller as deemed necessary by Central Government.

Appointment of Controller and Other Officers

(1) The Central Government, by notification in the Official Gazette, appoints a Controller of Certifying Authorities and such number of Deputy Controllers and Assistant Controllers as it deems fit.

(2) The Controller shall discharge his functions under this Act subject to the general control and directions of the Central Government.

(3) The Deputy Controllers and Assistant Controllers shall perform the functions assigned to them by the Controller under the general superintendence and control of the Controller.

(4) The qualifications, experience and terms and conditions of service of Controller, Deputy Controllers and Assistant Controllers shall be such as may be prescribed by the Central Government.

(5) The Head Office and Branch Office of the office of the Controller shall be at such places as the Central Government may specify, and these may be established at such places as the Central Government may think fit.

(6) There shall be a seal of the Office of the Controller.

Functions of Controller

The Controller may perform all or any of the following functions, namely:

(a) exercising supervision over the activities of the Certifying Authorities;

(b) certifying public keys of the Certifying Authorities;

(c) laying down the standards to be maintained by the Certifying Authorities;

(d) specifying the qualifications and experience the employees of the Certifying Authorities should possess;

(e) specifying the conditions subject to which the Certifying Authorities shall conduct their business;

(f) specifying the contents of written, printed or visual materials and advertisements that may be distributed or used in respect of a Digital Signature Certificate and the public key;

(g) specifying the form and content of a Digital Signature Certificate and the key,

(h) specifying the form and manner in which accounts shall be maintained by the Certifying Authorities;

(i) specifying the terms and conditions subject to which auditors may be appointed and the remuneration to be paid to them;

(j) facilitating the establishment of any electronic system by a Certifying Authority either solely or jointly with other Certifying Authorities and regulation of such systems;

(k) specifying the manner in which the Certifying Authorities shall conduct their dealings with the subscribers;

(l) resolving any conflict of interests between the Certifying Authorities and the subscribers;

(m) laying down the duties of the Certifying Authorities;

(n) maintaining a data base containing the disclosure record of every Certifying Authority containing such particulars as may be specified by regulations, which shall be accessible to public.

10.9 APPOINTMENT OF CERTIFYING AUTHORITIES TO ISSUE DIGITAL SIGNATURE CERTIFICATES

The person to whom a licence has been granted by the Controller to issue Digital Signature Certificate is termed as Certifying Authority (Certification Authority).

Any person can make an application to the Controller for grant of licence to issue Digital Signature Certificate. A licence is granted provided he fulfills the requirements in respect of qualification, expertise, manpower, financial resources and other infrastructure facilities, which are necessary to issue Digital Signature Certificate as may be prescribed by the Central Government. The licence is valid for such period as may be prescribed by the Central Government.

The Need for a Certification Authority

People use public keys to verify signatures or encrypt messages. But how can one be sure about the owner of the public key? For a public key cryptography system to function, an independent trusted third party is needed to authorise people's names and addresses with their public keys and sign the bundle with its own private key. Such parties are called Certification Authorities (CA).

Application for Licence: The application for issue of licence shall be in the prescribed format, prescribed by the Government and is to be accompanied by:

(a) a certification practice statement;

(b) a statement including the procedure with respect to the identification of the applicant;

(c) payment of fee, not exceeding rupees twenty-five thousand rupees as may be prescribed by the Central Government, and

(d) such other documents as may be prescribed by the Central Government.

Certifying Authority to follow certain Procedures

Every Certifying Authority has to follow certain procedures relating to security of system, in performance of its services.

Duties of Certifying Authority

The Certifying Authority has the following duties:

1. To ensure that every person employed or otherwise engaged by it complies, in the course of his employment or engagement, with the provisions of the Act, rules, regulations and orders made thereunder.
2. To display its licence at a conspicuous place of the premises in which it carries on its business.
3. To surrender the licence to the Controller, immediately, after its suspension or revocation.
4. To make reasonable efforts to notify any person who is likely to be affected by the occurrence of any event, which, in the opinion of the Certifying Authority, may materially and adversely affect the integrity of its computer system or the conditions subject to which a Digital Signature Certificate has been granted. He may also act in accordance with the procedure specified in its 'certification practice statement' to deal with such event or situation.

Certification Practice Statement

Certification Practice Statement is a statement issued by the Certifying Authority specifying the practices it would employ while issuing Digital Signature Certificates.

Display of Licence

Every Certifying Authority shall display its licence at a conspicuous place of the premises in which it carries on its business.

Surrender of Licence

(1) Every Certifying Authority whose licence is suspended or revoked shall, immediately, after such suspension or revocation, surrender the licence to the Controller.

(2) Where any Certifying Authority fails to surrender a licence, the person in whose favour a licence is issued, shall be guilty of an offence and shall be punished with imprisonment which may extend up to six months or a fine which may extend up to ten thousand rupees or with both.

Service Charges

The service providers may be authorised by the Central Government or the State Government to set up, maintain and upgrade the computerized facilities and also collect appropriate service charges for providing such services at such scale as may be specified by the Central Government or the State Government.

10.10 PROCEDURE TO BE FOLLOWED BY CERTIFYING AUTHORITIES TO ISSUE DIGITAL SIGNATURE CERTIFICATES

Every certifying authority has to follow certain procedures relating to security of system in performance of its services.

1. Every Certifying Authority shall make use of hardware, software and procedures that are secure from intrusion and misuse.
2. It has to provide a reasonable level of reliability in its services, which are reasonably suited to the performance of intended functions.
3. The Certifying Authority has to ensure that the security and secrecy of the digital signatures are assured.
4. The Certifying Authority has to observe such standards as may be specified by the Information Technology (Certifying Authorities) Regulations.
5. Digital Signature Certificate shall be granted after the Certifying Authority is satisfied that
   (a) the applicant holds the private key corresponding to the public key to be listed in the Digital Signature Certificate;
   (b) the applicant holds a private key, which is capable of creating a digital signature and
   (c) the public key to be listed in the certificate can be used to verify a digital signature affixed by the private key held by the applicant.
6. A Certifying Authority, while issuing a Digital Signature Certificate, shall certify that
   (a) it has complied with the provisions of this Act and the rules and regulations made thereunder,
   (b) it has published the Digital Signature Certificate or otherwise made it available to such person relying on it and the subscriber has accepted it;
   (c) the subscriber holds the private key corresponding to the public key, listed in the Digital Signature Certificate;
   (d) the subscriber's public key and private key constitute a functioning key pair,
   (e) the information contained in the Digital Signature Certificate is accurate; and
   (f) it has no knowledge of any material fact, which if it had been included in the Digital Signature Certificate would adversely affect the reliability of the representations made in clauses (a) to (d).

The certifying authority shall reject no application unless the applicant has been given a reasonable opportunity of showing cause against the proposed rejection.

10.11 DUTIES OF SUBSCRIBERS

The duties of the subscribers, while availing digital signature certificate, are as under:

(A) Generating key pair

Where any Digital Signature Certificate (the public key, which corresponds to the private key of that subscriber which is to be listed in the Digital Signature Certificate) has been accepted by a subscriber, then the subscriber has to generate the key pair by applying the security procedures. The subscriber has to generate the 'private key' to correspond with the 'public key' listed in the digital signature certificate.

(B) Acceptance of Digital Signature Certificate

A subscriber shall be deemed to have accepted a Digital Signature Certificate if he publishes or authorises the publication of a Digital Signature Certificate —

(a) to one more persons

(b) in a repository; or otherwise demonstrates his approval of the Digital Signature Certificate in any manner.

By accepting a Digital Signature Certificate, the subscriber certifies to all who reasonably rely on the information contained in the Digital Signature Certificate that –

(a) the subscriber holds the private key corresponding to the public key listed in the Digital Signature Certificate and is entitled to hold the same ;

(b) all representations made by the subscriber to the Certifying Authority and all material relevant to the information contained in the Digital Signature Certificate are true ;

(c) all information in the Digital Signature Certificate that is within the knowledge of the subscriber is true.

(C) Control of private key

Every subscriber has to exercise reasonable care to retain control of the private key corresponding to the public key listed in his Digital Signature Certificate. He has to take all steps to prevent its disclosure to a person not authorised to affix the digital signature of the subscriber.

If the private key corresponding to the public key listed in the Digital Signature Certificate has been compromised, then, the subscriber shall communicate the same without any delay to the Certifying Authority in prescribed manner. The subscriber shall be liable till he has informed the Certifying Authority that the private key has been compromised.

10.12 THE CYBER REGULATIONS APPELLATE TRIBUNAL

The IT Act, 2000 deals with the establishment of one or more Appellate Tribunals to be known as

Cyber Regulations Appellate Tribunal or Cyber Appellate Tribunal to exercise jurisdiction, powers and authority as conferred under the Act.

Appeal to Cyber Appellate Tribunal

1. Any person aggrieved by an order made by Controller or an adjudicating officer under this Act may prefer an appeal to a Cyber Appellate Tribunal having jurisdiction in the matter.
2. Every appeal has to be filed within a period of forty-five days from the date on which a copy of the order made by the Controller or the adjudicating officer is received by the person aggrieved and it shall be in such form and be accompanied by such fee as may be prescribed.

   Provided that the Cyber Appellate Tribunal may entertain an appeal after the expiry of the said period of forty-five days if it is satisfied that there was sufficient cause for not filing it within that period.
3. On receipt of an appeal, the Cyber Appellate Tribunal may, after giving the parties to the appeal, an opportunity of being heard, pass such orders thereon as it thinks fit, confirming, modifying or setting aside the order appealed against.
4. The Cyber Appellate Tribunal shall send a copy of every order made by it to the parties to the appeal and to the concerned Controller or adjudicating officer.
5. The appeal filed before the Cyber Appellate Tribunal shall be dealt with by it as expeditiously as possible and endeavour shall be made by it to dispose of the appeal, finally, within six months from the date of receipt of the appeal.

PROCEDURE AND POWERS OF THE CYBER APPELLATE TRIBUNAL

(1) The Cyber Appellate Tribunal shall not be bound by the procedure laid down by the Code of Civil Procedure, 1908 but shall be guided by the principles of natural justice and, subject to the other provisions of this Act and of any rules. The Cyber Appellate Tribunal shall have powers to regulate its own procedure including the place at which it shall have its sittings.

(2) The Cyber Appellate Tribunal shall have, for the purposes of discharging its functions under this Act, the same powers as are vested in a civil court under the Code of Civil Procedure, 1908, while trying a suit, in respect of the following matters, namely:-

(a) summoning and enforcing the attendance of any person and examining him on oath;

(b) requiring the discovery and production of documents or other electronic records;

(c) receiving evidence on affidavits;

(d) issuing commissions for the examination of witnesses or documents;

(e) reviewing its decisions;

(f) dismissing an application for default or deciding it ex parte;

(g) any other matter which may be prescribed.

(3) Every proceeding before the Cyber Appellate Tribunal shall be deemed to be a judicial proceeding and for the purposes of section 196 of the Indian Penal Code and the Cyber Appellate Tribunal shall be deemed to be a civil court for the purposes of section 195 and Chapter XXVI of the Code of Criminal Procedure, 1973.

Civil Court not to have Jurisdiction

No court shall have jurisdiction to entertain any suit or proceeding in respect of any matter which an adjudicating officer appointed under this Act or the Cyber Appellate Tribunal constituted under this Act is empowered by or under this Act to determine and no injunction shall be granted by any court or other authority in respect of any action taken or to be taken in pursuance of any power conferred by or under this Act.

Appeal to High Court

Any person aggrieved by any decision or order of the Cyber Appellate Tribunal may file an appeal to the High Court within sixty days from the date of communication of the decision or order of the Cyber Appellate Tribunal to him on any question of fact or law arising out of such order.

The High Court may, if it is satisfied that the appellant was prevented by sufficient cause from filing the appeal within the said period, allow it to be filed within a further period not exceeding sixty days.

10.13 COMPUTER CRIMES

While there is no precise definition for a computer crime, it includes the illegal use of or the unauthorized entry into a computer system or computer data to tamper, interfere, damage, or manipulate the system or data.

Computer crimes are constantly on the increase. Criminals, using sophisticated technology, are increasingly trying to burst into computer systems to make a fast buck or to serve other nefarious designs. Sometimes they are even better equipped than the security professionals. Some statutes like Sarbanes Oxley Act require that the data, especially those concerning with privacy issues, be protected by the Management.

Computer crimes are happening everyday across the globe.

What's a Computer Crime?

Computer crimes include illegal use of or the unauthorized entry into a computer system or computer data to tamper, interfere, damage, or manipulate the system or data.

While there is no precise definition for a computer crime, it can be categorized into one of the following three areas:

1. **A computer may be the target of the offence.** In these cases, the criminal's goal is to steal information from, or cause damage to a computer. This includes tampering and altering data, adding fraudulent data etc. For example the DOS attack or stealing credit card information or bank account information.
2. **The computer may be a tool of the offence.** This occurs when an individual uses a computer to facilitate some traditional offence such as fraud or theft (for example, a bank employee may use a computer program to skim small amounts of money from a large number of bank accounts, thus generating a significant sum for personal use). This also includes use of one computer to access another computer. For example, telecommunication and computer manipulation crimes. Loss of intellectual property is also a major crime and in most cases it results in irreversible loss.
3. **Computers are sometimes incidental to the offence.** But, significant to law enforcement because they contain evidence of a crime. Narcotics dealers, for example, may use a personal computer to store records pertaining to drug trafficking instead of relying on old-fashioned ledgers.

Thus, any type of computer crime falls into one of the above categories. Although the above definitions seem very simple, the actual impact of such crimes is far beyond imagination.

Scenario – 2006

Role of Spam and Phising Attacks

There had been an unprecedented increase in the computer crimes mainly junk e-mails (spam) and sophisticated on-line attacks during 2006.

Phising attacks, involving **Social Engineering** (behavioural exploitation of individuals), were one of the primary methods used to extract personal information through junk mails. Computer criminals use spoofed websites to trick the consumers to divulge personal information. In corporate world, unprotected web servers are the main targets of these attackers. Two main reasons are attributed to this kind of attacks:

(A) Huge increase in the number of security holes identified in various software products, and

(B) Inadequate training or awareness among the employees and persons.

When sophisticated junk mail filters have been employed to detect such mails, the spammers even have begun embedding their messages in images, which the filters fail to detect. Usually filters look for only words or phrases.

What is New?

Many security professionals are speaking about Microsoft's **Vista** —the newest version of windows. It has more sophisticated features like hardened web browser which includes new anti-fraud tools and operating level changes. This, they claim, would prevent any spy-ware or viruses to make unwanted changes to the key settings and files. If the new version works foolproof, it would be a worthwhile solution.

> **It is indeed, a real challenge for the computer experts and security professionals to keep pace with today's computer criminals, using latest technology to crack the computers and steal valuable data from them. Obviously, the criminals are, often, better prepared than the security professionals.**

Challenges Ahead

Information Technology has to gear up with the emerging challenges. The best way is to be ready, abreast with the developments, problems and visualizing the anticipated moves of computer criminals, for changing the law, swiftly, in line with the moving trends to compete and beat them in their own way.

Check Your Understanding

State whether the following statements are True or False

1. The Information Technology Act has been enacted in the year 2000 to give a boost to e-commerce and provide mechanism for e-governance.
2. The basic objective of 'The Information Technology Act' has been to provide legal recognition to the transactions carried out by means of electronic data interchange and other means of electronic communication, commonly referred as "Electronic Commerce".
3. Digital signature means authentication of any electronic record by means of an electronic method or procedure by a subscriber.
4. Identity, while sending reports or messages, cannot be established by any means, other than physically.
5. A digital certificate can be presented electronically to prove identity, access information or services on the Internet or sign certain documents, digitally.
6. Digital signature is the electronic equivalent of the handwritten signature.
7. The public and private keys are not unique to each subscriber.
8. Encryption stands for coding and decryption for decoding.
9. Digital signature does not serve the same purpose what a written signature does on documents for evidence in a court of law.
10. Authentication of the electronic record is effected by the use of 'asymmetric crypto system' and 'hash function'.
11. The public and private keys are unique to each subscriber and constitute a functioning key pair.
12. 'Asymmetric crypto system' protects from tampering the messages during transmission from sender to the receiver.
13. Decryption stands for coding and encryption for decoding.
14. The Information Technology Act, 2000 is the first Cyber law in India.
15. Certification Practice Statement is a statement issued by the Certifying Authority specifying the practices it would employ while issuing Digital Signature Certificates.

16. Electronic documents are not accepted as evidence in a court of law.
17. Digital Signature Certificates are not the digital equivalent of physical or paper certificates.
18. Digital signature uses 'asymmetric crypto system' and 'hash function' to transform the initial electronic record into another electronic record.
19. Public key and private key are used to encrypt and decrypt the messages, respectively.
20. The controller exercises supervision over the activities of the Certifying Authorities.
21. Private key is used to create a digital signature while Public key is used to verify a digital signature, listed in the Digital Signature Certificate.
22. The person to whom a licence has been granted by the Controller to issue Digital Signature Certificate is termed as Certifying Authority.
23. People are aware of the advantages of Information Technology; however, many are reluctant to conduct the business in the electronic form due to fears about foolproof infrastructure and legal support.
24. Private Key is confidential, while the subscriber shares public key.
25. After registration, each subscriber will have a public key as well as private key.

Answers:

1. True	2. True	3. True	4. False	5. True
6. True	7. False	8. True	9. False	10. True
11. True	12. True	13. False	14. True	15. True
16. False	17. False	18. True	19. True	20. True
21. True	22. True	23. True	24. True	25. True

Descriptive questions

1. What is meant by the term 'Information Technology'? Explain the rationale and need for enacting the Information Technology Act. **(10.1 and 10.2)**
2. Explain the terms "e-commerce" and "e-governance" with reference to Information Technology Act, 2000. **(10.1 and 10.2)**
3. What, in your view, are the objectives of the Information Technology Act?**(10.1 and 10.3)**
4. Explain the changes that have been made in Information Technology Act, 2000 after its promulgation. **(10.1 and 10.4)**
5. Write a note on issue, security of Digital Signature, with a practical example of its working. **(10.1, 10.5 and 10.6)**
6. Discuss the provisions of Information Technology Act, 2000 relating to "Digital Signature Act". **(10.1, 10.5 and 10.6)**
7. How Digital Signature acquires legal recognition? **(10.1, 10.5 and 10.6)**
8. Define the following terms used in the Information Technology Act, 2000. **(10.7)**

   (A) Asymmetric cryptic network

(B) Digital Signature

(C) Key pair

(D) Originator

(E) Private key and public key

9. How is Controller or Certifying Authority appointed? What are his powers and functions under the Information Technology Act, 2000? **(10.8)**
10. Explain the matters related to appointment of Certifying Authorities to Issue Digital Signature Certificates? **(10.9)**
11. Describe the duties of Certifying Authority while issuing digital signature certificate? **(10.9)**
12. Elaborate the procedure to be followed by Certifying Authorities to Issue Digital Signature Certificates? **(10.10)**
13. What are the duties of Subscribers while accepting digital signature certificate? **(10.11)**
14. How is Cyber Appellate Tribunal appointed? What are its powers? **(10.12)**
15. What is a computer crime? Describe the different types of computer crimes and bring out the current scenario on this area? **(10.13)**